# DATA PROCESSING PROJECT MANAGEMENT

# DATA PROCESSING PROJECT MANAGEMENT

## Thomas R. Gildersleeve

**VNR** VAN NOSTRAND REINHOLD COMPANY

NEW YORK    CINCINNATI    ATLANTA    DALLAS    SAN FRANCISCO
LONDON    TORONTO    MELBOURNE

Van Nostrand Reinhold Company Regional Offices:
New York    Cincinnati    Chicago    Millbrae    Dallas

Van Nostrand Reinhold Company International Offices:
London    Toronto    Melbourne

Library of Congress Catalog Card Number: 74-8029
ISBN: 0-442-25309-5
ISBN: 0-442-25656-6 pbk.

Manufactured in the United States of America

Published by Van Nostrand Reinhold Company
135 West 50th Street, New York, N.Y. 10020

Published simultaneously in Canada by Van Nostrand Reinhold Ltd.

15  14  13  12  11  10  9  8  7  6  5

**Library of Congress Cataloging in Publication Data**

Gildersleeve, Thomas Robert.
    Data processing project management.

    1. Electronic data processing departments—Manage-
ment.   I. Title.
HF5548.2.G53        658'.05'4        74-8029
ISBN 0-442-25309-5
ISBN 0-442-25656-6 pbk.

*To my father*
*Robert W. Gildersleeve*

# CONTENTS

# DATA
# PROCESSING
# PROJECT
# MANAGEMENT

# INTRODUCTION

This book is written for data processing personnel who are about to assume or who already have management responsibility for the development of a data processing system.

I was introduced to project management in all too common a way. One day I was happily analyzing user requirements, designing data processing systems, and developing programs. The next day the location manager called me into his office, told me that my project manager was leaving for another assignment, and announced that I was going to take over responsibility for the project.

Actually, I was lucky. My project manager had one week to brief me before he left, so I did get some project management training, informal though it was, before moving into the job. To this day most of my contemporaries don't get this much training before they're thrown in the water to sink or, by some combination of luck and native intelligence, swim.

The purpose of this book is to both prevent and correct this situation. For those who have not yet assumed project management responsibility, this book is designed to sensitize you to the common pitfalls that lie in wait for the novice and unwary project leader. For those who have already been through some amount of project management, who have managed to survive to tackle a succeeding assignment, and whose experience leads them to suspect that there is an organized, consistent way to manage a data processing project, this book is here to reinforce that feeling. For both the experienced and the inexperienced, this book presents a systematic approach to project management.

This book assumes, on your part, enough data processing system development experience, either as a member of a Systems and Programming Department or as a member of a user organization a function of which was automated, to recognize the various problems of project management as they are described. It does not assume any knowledge of a consistent, organized approach to the solution of these problems.

This book is organized into six main sections.

1. Without certain prerequisites in the environment in which he works, the project leader faces an insurmountable job no matter how skilled he is. Section I of this book describes these prerequisites.

2. Section II tells you what project management is and why your manager might select this type of management for the development of a data processing system.

3. Section III tells how the project leader can carry out his planning responsibility.

4. The project leader not only plans the project activities, he also directs them. He must see that his project members stay on the schedule implied by his plans. But not only must project members stay on schedule. Their performance must also produce the desired results. Section IV addresses the project leader responsibilities of monitoring the schedule and gaining control over project member performance.

5. As a project leader, not only must you plan, monitor and control—you must also serve as the primary hub for communication with respect to your project. This is the subject of Section V.

6. Section VI is our residual category. It takes up a variety of topics consisting of time reporting systems, motivation, construction considerations, and standards and procedures.

We've written this book to make it easy and educational to read. The principles we adopted are as follows.

1. The body of the book discusses concepts. They are presented in a down-to-earth, easy-to-read way. More extensive, formal presentations appear as appendices. This isn't an invitation not to read the appendices. To the contrary, the appendices are an essential part of your education. The book is organized in this fashion so you can read about concepts without wading through a lot of detail; you are then supposed to read the applicable appendices to see how

these concepts are applied. The text directs you to the appendices at the appropriate points.

2. Programmed instruction is a sound educational concept. Yet most books that hew to a programmed instruction format are deadly dull, which defeats the purpose intended. Consequently, most of this book is text. Nevertheless, at those points in this book where you should think out the concepts presented before moving on, the book switches to a programmed instruction format. Thus, at certain points throughout this book you will find a question followed by an admonition not to continue in the text until you have formulated your own answer to the question. To get the most out of this book, you should do just that.

3. At the end of most chapters are one or more exercises designed to give you the opportunity to apply what you have learned in the chapter. This gives the book the appearance of a school text, which publishers love, because the school market is clearly defined and relatively easily reached. And if this book is adopted as a text, we can only be pleased. However, the exercises are not in the book for this purpose, but because the book is designed to teach you how to be a project leader, and you won't learn these skills by just reading about them, no matter how well the book is written. To learn skills you must practice them. The exercises are designed to give you this practice. Consequently, if you're sincere in your desire to acquire project management skills, we cannot urge you too strongly to work out each exercise before going on in the book. To give you something to check your exercise solutions against, school solutions to the exercises are presented at the end of this book. (For those of you who won't take the time to work out the exercises no matter how much we implore you, at least read the exercise solutions as you go along—some of the text of this book is incorporated in these solutions.)

To give us a common ground for discussing project management, the rest of this introductory chapter consists of a case study of a data processing project in which all things don't go right.

The saga of Larry Leadpants sprawls in its unforgettable enormity across the next 40 pages.

Read on.

REQUEST FOR SERVICES

Date:  May 2, 1983

Requesting Department:  Demitak

Department Head:  Marvin Melonhead

Problem Statement:

The data processing involved in the correscoping of
our framistans is on the verge of complete breakdown.
This processing is currently completely manual in
nature.  We now have 69 girls on the floor to do
the paper shuffling, and the projections in our
three year plan indicate that we'll need a 100%
increase in this workforce in the next two years
just to maintain the level of operation we currently
experience, a level of operation that is of questionable
acceptability as it is.  Summary reports of our operations
always lag closing dates by at least two months, and
special reports are practically impossible to get.
As a result we're managing our operation basically by
the seat of our pants, have no real knowledge of our
current position, and are often surprised by develop-
ments we had no idea were in the making.  We're con-
tinually barraged by complaints on foulups in our
recordkeeping, and the complete loss of a record is
not an uncommon occurrence.  Meeting the deadlines
imposed on us by government regulations always pre-
cipitates a department effort that invariably reaches
crisis proportions before being resolved.

Objectives:

1.  Eliminate the loss and erroneous modification of our
    historical records.

2.  Produce summary reports at a maximum of 10 working days
    after closing.

3.  Be able to get special reports with a 48 hour turnaround
    on a normal basis, 24 hours on an expedited basis.

4.  Produce required government reports as a standard
    operating procedure.

Scope:

The data processing system developed will be strictly
for the use of the Demitak Department.  There will
be no impact on any of the other operations of the
Quasi Corporation.

Benefits:

1.  Reduction in administrative expense.

2.  Improvement in department:

    a.  Management
    b.  Operations
    c.  Public relations

Date Desired:  January 2, 1984.

Date:  May 11, 1983

Memo To:  William Bluster
          Manager
          Systems and Programming

From:  Larry Leadpants
       Analyst
       Systems and Programming

On May 10 a meeting was held to discuss the features of
the Correscoping System called for in Marvin Melonhead's
Request for Services of May 2.  Attending the meeting were:

1.  William Bluster, Manager, Systems and Programming
2.  Marvin Melonhead, Department Head, Demitak Department
3.  Archibald Anarchist, Assistant Department Head in
    charge of framistans, Demitak Department
4.  Larry Leadpants, Analyst, Systems and Programming

At this meeting Messrs. Melonhead and Anarchist presented
us with:

1.  A general description of the record processing done
    with respect to the correscoping of framistans.
2.  Samples of the reports presently prepared by the
    current manual correscoping system together with:

    a.  Closing and delivery dates for these reports
    b.  Suggestions on how these reports could be improved

3.  A broad list of the special reports the Demitak Depart-
    ment might like to get from the Correscoping System on
    an ad hoc basis.

Summaries of this information are attached to this memo.

Bill, it looks to me like I ought to be able to get the
analysis and design on this system done in a couple of months
by myself.  Then with the help of three programmers for three
or four months we ought to be able to put the Correscoping
System into shape for operation by Demitak on January 2, 1984
with no trouble.

```
Date:  May 16, 1983

Memo to:  Marvin Melonhead
          Department Head
          Demitak Department

From:  William Bluster
       Manager
       Systems and Programming

Copy to:  Larry Leadpants
          Analyst
          Systems and Programming
```

Marv, I've just made our final review on your service request
for a Correscoping System for your framistans.  We're up to
our ears here in Systems and Programming, but I can see that
you've got a real problem, and we're here to help you out.
I've appointed Larry Leadpants as project leader for the
development of your system, and I've assigned project number
666 to the project.  Our price for this project will be
$72,000, and we don't see any reason why we can't meet your
January 2 deadline.  If all this is agreeable with you, just
let us know, and we'll get Larry on the job.

Mary says she's looking forward to attending our reunion at
Miasma U with you and Helen.  It sure will be good to see
the old frat house boys after 15 years, won't it?

Date:  May 23, 1983

Memo to:   William Bluster
           Manager
           Systems and Programming

From:   Marvin Melonhead
        Department Head
        Demitak Department


Bill, you're figures look OK to me.  If it will get us
out of the mess we're in, $72,000 is cheap, especially
when it's Chinese dollars.  Tell Larry he's got my OK
to speak to anyone on my staff to get the information
he needs.  I can hardly wait to start using the new system.

Date:   June 24, 1983

Status Report

To:        William Bluster
           Manager
           Systems and Programming

From:      Larry Leadpants
           Analyst
           Systems and Programming

Project Number 666

A Correscoping System for the Demitak Department

I think we can say that the analysis on this project is
just about over.  Frankly, I didn't get a lot of cooperation over at the Demitak Department.  This guy Anarchist
is probably the most disorganized person I've ever run
across.  Most of the time when I tried to see him he was
busy with something else, and when we did sit down to talk
he was always hopping up to handle the crisis de jour.

However, I've gotten a pretty good insight into the
correscoping operation, and frankly, it's just another file
maintenance job.  Everybody over there seems to think they've
got some unique problems, but you know how users are.

It looks like we're right on schedule.  This week I'm going
to start laying out the design, and if everything goes
according to plan, in a month I'll have the system spec'ed
out.

Date:   July 21, 1983

Memo to:   Larry Leadpants
           Analyst
           Systems and Programming

From:   William Bluster
        Manager
        Systems and Programming


Frankly, Larry, I never got a chance to look at your status
report before I went on vacation the end of June, and you
know what a guy's desk looks like when he gets back after
two weeks away from the shop.  Consequently, I didn't read
your report till yesterday.

By now you must have the design of the Correscoping System
just about done.  I'm sorry I didn't get into the act earlier.
I sure would have liked to get my hand in on the system layout.
However, it's too late now.  I've got all the confidence in
the world in you, Larry.  I know you'll do a great job for
Demitak.  Go to it, boy!

Date:   July 29, 1983

Status Report

To:   William Bluster
        Manager
        Systems and Programming

From:   Larry Leadpants
          Analyst
          Systems and Programming

Project Number 666

A correscoping System for the Demitak Department

I'm putting the finishing touches on the system design
this week.  We'll be ready to put programmers on the
job by Wednesday.

```
Date:   August 4, 1983

Memo to:   William Bluster
           Manager
           Systems and Programming

From:   Larry Leadpants
        Analyst
        Systems and Programming

Bill -- where are my programmers?
```

```
Date:  August 8, 1983

Memo to:  Larry Leadpants
          Analyst
          Systems and Programming

From:  William Bluster
       Manager
       Systems and Programming

Chriminettles, Larry, give me a chance.  You don't
expect me to whomp up programmers out of thin air,
do you?  I'll get you some people as soon as I can.
```

```
Date:  August 11, 1983

Memo to:  Larry Leadpants
          Analyst
          Systems and Programming

From:  William Bluster
       Manager
       Systems and Programming

Beginning Monday, August 15, the following programmers
will be assigned fulltime to the development of the
Correscoping System, project number 666.

1.  Frederick Faithful
2.  Elaine Eager
```

Date:   August 12, 1983

Memo to:   William Bluster
            Manager
            Systems and Programming

From:   Larry Leadpants
         Analyst
         Systems and Programming

Holy cow, Bill, what are you trying to do to me?
You know that in the ten years Fred Faithful's been
with us, he's never met a deadline.   And Elaine Eager
is right out of our entry level training program.
At this rate, who can tell when we'll finish this
project?

Not so incidently, we need three programmers, not
two.   When can I expect the third member of my team?

Date:  August 16, 1983

Memo to:   Larry Leadpants
           Analyst
           Systems and Programming

From:   William Bluster
        Manager
        Systems and Programming

I'm really sorry about all this, Larry, but you know
the problems we've got right now -- we're putting in
more new systems than ever before, maintenance work
seems to be skyrocketing, and the brass is holding
our budget to last year's level.  Frankly, at this time
Faithful and Eager are the only people I can spare.
I'll admit you've a few problems there, but it's
nothing that a little supervision can't solve.

I'll try to get you a third man just as soon as I
can.  In the meantime, Larry, perhaps you'd better
roll up your sleeves and really dive into that programming work yourself.

I've got all the confidence in the world in you, Larry.
I know you'll do a great job for Demitak.  Go to it,
boy!

```
Date:  August 17, 1983

Memo to:  Wallace Wheeler
          Manager
          Computer Center

From:  Larry Leadpants
       Analyst
       Systems and Programming
```

Boy, Wally, this almost slipped my mind.  As you may know, we're working on the Correscoping System, and in a week or two we're going to start needing some computer time for debugging.  Any problem?

```
Date:  August 22, 1983

Memo to:  Larry Leadpants
          Analyst
          Systems and Programming

From:  Wallace Wheeler
       Manager
       Computer Center

I can't see any problems, Larry.  When you're ready
for some computer time, we ought to be able to fit
you in.  We'll be hearing from you.
```

Date:   September 6, 1983

Memo to:   Larry Leadpants
           Analyst
           Systems and Programming

From:   William Bluster
        Manager
        Systems and Programming

Beginning Wednesday, September 7, Suki So-so will be
assigned fulltime to the development of the Correscoping
System, project number 666.

```
Date:  September 12, 1983

Memo to:  Larry Leadpants
          Analyst
          Systems and Programming

From:  William Bluster
       Manager
       Systems and Programming

Larry, what's going on?  For the past month you've
been bugging me for another programmer.  So even
though it's hurting, I took So-so off the Pulsitran
System and gave him to you.  Today I walk past Suki's
desk, and he's working crossword puzzles!!!  Larry,
what's going on?
```

Date:  September 12, 1983

Memo to:  William Bluster
          Manager
          Systems and Programming

From:  Larry Leadpants
       Analyst
       Systems and Programming

Sorry about this So-so business, Bill.  Frankly, since
you gave me Suki last Wednesday, I've been:

1.    Keeping on Faithful's tail so he stays out of
      the coffeeshop and finishes up the Edit Program
      he was supposed to have coded two weeks ago.

2.    Working with Elaine Eager a couple of hours every
      day to teach her enough programming to get her
      work done.

3.    Trying to get enough done on the Update Program
      (for which I assumed the responsibility in the
      absence of any other programmer on the team) so
      it wouldn't slip so far behind that it would hold
      up Fred and Elaine when they need it.

I just haven't had enough time left over to brief Suki
on the job I have for him.  However, even though it will
hurt, I'll ignore these other responsibilities for a few
days and get Suki into the Phase Three Program, which
as you know, is the heart of the Correscoping System.

Bill, I did want to say that I appreciate your assigning
Suki to the team.  He's just the man to handle the Phase
Three Program, and it's a weight off my mind.

Date:   September 23, 1983

Status Report

To:   William Bluster
      Manager
      Systems and Programming

From:   Larry Leadpants
        Analyst
        Systems and Programming

Project Number 666

A Correscoping System for the Demitak Department

Well, things are beginning to look up.  I still have
to dog Faithful to keep him on the job, and we're
really not getting the turnaround on our test shots
that we need, but Elaine Eager is beginning to shape
up into a real programmer.  I'm beginning to rely on
her more and more heavily.  And Suki So-so has sure
torn into the Phase Three Program.  He's already taken
it far beyond the point to which I had it worked out,
and although, I sometimes worry about the fact that he
carries so much of what he's doing around in his head,
he certainly is turning out the code.

Date:   September 26, 1983

Memo to:   Larry Leadpants
           Analyst
           Systems and Programming

From:   William Bluster
        Manager
        Systems and Programming

Larry, I really hate to do this to you, but over the
weekend the Pulsitran System blew up higher than a
kite, the boys seem to think the trouble is in Suki's
program, and you know the kind of documentation he
leaves behind.   I'm afraid I'm going to have to pull
Suki off the Correscoping System till we get the
Pulsitran System straightened out.   It may be a week
or two.   Larry, I'm sorry.

```
Date:   September 26, 1983

Memo to:  William Bluster
          Manager
          Systems and Programming

From:   Larry Leadpants
        Analyst
        Systems and Programming


...help!
```

Date:  October 7, 1983

Status Report

To:  William Bluster
     Manager
     Systems and Programming

From:  Larry Leadpants
       Analyst
       Systems and Programming

Project Number 666

A Correscoping System for the Demitak Department

Here's the situation.

1.  Faithful is performing in his usual manner, which
    means that he keeps falling behind.  At least the
    work he does turn out is pretty reliable, and I'm
    keeping after him.

2.  Elaine Eager is really beginning to blossom.  As
    soon as she finishes the scut work she's been doing,
    I'm going to assign her to the Phase Two Program.

3.  Suki finally returned to us Wednesday and is now
    back hard at work.  Nevertheless, we've lost about
    another two weeks on Phase Three.

In general, we're somewhat behind, and we're just going
to have to start putting in some overtime.  Computer
turnaround still isn't what it should be either, but
so far this hasn't hurt us too much.

Date:    October 19, 1983

Memo to:    William Bluster
            Manager
            Systems and Programming

From:    Larry Leadpants
         Analyst
         Systems and Programming

Copy to:    Wallace Wheeler
            Manager
            Computer Center

Bill, as you know, we're going forced draft to get the
Correscoping System done on schedule.  Everyone is
working overtime, and we're really turning out the
code.  However, the computer room is beginning to
create a real bottleneck for us.  I told Wallace back
in August that we'd need debugging time, but we're
not getting the turnaround we need.  If things don't
change, we're going to be in a real bind.  Is there
anything you can do to help us out?

```
Date:   October 20, 1983

Memo to:  William Bluster
          Manager
          Systems and Programming

From:   Wallace Wheeler
        Manager
        Computer Center

Copy to:  Benjamin Bigdome
          Director
          Data Processing

          Larry Leadpants
          Analyst
          Systems and Programming
```

With reference to Larry Leadpants' memo of October 19, 1983 to you, a copy of which is attached:

Bill, you know we've done our level best to give your programmers the service they need.  The facts are that, in addition to our normally heavy production workload, the fiscal year ended on September 30, and we're trying to get our yearend work out of the way.  In spite of all this, we do set aside as much time as we can to handle debugging shots.

I'm attaching a copy of Mr. Leadpants' memo of August 17 to me.  As you can see, all he asked for was "some computer time", and that's what he's getting, just like all the other programmers in your shop.  We never expected Mr. Leadpants' work to peak like it has.

Nevertheless, I want to do my best to cooperate.  The 12 midnight to 8 am shift on Saturday nights is open, and if Mr. Leadpants wants to use this time, I'll assign an operator to the shift.

```
Date:  October 24, 1983

Memo to:  Larry Leadpants
          Analyst
          Systems and Programming

From:  William Bluster
       Manager
       Systems and Programming

I just got back from a meeting with Ben Bigdome.
Frankly, he was a little hot under the collar.  The
boys upstairs have been giving him some heat about
the yearend reports being late, and at this point
he doesn't want to get Wallace Wheeler all stirred
up.  Consequently, I think you'd better cool it on
the computer turnaround for a while.

I know a block of 8 solid hours isn't the kind of
computer time you need, but Ben wasn't in the mood
to listen to reason.  Maybe you better try to use
that Saturday night time.  Nuff said?
```

Date:   October 31, 1983

Memo to:   William Bluster
           Manager
           Systems and Programming

From:   Marvin Melonhead
        Department Head
        Demitak Department

Bill, Archie Anarchist has just come up with a brilliant
idea for improving our framistan operation.  He hasn't
got all the details worked out yet, but before you get
the Correscoping System cast in concrete, why don't you
have Larry Leadpants get together with Archie to see
what, if any, effect his ideas will have on the system?

Bill, I can't tell you how much we're looking forward
to the beginning of the year when we'll start using your
new data processing system to bail us out of the paperwork mess were in now.  I only wish I could have been
closer to the whole thing.  However, I've got all the
confidence in the world in you, Bill.  I know you'll
do a great job for Demitak.  Keep up the good work!

```
Date:  November 3, 1983

Memo to:  Marvin Melonhead
          Department Head
          Demitak Department

From:  William Bluster
       Manager
       Systems and Programming

Copy to:  Larry Leadpants
          Analyst
          Systems and Programming

Marv, it's good to hear those kind words.  Of course,
we'll see what we can do to help out Archie Anarchist.
After all, if we don't provide service, what are we
for?

By copy of this memo I'm asking Larry to get together
with Archie and find out what Archie's thoughts are
on the framistan operation.
```

Date:   November 8, 1983

Memo to:   William Bluster
           Manager
           Systems and Programming

From:   Larry Leadpants
        Analyst
        Systems and Programming

Bill, I finally got together with Archie Anarchist,
and does he have ideas!  The way he's talking now,
a good bit of the work we've done on the Update
Program and almost everything we've put into Phase
Three is down the drain.

We're just not going to meet that January 2 date,
Bill.  I recommend that we tell Demitak now, so they
can adjust to the change.

```
Date:   November 9, 1983

Memo to:   Larry Leadpants
              Analyst
              Systems and Programming

From:   William Bluster
            Manager
            Systems and Programming

Larry, I'm trying to get my five year plan past Ben
Bigdone's desk.  All I need now is a big slip on a
major project.

For Pete's sake, get in there with Archie Anarchist
and get these changes nailed down, and then pour on
the coal!  In the meantime, I'll see if I can get you
another pair of hands.
```

Date:  November 25, 1983

Status Report

To:  William Bluster
     Manager
     Systems and Programming

From:  Larry Leadpants
       Analyst
       Systems and Programming

Project Number 666

A Correscoping System for the Demitak Department

In the past two weeks the functional specifications
for this system have undergone major revision three
separate times.  However, I think we've finally got
them the way Anarchist wants them, and we're now back
trying to recover lost time.  I'm afraid overtime has
become a way of life on the project.

I want to thank you for the extra man you assigned to
the project and also for interceding for me with Wally
Wheeler.  He's speaking to me again, although rather
distantly, and computer turnaround is beginning to
improve.

Elaine Eager has finished Phase Two, and I've got her
helping Suki with Phase Three.  That girl is really a
comer, but of late her work has been getting a little
ragged.  She tells me her boyfriend has broken up with
her and she has headaches almost everyday.  She says if
overtime doesn't stop soon, she's going to quit.

```
Date:   December 5, 1983

Memo to:   William Bluster
           Manager
           Systems and Programming

From:   Larry Leadpants
        Analyst
        Systems and Programming

Bill, we need a replacement for Elaine Eager.
```

```
Date:  December 23, 1983

Status Report

To:  William Bluster
     Manager
     Systems and Programming

From:  Larry Leadpants
       Analyst
       Systems and Programming

Project Number 666

A Correscoping System for the Demitak Department

We're putting the final touches on the programs and
are ready to go into system test.  Unfortunately, I
haven't yet had time to prepare the system test data.
I'm going to give the team the holidays off, and I'll
use the time to put the data together.

Any day now we should probably tell Demitak we aren't
going to make the January 2 date.

It also just occurred to me that, to put the system on
the air, we're going to have to convert all those
ledger cards over there in Demitak to mag tape.  That's
no mean task, and we better institute a crash effort
to get the job done.  I figure that two more men in
addition to the project team ought to be able to do
the job in three weeks.
```

Date:    December 28, 1983

Memo to:    All Vice Presidents, Department Heads, and
            Managers

From:    Peter Pompous
         President
         Quasi Corporation

It is with regret that we announce that Marvin Melonhead,
our good friend and former Head of the Demitak Department,
has resigned his position to take on new and challenging
work.  However, Quasi Corp. has never been unmindful of
its larger responsibilities to the society that nourishes
us all, and we are happy to know that, in some small measure, we have prepared Marv for his new venture.  Therefore,
it is with mixed feelings of regret and pride that we
wish Marv Godspeed and good luck in his new position as
Head Janitor at Miasma University.

We are fortunate in being able to replace Marv with a
man who brings many years of experience to his job.  It
is my pleasure to announce the appointment of Warren
Windy to the Position of Department Head, Demitak Department.  I know you will all show Warren the courtesy for
which Quasi is famous and give him your utmost in cooperation.

Warren comes to us from a series of responsible positions
at Miasma University, the last of which was as Head
Janitor.

Date:   January 5, 1984

Memo to:   William Bluster
           Manager
           Systems and Programming

From:   Warren Windy
        Department Head
        Demitak Department

It has recently been brought to my attention that
there is in development in your shop a "Correscoping
System" for our framistan operation.  Since I'm rather
new on the job, I'm wondering if we can't get together
someday soon, perhaps over lunch, to discuss this
system.  I've reviewed the correspondence, but I'm
not sure I quite grasp the system's purpose.

Date:  January 10, 1984

Memo to:  Larry Leadpants
          Analyst
          Systems and Programming

From:  William Bluster
       Manager
       Systems and Programming

Larry, I just got back from a long and rather uncom-
fortable luncheon with Warren Windy.  He doesn't seem
to be at all convinced that our Correscoping System is
what his framistan operation needs.  However, I did
manage to get him to agree that the major investment
in system development has already been made and that it
would be unjustified to not go ahead and finish the
work we've started.  Consequently, it looks like we've
got the green light.

You're doing a great job, Larry.  Keep up the good work!

```
Date:  February 15, 1984

Memo to:  Archibald Anarchist
          Assistant Department Head
          Demitak Department

From:  Larry Leadpants
       Analyst
       Systems and Programming

As you know, Archie, we completed the conversion of
your master file last Wednesday.

Last night our system processed the test data we
developed for it without a hitch.

Consequently, we'd like to cut over to the new system
on Monday and have you take the responsibility for the
operation of the system.
```

Date:    February 17, 1984

Memo to:    William Bluster
            Manager
            Systems and Programming

From:    Archibald Anarchist
         Assistant Department Head
         Demitak Department

Copies to:    Warren Windy
              Department Head
              Demitak Department

              Benjamin Bigdome
              Director
              Data Processing

With reference to Mr. Larry Leadpants' memo of February
15, 1984, a copy of which is attached:

The chaos in our operation that has resulted from the
conversion of our historical data to magnetic tape
leaves us with no alternative but to acquiesce in the
February 20 cutover to the new Correscoping System.
However:

1.    A preliminary review of the system test results
      supplied to us by Mr. Leadpants indicates that
      the designers of the new system suffered under
      some gross misconceptions as to procedures in
      the framistan operation.  Documentation to support
      this contention is attached.  Review of system
      results by the Demitak Department will continue,
      and periodically you will be informed of all other
      deficiencies unearthed.

2.    The Demitak Department is totally without the facil-
      ities to operate the new Correscoping System.  No
      written procedures for the new system exist, and
      none of our personnel have received any briefing,
      let alone training, on how to carry out their new
      responsibilities.  As a consequence, until procedures
      are documented and the personnel are trained, our
      staff will follow the old procedures, and your
      department will have to effect the required adjust-
      ments to make our operation compatible with the new
      system.

Until these operational, documentation and educational
difficulties are cleared up, responsibility for the
Correscoping System must remain with the Data Processing
Department.

Date:  April 13, 1984

Report

Post-Installation Review

To:  William Bluster
     Manager
     Systems and Programming

From:  System Review Committee

Project Number 666

A Correscoping System for the Demitak Department

This project was officially closed on March 30, 1984.
On that date, by direction of Mr. Peter Pompous,
President of Quasi Corporation, the Demitak Department
accepted responsibility for the Correscoping System.
Mr. Pompous accounted for his action by saying that
he felt the remaining problems with this system would
be cleared up more quickly if responsibility for the
system were in the hands of the operating department
originally requesting the system.  In accepting the
system, Mr. Warren Windy, Operating Head of the Demitak
Department, said that he did so under protest, that he
didn't see why he should have to clean up someone else's
mess, and he swore he would never let the Data Processing
Department do anything for him again.  He said he'd
rather hire his own programmers, if that's what it took.

Thus, the Correscoping System was officially delivered
exactly three months after its committed delivery date,
although troubles with the system remain, and it is
expected that, for a period of at least six months, the
maintenance load for this system will be high.

Development cost for this project overran the Data
Processing Department's original quotation by 95%.

A comparison of the operation of this system with the
original objectives set forth for it reveals the
following.

1.    The normal file maintenance operation of the system
      is performing about as the previous manual system.
      Mistakes still occur, but since March 7, when
      27,534 master records were misplaced, no loss of
      information has occurred.  It's expected that
      these difficulties are temporary and that normal
      maintenance operations will clear them up.  The
      Demitak Department now estimates that, in the next
      two years, they will have to increase their clerical
      work force by only 50% rather than by 100%.  They
      are dissatisfied with this reduction, but it's
      impossible to tell whether the system has met its
      objective in this area, since the objective was
      never quantified.

Continued on opposite page.

2.  The lag between closing and production of summary
    reports has been reduced to an average of 22 working
    days.  Most of the delay in this area can be attri-
    buted to the need for reruns because of inconsisten-
    cies found in the reports produced.  It is expected
    that, when the system is shaken down, the goal of a
    maximum lag of 10 working days will be realized.

3.  As near as the committee can determine, the system's
    ability to produce special reports appears to have
    met the objective originally set for it.  The
    reason why it is necessary to be hazy in this area
    is because this feature has never been subjected
    to a real-life test.  Demitak personnel are so
    disenchanted by their initial experiences with the
    system that they now refuse to use it.  Management
    continues to run the framistan operation the way
    they always have.

4.  The system has managed to reduce, but not yet elimi-
    nate, the crisis associated with production of
    government reports.  As bugs in the system are
    corrected, continued performance improvement in
    this area is anticipated.

In summary, it must be said that, despite its difficulties,
the Correscoping System is not a bad system.  As soon as
its current error rate is reduced through continued maintenance, it will undoubtedly be of some benefit to the
Demitak Department.  However, it was not designed to fit
in smoothly with the framistan operation; as a consequence,
it is somewhat awkward to use; and this, coupled with the
series of disasters to which the Demitak personnel were
subjected during the development and installation of the
system, has largely eliminated, in their eyes, any benefits
to be gained from the system.  The system has not made any
friends for the Data Processing Department; DP has certainly
gained some short-term, if not longterm enemies; and if
Demitak had it to do over again, they would probably
decide to stick with their old system.

On top of the difficulties in the Demitak Department,
the Correscoping System has also caused operating
problems on a corporate-wide basis.  The auditors say
that the system has been put together in such a way
that it's practically impossible to establish an audit
trail.  Also, the figures produced by the system are
not compatible with corporate general ledger accounting
practices, so at present, considerable manual manipulation of these figures must be done before they can be
passed on to the accountants.  In DP's defense, it must
be said that the original Request for Services prepared
by Demitak did specifically eliminate such corporate
considerations from the scope of the system.  But as the
new Demitak Department Head points out, only an incompe-
tent department head could have taken it on himself to
establish such limitations, and in the general difficulties
in which the Data Processing Department finds itself, it
seems to have been awarded full responsibility for these
corporate difficulties by not being smart enough to
ignore the limitations of scope mistakenly imposed on
the system by the former Demitak Department Head.

Date:  April 16, 1984

Memo to:  Benjamin Bigdome
          Director
          Data Processing

From:  William Bluster
       Manager
       Systems and Programming

I'm enclosing a copy of the Post-Installation Review
Report prepared by the System Review Committee on
Project 666, The Correscoping System.

As you can see, we didn't cover ourselves with glory.

I don't think it's too hard to pinpoint our difficulty.
Frankly, I never did have much confidence in Larry
Leadpants, but at the time of Demitak's request, he
was the only man available to assign to the job.

```
Date:  May 16, 1984

Memo to:  Larry Leadpants
          Analyst
          Systems and Programming

From:  Personnel Department

This is to inform you that your exit interview will
be conducted at 11 am on Friday, May 18 at these
offices.  At that time your termination check will
be available for you to pick up.
```

The fundamental question is: Where did Larry Leadpants go wrong?

Why don't you formulate your own answer to this question? (You can make your notes on the bottom of this page.)

Look at the following page to get our opinion.

Some people say Larry's fundamental mistake was in working for the wrong company. Now, Bluster has the earmarks of a scoundrel, and Demitak's role in the development of the Correscoping System was, at best, confused. We're even willing to admit that, in fabricating this data processing tragedy, we've overstated the situation to the point of absurdity. But exaggerated though they may be, we defy anybody to examine the regrettable and unsavory traits exhibited by the personae who collectively contributed to Larry's downfall and to deny that they exist within the ranks of data processing management and user personnel. Fortunately, all these faults and failings do not typically cluster in any one person, but everyone must be prepared for the likelihood that the people with whom he deals will be less than perfect in one or more ways. Given the general defectiveness of the world in which we live, each of us has a responsibility to protect himself from the failures of those around him, and consequently, no one can justifiably lay the blame for a catastrophe that has befallen him at another person's door. The object is not so much that every person has to look out for his own hide (although that's not a bad idea), as it is that, if we each individually protect ourselves against the failures of others, we protect ourselves collectively from common disaster.

Specifically, we fault Larry for the following failures:

1. He accepted a fixed delivery date and budget before he knew what it was he had to deliver. Also, he never came to an agreement with the user as to what it was he was supposed to deliver. As a consequence, he missed his delivery date by three months, and he overran his budget by 95%.

2. The design of the system was never reviewed by the people in the corporation who are concerned with the design of all data processing systems regardless of user. Consequently, these people couldn't live with the new system (the auditors couldn't establish an audit trail).

3. He didn't get prior agreement with the user as to what constituted acceptable system operation. As a consequence, when he decided the system was acceptable and tried to turn it over to the user, he found that the user would not accept it.

4. He didn't plan the resources required to accomplish the goals set for him. As a consequence:

    a. He was frequently surprised by the need to perform some major task (file conversion, procedure manual writing, user training) for which he had made no provisions.

    b. He found himself trying to accomplish tasks for which he had inadequate resources (not enough manpower, insufficiently skilled manpower, not enough computer time), and not uncommonly, he had even these insufficient resources yanked out from under him with no relaxation as to his commitments.

c. He found himself personally overcommitted on detailed tasks (coding a major program), with the result that he couldn't adequately handle his project leader responsibilities.

d. He subjected his staff to unreasonable demands (overtime as a way of life, debugging on the Saturday night graveyard shift).

In all justice, we must admit that Larry suffered under one handicap over which he had no control. Between the time the project was initiated and the time the system was defined, the definition of the user changed. As a consequence, people (the corporate accountants), whose needs were never considered when the system was designed, became dissatisfied when their needs weren't met.

You may think Larry's experience was a total disaster. To the contrary, Larry stumbled into only a few of the pitfalls that lie in wait for the unwary project leader.

The purpose of this book is to acquaint you with the more common mistakes a project leader can make and to show you how you can go about avoiding them. It is hoped that, thus armed, you can carry out your project leader responsibilities without experiencing disaster.

The negative phrasing of this book's purpose is intentional. We want in no way to imply that use of the techniques recommended in this book will make project management a breeze, nor do we mean to infer that use of these techniques in itself is easy. By definition, to undertake a project is to try something that, to some extent, has never been done before, and you can expect such a job to be fraught with frustration, aggravation, problems, and setbacks (as well as the chance to enjoy a feeling of accomplishment, a better salary, and an increasingly responsible position). If you don't want to subject yourself to this kind of heat, then take President Truman's advice and stay out of the kitchen. However, if you're willing to wrestle with the problems of project management, there's no reason why your efforts should result in catastrophe. This book will show you how to be a project manager, how to deliver on your commitments, and how to keep your reputation intact.

# PROJECT PREREQUISITES

# THE USER

The data processing department is a service organization. Its functions produce no direct revenue. Its contribution is to help other departments cut costs and increase revenue. The success of the data processing department depends on its ability to satisfy its customers, the users of its data processing services. Your ability to perform as a project leader depends on a firm identification of the user of your product and an understanding of his needs. Production of the right product for the wrong customer spells failure.

User identification is not a project leader responsibility. This is a decision that must be made for you.

The best way to identify the customer is to determine who is going to pay. A data processing department in which every cost is billed back to the department that stands to benefit from the service rendered is an environment in which a project leader's chance for success is significantly enhanced.

Now for several caveats: The purpose of this book is not to discuss billback systems and ways of identifying users, and we are not going to get sucked into addressing these subjects here. We are willing to admit that:

1. The departmental lines of groups served by data processing systems are not always clearcut or simple, and identifying the user is sometimes not an easy task.

2. Not every activity performed in a data processing department can be considered to be for the benefit of a particular user, and therefore, some burden must be prorated over costs that are chargeable to individual clients.

3. It is not always easy to distribute chargeable costs between users on an equitable basis.

Nevertheless, these problems are not insurmountable, and anyone who is willing to assume the responsibility for a data processing department or a company should be willing to face them and to provide solutions. (For example, user identification, with or without a billback system, is clearly a company responsibility, and the steering committee appears to be the best solution to this problem.)

All we want to say in this book is:

1. The project leader who does not know who his user is, is in danger of disaster.

2. Ideally, the user should be identified in terms of whom you, the project leader, are to bill your charges to.

3. In any case, the user should be identified by the company, not by the data processing department.

4. If the company won't accept the responsibility of defining your user, and your manager won't force the issue, ask your manager to identify your user for you.

5. If your manager won't identify your user for you, make the identification yourself and ask your manager to approve your identification.

6. If your manager won't give positive approval to your user identification, make it clear that lack of disapproval constitutes approval. ("In the absence of notification to the contrary on or before the specified date, the following user identification is considered approved.")

7. Once the user is identified, any subsequent change in user definition must be considered sufficient grounds for relieving you of any and all commitments you've made up to the point of change. (This doesn't mean you're going to renege on all your commitments—it just means you have the right to withdraw any that you feel have been made untenable.) Be sure everybody understands this.

If you think this is being hardnosed, ask yourself if anyone could be considered wrong, or even unreasonable, for taking such a position. If you do take such a position and someone does accuse you of being unreasonable, then perhaps you should begin to ask yourself if you are working for the right company.

The rest of this book assumes that the project leader is working in a billback environment.

## EXERCISES

1. Your company treats all data processing costs as part of company overhead. Your project is to develop a production control system. Who is your user?
2. Your company has 67 branch offices. Your project is to develop a common order entry system for all 67 branches. You charge all project expenses to the home office marketing department. Who is your user?
3. You work for a computer manufacturer. Your project is to build a software package for a computer system manufactured and marketed by your company. Who is your user—your company or your company's customers?

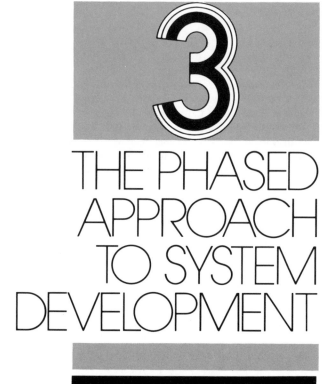

# THE PHASED APPROACH TO SYSTEM DEVELOPMENT

One of Larry Leadpants' problems was that he committed himself to a fixed budget before he knew what it was he had to deliver. The hardnosed solution to this problem is for the project leader to say, "I won't make any budget or other financial evaluation until I know exactly what it is I have to do."

But let's look at the situation through the user's eyes for a moment. He's saying, "You, Mr. Data Processing Man, want me to set up an account against which you can charge large numbers of hours at outrageous rates; you want to come into my department, disrupt my operations, and tie up my key personnel in long interviews; and you want me to do all this without knowing whether it's even remotely worthwhile starting down this road." One can hardly say the user doesn't have a point.

This is a clasic case of dilemma. *X* (the user) is saying to *Y* (the data processing department), "I can't give you *A* (a definition of the system) until you give me *B* (the development and operating costs of the system)," and *Y* is saying to *X*, "I can't give you *B* until you give me *A*." The solution to this type of problem is a phased approach in which reciprocal commitments are made in a graduated manner that allows each side to provide useful information to the other without prematurely overcommitting either party.

In general, the development of a data processing system goes through five phases.

1. *Conceptual*  All systems not developed or in some other development phase are in the conceptual phase—that is, waiting to be conceived. A system moves from the conceptual phase into the initiation phase when the user decides it's worth going through at least one iteration in the attempt to determine whether the system is feasible.

2. *Initiation*  In the initiation phase, the user and the data processing department invest the minimum amount of resources possible to provide the user with enough information to decide whether he has any real interest in pursuing the development of the system further.

3. *Analysis*  The user and the data processing department agree on what the system is going to do.

4. *Design*  The data processing department decides how the system is to be constructed.

5. *Construction*  The data processing department constructs and installs the system.

Obviously, the initiation phase culminates in the user making a feasibility decision. What may not be so clear is that, if this decision is positive, the decision made is to undertake the analysis phase only, not to undertake all of the remaining phases in the development process.

At the end of the analysis phase the user once more makes a feasibility decision. If this decision is positive, the decision is to undertake the design phase only.

At the end of the design phase, the user makes a feasibility decision one more time. If this decision is positive, then the construction phase is entered.

Thus, the user's feasibility decision is not a one-time thing. Instead, he makes it at least three times—at the end of each of the initiation, analysis, and design phases. If at any one of these points the decision is negative, then all work on the system is discontinued, and it returns to the limbo of the conceptual phase. (Some installations divide the construction phase into two phases—construction and installation—and they conduct a fourth feasibility evaluation after the system is constructed but before it is installed. The idea is that, for a decentralized organization, the installation cost may be significant enough to kill development of a system if, after construction, it proves to be unfeasible.)

The idea behind multiple feasibility decisions is that, with the completion of each phase in the development of the system, there should be improvement in the user's ability to estimate the benefits and costs of the system. The theory is that what might have looked attractive in broad terms may, with the benefit of investigation, turn out to be undesirable.

Some of the crucial input to the user's feasibility decisions is the data processing department's estimates of system development and running costs. The data processing department estimates these costs at the end of each phase, and, with each successive phase, the confidence the user can place in these estimates improves. For example, at the end of the initiation phase, the possibility for error in the data processing department's estimates might be in the range of 100%, at the end of the analysis phase in the range of 50%, and at the end of the design phase in the range of 10%. Thus, if doubling the data processing department's estimates at the end of the initiation phase puts the system outside the range of feasibility, then system feasibility is not eliminated, but it does become questionable.

How can the data processing department provide increasingly reliable cost estimates as the system development phases pass? It can because, with each passing phase, the system specifications become progressively more firm. At the end of the initiation phase there are only broad statements of scope and objectives on which to base estimates. However, at the end of the analysis phase, what the system is going to do is spelled out. And at the end of the design phase, how the system is going to be constructed has been defined.

And how can the data processing department be assured that this progressive firming of systems specifications is actually taking place? Because at the end of each phase the specifications are documented and the parties involved in these specifications have approved them. In this book we will call the specifications produced at the end of the analysis phase functional specifications, and the specifications produced at the end of the design phase design specifications.

Functional specifications are approved by the user. In making this approval, the user attests that the functional specifications do, in fact, describe the system he wants.

Design specifications are approved by a design review committee. Every part of the company with an interest in the design of its data processing systems should be represented on the design review committee. Four such groups are as follows.

1. The Systems and Programming Department: The design review committee member from this department must attest to the technical acceptability of the design—is it "state of the art"?

2. The Computer Center: The member from this department must attest to the conformance of the system to computer center operating standards and facilities. Among the items reviewed by the computer center representative are:

   a. Central processor time.
   b. Maximum memory requirements.
   c. Number and type of input-output devices required.
   d. Channel utilization.

   e. Files:

      (1) Consolidation and separation needs.

      (2) Security requirements.

   f. Teleprocessing facilities:

      (1) Volumes of data and response time.

      (2) Schedule of use.

      (3) Use procedures.

   g. Special software and libraries required.

3. The Maintenance Department: This member must attest to the maintainability of the system.

4. The company auditors: This member must attest that the design does permit all auditing functions, both internal and external, to be performed.

As a consequence, as a project leader you can always tell what phase the system you are developing is in by taking a quick pass through the decision table shown in Fig. 3-1.

| | 1 | 2 | 3 |
|---|---|---|---|
| Has the user approved the functional specifications? | Y | Y | N |
| Has the design review committee approved the design specifications? | Y | N | – |
| The system is in the construction phase | X | – | – |
| Error range on estimates is 10% | X | – | – |
| The system is in the design phase | – | X | – |
| Error range on estimates is 50% | – | X | – |
| The system is in the analysis phase | – | – | X |
| Error range on estimates is 100% | – | – | X |

**Fig. 3-1  Phase determination.**

Design specifications consist of system flow charts and applicable backup documents—file and record layouts, and program descriptions. A set of standards for design specifications is given in Appendix A.

Functional specifications describe what the system is going to do. Functional specifications should be comprehensive enough so that:

1. When a question arises as to what the system is going to do, everyone's first inclination is to look for the answer in the functional specifications.

2. When a change is going to be made in the function of the system, the first step in making the change is to modify the functional specifications.

Functional specifications should be written in the user's language. Stated negatively and perhaps more powerfully, functional specifications should *not* contain data processing jargon. They should be easy for the user to read.

Functional specifications should spell out what the system is going to do for the user. They should describe every input the user can introduce to the system, both valid and invalid, and the response of the system to each possible input. In particular, in those cases where introduction of input into the system causes the production of output, functional specifications should describe, in functional terms, how the input is manipulated to produce the output.

Functional specifications should include examples. As a matter of fact, part of the development of functional specifications should be simulation of the system operation. Thus, if the user interface is by terminal, the user should be encouraged to use a terminal to submit definitive data, and the terminal should be controlled to simulate the system's response to the data. If the user submits source documents to the system and receives reports from it, this user-system interaction should be simulated. Such simulation will give the user a better feel for what the functional specifications call for, he will thus be in a better position to specify optimum system operation, and the data used for simulation purposes can make up the examples that will give the functional specifications substance.

A set of standards for functional specifications is given in Appendix B.

Functional specifications will be a voluminous document. The only way the user can in good faith approve this document is to have participated actively at a high level in its development from its inception. This, of course, is a truism, and the basic question is, "How do you get the user involved actively at a high level?" It is not the purpose of this book to explore this question, but briefly, two effective ways are:

1. Have a company policy that spells out what the user's responsibilities in the development of systems are.

2. Educate the user on his responsibilities and how he can carry them out.

User approval of functional specifications means the specifications are frozen. This doesn't mean the specifications can't be changed. It does mean that you, the project leader, are going to make your plans, schedules, and cost estimates for the remainder of the system development on the basis of the approved functional specifications, and if the user changes the specifications, you must have the right to adjust your plans, schedules, and estimates appropriately. Consequently, to the user, approval of the functional specifications means he agrees that any subsequent changes to the specifications must follow a request for change procedure which incorporates the following features.

1. All requests for change must be made in writing by filling out a request for change form. This form requires the documentation of the following information.

    a. A description of the requested change.

    b. A listing of the benefits to be derived from the change.

    c. A classification of the change into one of the following two categories.

       (1) Changes that must be immediately incorporated into the design.

       (2) Changes that are desirable, but which can wait for implementation until the initial system is installed.

2. Postponable changes are tabled until after the initial system is installed.

3. Changes that require immediate attention are handled in the following way.

    a. The project leader spells out the impact of the change on the system and the project, and estimates the change in schedule and budget required to institute the change in specifications.

    b. This information is transmitted to the user.

    c. Implementation of the specifications change is not begun until the user approves the changes in schedule and budget.

A sample request for change form is shown in Appendix C.

An objection sometimes raised to the phased approach to system development is that, in some systems, it is impossible to specify with any accuracy what a system is supposed to do until after it has been installed and experimented with. This objection is most frequently raised by people who work in operations research.

People who raise such an objection are both right and wrong. They are right in that a phased approach won't work for the type of system they posit, and they are wrong to reject the phased approach on this basis. The type of work they are describing is *research*, where the outcome of the work is unknown beforehand. We are proposing a phased approach for project work only, where the goal to be reached can be predetermined. Only if this is the case can you project what the cost to reach the goal will be, and then and only then is project management appropriate. Research is a worthwhile undertaking, but it is not managed on a project basis. Your company cannot have its cake and eat it also. Either they want to leave the end goal undefined, in which case costs and deadlines are by definition indeterminable, or else they want a system developed on a project basis, in which case they must be willing to come to a detailed agreement as to the system specifications before the system is designed and constructed.

## EXERCISES

1. You are negotiating with your user as to what the system is going to do. You discover that, to determine whether the system can be constructed to do what the user wishes, you must design the system in great detail. Are you in the analysis or design phase?

2. All six of the people working on your project are writing programs. What phase are you in?

3. Your manager tells you that Charlie Brown has been promoted to Programming Su-

pervisor and you are going to replace Charlie as project leader on the inventory system development project. Your manager tells you that the development of the system has just entered the construction phase. What is your response to this statement?

4. In Appendix D is a case study. In what development phase is the system described in this case study?

5. When does the analysis phase end and the design phase begin?

6. As a project leader, what should you do if the user requests that a change be made to the functional specifications he has previously approved?

7. When does the user make a decision on the feasibility of developing a data processing system?

8. Why does the user make a decision on the feasibility of developing a data processing system more than once?

9. Why can more confidence be placed in the development and operating cost projections for a data processing system at the end of each successive phase in the development of the system?

10. How do you know that, with each passing phase in the development of a data processing system, the specifications for the system are becoming more firm?

11. Who signs off on the design specifications for a data processing system?

12. Who sits on the design review committee?

13. What would be some typical groups represented on the design review committee?

14. What would be a good way to develop the examples to be included in the functional specifications of a data processing system?

# THE ACCEPTANCE TEST

To plan the development of a system, you must know what constitutes the end of system development. An effective method for marking the end of system development is to have the system pass an acceptance test.

The acceptance test is a test procedure that the user develops or approves. The user agrees, prior to the running of the test, that if the system passes the test, the system is accepted as operational.

Examples of acceptance tests are:

1. Benchmarks: Specially developed tests.

2. Pilot tests: The system is installed on an extremely limited basis.

3. Parallel operation: The system is installed but the previous system is not discontinued.

In all instances, it is necessary to specify not only what the acceptance test will be, but also what constitutes successful completion of the test, which may be predetermined results in the case of a benchmark or specification of what constitutes equivalent operation in the case of parallel operation.

The checking for equivalent results in parallel testing is a large-scale job for which adequate plans must be made. In some instances, special computer programs or unit record equipment plugboards can be constructed to automate part of the comparison procedure. Decisions concerning whether checked out totals are sufficient or whether details must be verified must be made.

Included in the acceptance test should be some demonstration of competence on the part of user personnel in the use of the system. As a consequence, formal user training must be completed prior to the acceptance test (although the acceptance testing period is an excellent time to follow up this formal training with simulated on-the-job experience), and to conduct an effective training program, user procedure manuals and all input forms must be available for use during the training program.

The proper time to develop the specifications for the acceptance test is at the time the functional specifications are being developed. Not only does such an approach satisfy the requirement that the user agree to the specifications of the acceptance test prior to the running of the test, it also forces the kind of nuts and bolts thinking necessary to come up with functional specifications in which the user has confidence. In this sense, development of the acceptance test is similar to the simulation of system operation that should be part of every functional specifications development effort, and the two might well be developed at the same time to the benefit of both the effectiveness of the simulation and the acceptance test, and the quality of the functional specifications in general.

## EXERCISES

1. What marks the end of the construction phase in the development of a data processing system?
2. When must the user and the data processing department agree on the specifications for the acceptance test?
3. What aspects of the acceptance test should the agreement between the user and the data processing department cover?
4. When is the best time to give the user practice in the operation of the system? Why?

# PROJECT ORGANIZATION

# 5
# PROJECT ORGANIZATION

This chapter is a diversion of sorts. It contains no information a project leader would apply directly to his job. Instead, it is concerned with the nature of project organization and why a manager might adopt such an organization. Consequently, it will be useful to you as a project leader only in the sense of giving you a perspective as to why your job exists.

The classic organization structure is functional. A schematic of a functionally organized systems and programming department is shown in Fig. 5-1.

The goal a manager strives for by adopting a functional organization is to develop and maintain expertise. By dividing his department along functional lines he encourages people to specialize and become experts in particular functions.

Not uncommonly, an organization is assigned the responsibility for attaining several goals, and to reach these goals on time, it is necessary for the organization to work on more than one of these projects at the same time. For example, a systems and programming department may be required to develop an order entry system, an inventory control system, and a production control system, all in the same general time frame.

If these concurrently running projects require the efforts of people from most

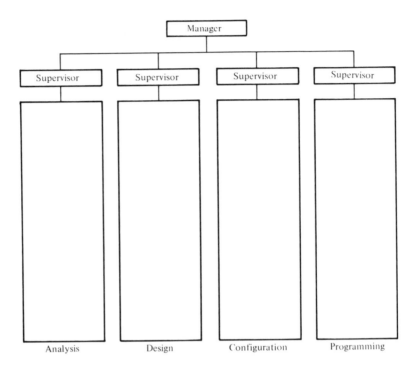

**Fig. 5-1  Functional organization.**

or all of the functional groups in the organization, then in a functionally organized department, the manager must personally coordinate each of these projects or project coordination becomes fragmented among the functional supervisors. The first alternative is usually not humanly possible, and the second is not desirable, since fragmented coordination is typically lack of coordination.

The manager solves this problem by delegating his responsibilities for a particular project to a project leader. In this way a project organization is superimposed on the functional organization. (A schematic of such an organization for a systems and programming department working on two concurrent projects is shown in Fig. 5-2.) In such an organization, the manager looks to his functional supervisors to maintain the professional quality of the work being done and to his project leaders to pursue thier individual project goals.

There are inherent conflicts between people with functional responsibility and people with project responsibility. For example, functional supervisors generally institute procedures for accomplishing various functions because they have discovered that these procedures give them the quality of results they want. As a consequence, functional managers generally insist that these procedures be followed no matter what. Project leaders sometimes feel that, because they are con-

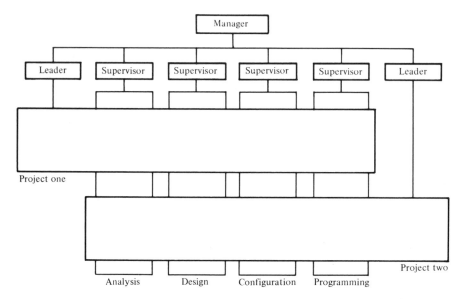

**Fig. 5-2   Project organization.**

cerned with coordinating many different functions to achieve project goals, the same quality can be maintained in less time-consuming ways, and they consider the functional manager's procedures to be a hindrance to achieving project goals.

Project organization institutionalizes these conflicts, brings them into the open, and allows the manager to resolve each one in the light of the overall situation as he sees it. All this is the case if the project leaders report to the manager either directly or through a line that does not involve functional supervisors. If the project leaders report to functional supervisors, the degree to which the manager is exposed to the project point of view is, to some extent, limited. The greater the significance of the project in terms of the benefits to be derived and/or the resources required, the more directly will the manager want the project leader to report to him.

Project organization can be carried out in one of two ways.

1. Individuals can be selected from the various functional groups for assignment to a project team. In this type of project organization, the project leader coordinates the activities of the team members, and the functional supervisors monitor the activities of their personnel to see that they conform to functional standards.

2. Each functional supervisor coordinates those project activities for which he has functional responsibility. The project leader monitors the activities of the

functional groups to see that they mesh in such a manner that the project goal is achieved.

Thus, under the first type of organization, a system and programming project leader would be assigned personnel from the analysis, design, configuration, and programming groups, he would coordinate the activities of these personnel, and each functional supervisor would see that his personnel carried out their activities in a professional way. The analysis supervisor would see that the analysts assigned to the project conformed to analysis standards in carrying out their analysis activities; the design supervisor would see that the designers assigned conformed to design standards; and so on.

Under the second type of organization, the analysis supervisor would coordinate the analysis activities for the project, the design supervisor would coordinate the design activities, and so on, and the project leader would see that the activities of the analysis, design, configuration, and programming groups mesh in such a manner that consistent and timely progress toward the project goal is made.

Thus, in the first type of organization, the project leader does the coordinating, and in the second type he sees that the coordinating is done in an integrated fashion. The first type of organization is typical of projects involving small numbers of people, the second of projects involving large numbers. The rest of this book assumes the first type of project organization.

The position of project leader for a particular project lasts only as long as the project lasts, and by definition, all projects end. Thus, a man may be project leader on one project at one point in time and a project member on another project at another point in time.

When a person isn't working on a project, he returns to the functional group in which his specialty lies, where he performs such functional tasks as procedure refinement, research into new techniques, self education, conduct of education for more junior personnel, and so on.

To recapitulate:

1. A project is an organized effort to reach a predefined goal. The goal has some aspect of uniqueness, the implication being that, once the goal is reached, the project is over. The landing of a man on the moon, the climbing of a challenging mountain peak, the turnover of a new model car to production, and the implementation of a new demand deposit data processing system are all projects. Note the orientation of the project toward a unique, terminal goal as contrasted with activities such as the mass production of cars and the updating of passbooks, which are activities done over and over again.

2. Projects are also to be distinguished from research efforts. Projects and research efforts share the common characteristic of uniqueness of goals. They

differ in that a project goal is predefined, whereas a research goal is necessarily vague. Research is concerned with developing new technologies; projects are concerned with using known technologies to reach predefined goals.

3. The essence of project management is that a single individual, the project leader, is given total responsibility for attainment of the project goal, on schedule, within cost, and according to specifications.

4. Attainment of a project goal requires the use of several different specialties.

5. Project organization doesn't replace functional organization. It's superimposed on functional organization.

6. Specialists are maintained by the functional organization. However, they can't remain detached in a staff advisory function, since they're committed to a project.

# PROJECT PLANNING

# PLANNING

Plans are necessary to:

1. Project schedules.
2. Project costs.
3. Direct activities in a coordinated fashion toward a predetermined goal.

As shown in Fig. 6-1, you, as a project leader, will, during the development of a data processing system, have to develop at least five plans.

Manpower will be involved in all five plans. Computer time will certainly be required for the construction phase and may be needed in the design and/or analysis phases.

EXERCISE

What are plans used for?

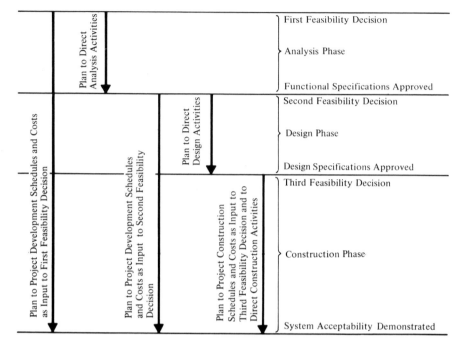

**Fig. 6-1   Project planning requirements.**

# MANPOWER PLANNING, PART ONE

Figure 6-1 shows the need to plan for five different "jobs".

1. The analysis, design, and construction of a system.
2. The analysis of a system.
3. The design and construction of a system.
4. The design of a system.
5. The construction of a system.

A plan for the manpower required to do any one of these jobs is developed as follows.

1. The tasks making up the job are enumerated.
2. The dependency between the tasks is determined.
3. The external restraints under which the job must be done are determined.
4. Personnel are allocated to the tasks.
5. The time required to do each task is estimated.
6. Allowance for contingencies is made.

## 7.1  ENUMERATING TASKS

The first step in developing a manpower plan is to make an exhaustive list of the tasks that must be done to complete the job at hand. Each task should be such that a man working on it full-time would need at least one week but not more than one month to complete it. In this way the job is subdivided into tasks of duration small enough to maximize the reliability of the estimate of the time required to do each task.

Jobs are subdivided into tasks on the basis of:

1. The functions performed by the system being developed.
2. The activities performed to get the job done.

For example, in the case study in Appendix D, each program performs a function. Thus:

Program 2:  Validates transaction data.
Program 4:  Updates the master file.
Program 7:  Does payroll calculations.

Consequently, the programs in the payroll system constitute a functional basis on which to isolate tasks. As another example, in an accounts receivable operation, the following functions are performed:

1. Opening new accounts.
2. Checking credit.
3. Posting credit sales.
4. Posting cash receipts.
5. Issuing statements.
6. Making billing adjustments.

Thus, listing the functions performed by a system requires comprehensive knowledge of the system being developed, which is why the confidence level in cost and schedule projections is so low before the system is specified.

On the other hand, the activities performed to get the job done remain relatively constant regardless of the system being developed. Thus, in the analysis phase, typical activities are:

1. Conducting interviews.
2. Analyzing existing reports, forms and records, etc.

In the construction phase, typical activities are:

1. Coding.
2. Converting files.
3. System testing.

The tasks needed to get a job done are enumerated by cross-referencing activities against functions. Thus, if the job were to analyze the accounts receivable operation, part of the grid on which tasks can be isolated would appear as shown in Fig. 7-1.

The big danger in developing the task list is that you may overlook one or more tasks. When listing functions you have nothing to rely on but your knowledge of the system, but when listing activities, you can use a checklist to remind you of the typical activities associated with each development phase. An example checklist is shown in Appendix E.

We are now going to develop an example of listing the tasks making up a job. In developing an example, there is characteristically a conflict between developing an example that is complicated but realistic and developing an example which emphasizes the points to be made but is simplified and unrealistic. We face this dilemma now and are going to opt for the example that is graphic but simplified, so be warned.

For example, suppose the job is to construct an assembler, linker, and loader for computer *X*. The functional and design specifications for this software package have been developed and approved. It is a design decision that the programs, most particularly the assembler, are to be written in computer *X* assembly code.

| Functions | Activities | | | | |
|---|---|---|---|---|---|
| | Conduct Interviews | Analyze Reports | Analyze Forms | Analyze Records | Etc. |
| Open New Accounts | | | | | |
| Check Credit | | | | | |
| Post Credit Sales | | | | | |
| Post Cash Receipts | | | | | |
| Issue Statements | | | | | |
| Make Adjustments | | | | | |
| Etc. | | | | | |

Fig. 7-1   Task grid, analysis of accounts receivable.

Consequently, it is decided to develop a "boot assembler" that will run on computer $Y$, a computer with an already existing software system. The boot assembler will run on computer $Y$, accept computer $X$ source code, and produce computer $X$ object code, but will be written in computer $Y$ source code so it can be assembled and run with the already existing computer $Y$ software. The system to be constructed thus performs the following functions:

1. Boot assemble.
2. Load.
3. Assemble.
4. Link.

Up to now the reality of the example has not been degraded by any simplification.

Now, let us suppose that the following activities must be performed to get the job done.

1. Code
2. Assemble.
3. Develop unit test data.
4. Perform unit test.
5. Perform system test.

A quick look at Appendix E is sufficient to demonstrate that the above activity list is a gross simplification. Many essential activities—such as preparing internal specifications, writing user procedure manuals, and developing the system test—have been left out. Such is the sacrifice we authors must make for the sake of clarity.

The function-activity grid for this project is then as shown in Fig. 7-2. The task list can then be read from this grid as follows.

1. Code boot assembler.
2. Code loader.
3. Code assembler.
4. Code linker.
5. Assemble boot assembler.
6. Assemble loader.
7. Assemble assembler.
8. Assemble linker.
9. Develop boot assembler unit test data.
10. Develop loader unit test data.
11. Develop assembler unit test data.
12. Develop linker unit test data.
13. Unit test boot assembler.
14. Unit test loader.
15. Unit test assembler.

| Functions \ Activities | Code | Assemble | Develop Unit Test Data | Perform Unit Test | Perform System testTest |
|---|---|---|---|---|---|
| Boot Assembler | X | X | X | X | – |
| Loader | X | X | X | X | X |
| Assembler | X | X | X | X | X |
| Linker | X | X | X | X | X |

**Fig. 7-2 Task grid, software package construction.**

16. Unit test linker.
17. System test.

## 7.2 DETERMINING TASK DEPENDENCY

Typically, when doing a job, some tasks must be finished before others can be started. For example, a program must be coded before it can be assembled, it must be assembled before it can be unit tested, and unit test data for the program must also be developed before the program can be unit tested. As another example, in our software construction project, the boot assembler must be debugged before the loader, assembler, or linker can be assembled. And as a second example from our software project, since the assembler and linker cannot be unit tested until they can be loaded, and since it is the loader which will load the assembler and linker, it follows that the loader must be unit tested before the assembler or linker can be unit tested.

You must rely on your knowledge of the system and your knowledge of the process of developing systems to determine the dependency between tasks. For example:

1. Your knowledge of the purpose of the boot assembler tells you that assembly of the loader, assembler and linker are dependent on the debugging of the boot assembler.
2. Your knowledge of the purpose of the loader tells you that unit testing of the assembler and linker are dependent on unit testing of the loader.

3. Your knowledge of the process of developing systems tells you that assembling a program is dependent on coding it and that unit testing a program is dependent on both assembling it and on the development of unit test data.

In addition, some task dependencies are a function of the approach you decide to take in doing your job. For example, if you decide to use the assembler to develop unit test data for the linker, then development of this test data is dependent on the debugging of the assembler, while if you decide to develop unit test data for the linker from scratch, then this task is independent of the debugging of the assembler.

A systematic way of ferreting out the dependency between tasks is to create a list of the tasks making up a job; number the tasks; and then, following each task in the list, enter the number of the tasks on which the given task directly depends. Figure 7-3 shows such a completed task list for our software project.

| Task | Dependencies |
|---|---|
| 1. CODE BOOT ASSEMBLER | — |
| 2. CODE LOADER | — |
| 3. CODE ASSEMBLER | — |
| 4. CODE LINKER | — |
| 5. ASSEMBLE BOOT ASSEMBLER | 1 |
| 6. ASSEMBLE LOADER | 2, 13 |
| 7. ASSEMBLE ASSEMBLER | 3, 13 |
| 8. ASSEMBLE LINKER | 4, 13 |
| 9. DEVELOP BOOT ASSEMBLER TEST DATA | — |
| 10. DEVELOP LOADER TEST DATA | — |
| 11. DEVELOP ASSEMBLER TEST DATA | — |
| 12. DEVELOP LINKER TEST DATA | — |
| 13. UNIT TEST BOOT ASSEMBLER | 5, 9 |
| 14. UNIT TEST LOADER | 6, 10 |
| 15. UNIT TEST ASSEMBLER | 7, 11, 14 |
| 16. UNIT TEST LINKER | 8, 12, 14 |
| 17. SYSTEM TEST | 15, 16 |

**Fig. 7-3   Task dependency list.**

Use of such a dependency list cannot, of course, guarantee that, after its use, you'll have identified all task dependencies. All it can do is assure that you've systematically contemplated each task with regard to the tasks on which it depends. However, the methodical nature of the approach is sufficient to recommend it—by using it you'll unquestionably recognize more dependencies than you would without its use.

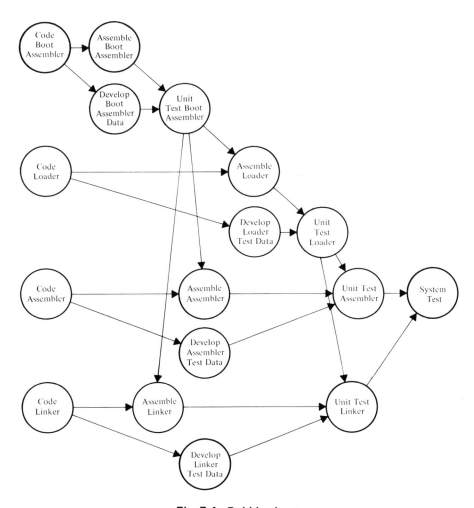

**Fig. 7-4  Bubble chart.**

A convenient way of summarizing the dependency between tasks is to construct a "bubble chart." A bubble chart for our example software project is shown in Fig. 7-4. On a bubble chart, the bubbles represent tasks and the arrows represent the dependencies between tasks.

The bubble chart really shows no information that isn't already presented on the task dependency list. However, the bubble chart presents this information in a more immediately meaningful way.

There are at least three reasons why you should always develop a bubble chart in the process of constructing a manpower plan.

1. Developing a bubble chart slows you down and forces you to spend more time thinking about task dependencies than you might otherwise. As a result, you're likely to recognize dependencies you might have otherwise overlooked.

2. Planning isn't a one-time thing. As development on your project proceeds, progress will deviate from plan. It then becomes necessary to modify your plan to retain your best posture toward your project goal. At the time you modify your plan, you'll want to refresh your memory as to task dependency. A bubble chart is a clear, concise method for documenting these dependencies for future reference.

3. After you develop your plan, you'll have to get your manager's approval of it, since he's the one who has to supply you with the manpower that both of you agree is needed to meet your goal. In getting his approval, one of the things of which you must convince him is the dependency between the tasks making up your job. (Have you ever negotiated with the manager who says, "Hum. So you need three men for a year. That's too long. Let's put six men on it and get it done in six months," when the dependency between tasks dictates that a year is as soon as you can get the job done no matter how many men are put on it?) A bubble chart is an effective presentation technique for getting across your task dependency situation.

## 7.3  DETERMINING EXTERNAL RESTRAINTS

Project activities are not carried out in a vacuum, but in a living environment that places limits on when and how these activities can be performed. These limits are what is referred to by the term "external restraints."

To develop a realistic plan, you must know what these external restraints are. But because it's in the future that you will contend with external restraints and because, by definition, they are beyond your control, the best you can do is get commitments from those who do control them as to what the external restraints under which you will operate will be.

External restraints fall into at least 3 classes.

1. Deadlines: In occasional contrast to the other two types of external restraints, you infrequently have difficulty getting commitments on deadlines. People to whom you're obligated to deliver products are generally quite explicit as to when they must have the products and display great resoluteness concerning these commitments as time passes.

2. Delivery dates: It may be necessary for someone else to deliver a product to you before you can get beyond a certain point in the development of your

system. For example, in our software project, we can't do any unit testing of the loader until we get access to the new computer or a reasonable facsimile thereof. Thus, availability on time of a prototype or existence of a simulator becomes an external restraint on our project.

3. Turnaround rates: System development requires some services of a repetitive nature. Debugging shots and keypunching are two examples of this type of service. Here it's not delivery date (the service is essentially always available)

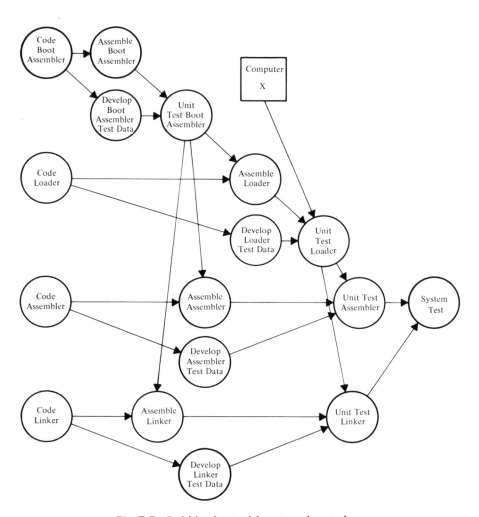

**Fig. 7-5  Bubble chart with external restraints.**

but turnaround that concerns you. For example, the actual number of hours it takes to debug a program is relatively fixed. However, the turnaround on debugging shots will determine the period of elapsed time over which the actual time is spread. For example, if turnaround is essentially instantaneous, actual time and elapsed time will be equivalent. However, if turnaround is 24 hours, a person will be able to spend an average of only half of each day in a debugging mode, and elapsed time will be "double" actual time.

The external restraints on which your plans are based should be an explicit part of your plans.

1. Deadlines will appear in your schedule.
2. Turnaround rates should be enumerated in a list that becomes a permanent part of your plan documentation.
3. Delivery dates can be put on your bubble chart.

The external restraint concerning availability of the new computer is shown in the bubble chart in Fig. 7-5. Use a symbol, which is different than a circle, to represent external restraints, so they can be clearly distinguished from your project tasks, which are represented by circles.

## EXERCISES

1. What are two bases on which to subdivide a job into tasks?
2. Name three kinds of external restraints.
3. What kind of external restraints can be shown on a bubble chart?
4. As you will recall in our answer to Exercise 4 at the end of Chapter 3, we agreed to consider the payroll system described in Appendix D as having just completed the design phase—that is, the design specifications have been completed and approved by the design review committee. You are project leader for the payroll system project, and it is now your responsibility to develop a manpower plan for the construction phase of this project. You are to plan the manpower required to take the system from its present design state to the point where the payroll department begins to use the system to generate the company's paychecks and to maintain its payroll records.

   An agreement has already been reached with the payroll department that the system acceptance test will consist of running the new payroll system in parallel with the old for four payroll cycles. The payroll system cycles twice a month. Therefore, you must process two months of payroll data in parallel. It is not necessary to conduct this parallel operation in "real time." That is, you may save up data from previous payroll cycles and then cycle the new system as frequently as you think you can to produce and check the parallel results.

   The decision has also been made to get the new payroll system on the air as rapidly as possible. As a consequence, it has been decided that only programs 1-5, 7-18, and 25 are to be included in the initial construction effort.

You are now going to take the first steps in developing the manpower plan for the construction phase of the payroll system project. Specifically, you are to develop:

1. A list of the tasks to be performed in the construction phase.
2. A bubble chart showing the dependence between these tasks.

# MANPOWER PLANNING, PART TWO

## 8.1 ALLOCATING PERSONNEL

Some general rules of thumb for allocating personnel to tasks are as follows:

1. There must be some relation between the demands of the task and the skills of the person assigned. Assigning a person to a task that underutilizes his skills has as many unfortunate consequences as assigning him to a task which is clearly beyond his abilities to perform.

2. Within the limitations in (1) above, it is desirable to assign a man tasks that give him an opportunity to widen both the range and extent of his skills.

3. Assign a person related tasks. At least two benefits accrue.

   a. The work will be more meaningful to the person.
   b. What the person learns in completing one task can be used to complete the other tasks more effectively.

   An obvious example is to assign the task of debugging a program to the person who wrote the program.

4. It is generally the case that certain tasks are more critical to the overall job than others. For example, in the payroll system, the system is handicapped if

program 13 will not run, but it is completely inoperable if either program 4 or 7 is down. It is also generally true that certain people are more reliable than others. To keep catastrophe to a minimum, it generally pays to assign the more reliable people to the more critical tasks.

One aspect of task assignment is the question of what tasks you, the project leader, assign yourself. In making this assignment, you must take into consideration the fact that, by virtue of being project leader, you have assumed certain responsibilities which will make demands on your time in rough proportion to the size of your project. One way to measure project size is in terms of the number of people assigned. As an upper limit, if your project is going to require the concurrent assignment of any more than 5 or 6 people, you should plan on having all your time consumed by your project leader responsibilities.

For projects of smaller size, you can assign yourself tasks that will consume some, but not all of your time. As project leader, you are the coordinator of the project as a whole. Consequently, the tasks you assign yourself should be ones that keep you oriented to the overall system, rather than making you an expert on some relatively small part of the system. Therefore, writing the user manual and developing the system test are examples of the type of tasks it would be preferable to assign yourself.

Most data processing system development projects are small enough so that, as project leader, you are a first line supervisor—that is, you are the first line of supervision in your organization. As a consequence, like any other first-line supervisor, you must have an appreciation of the skills your people use at their work, because when they run into trouble (that is, when they reach the limit of their current skill level), it is to you that they will look for help; they will expect you to either provide the help directly or know where to go to find the help. All this raises the question:

To perform this first-line supervisor function of skills enhancement, you are going to have to maintain your analysis, design, and programming skills at a high enough level to perform this function. This doesn't mean you have to be the greatest analyst, designer, or programmer that ever lived. It does mean that you must keep yourself current in these areas, so you can understand the team members when they explain their problems to you. How are you going to maintain this skill level if you don't periodically assign yourself a detailed task?

The answer to this question is that, if you have assigned people according to the principle that their tasks will require them to expand their skills, then it will frequently be the case that a project member will encounter difficulty in completing his task and will come to you for help. Providing this assistance will give you plenty of opportunity to remain in contact with the skills being used by the project members. The point is not that, as a project leader, you should not get involved in detail work—to the contrary, you should. The point is that you should not tie yourself down for long periods of time to a specific detailed task. Instead, you should keep yourself flexible, so you can work on detail with the project member who needs your help today. As soon as you have helped him solve his problem, the chances are some other project member will then have developed a problem, and you should be free to move over and assist him.

## 8.2  TIME ESTIMATING

Two of the main factors determining the time required to do a task appear to be:

1. The complexity of the task.
2. The capability of the person assigned to the task.

Practice indicates that there are three main methods for evaluating these factors to determine task time.

### 8.2.1  Professional Judgment

With this method, a person relies on his memory of his and his acquaintances' experience and on his unformulated impressions of the relative importance of various factors to come up with an estimate. If the person is experienced in the applications area for which the estimates are being made, he may be able to come up with relatively precise estimates. The disadvantages of this technique are:

a. It can't be used unless you have access to someone experienced in the applications area in which you are working.
b. The technique is inclined to give insufficient consideration to variations in capability. That is, the estimator tends to come up with an estimate of how long it would take him personally to do the task regardless of who's actually going to be assigned to the task.

### 8.2.2  Historical Technique

The question is: How long will it take person $A$ to do task $X$? The approach is to find some other task (task $Y$) that has been done in the past that resembles task $X$ as closely as possible, and that was done by a person (person $B$) who has capabilities in common with person $A$. The time it took person $B$ to do task $Y$ is then adjusted on the basis of significant differences between tasks $X$ and $Y$ and between the capabilities of persons $A$ and $B$, and this adjusted time is used as the estimate of the time it will take person $A$ to do task $X$. The major drawback to the historical approach is that few installations have enough reliable historical data to allow use of the technique.

### 8.2.3  Use of Standards

A standard involves the methodical assignment of values to various characteristics of the task to be done and the person assigned to do it. These values are then combined in a standard way to yield an estimate. The drawback to standards is that the ones in existence are primitive and gross. Their main attraction is that they are the only technique which promises the possibility for systematic improvement of estimating skills. Some examples of estimating standards are given in Appendix F.

Since only the standards method spells out a procedure for arriving at a time estimate, it alone offers the possibility that repeated comparison of estimated against actual time will reveal inadequacies in the procedure, which can then be corrected. Of course, for this to happen we must be able to collect reliable information on the time actually spent on various tasks. And this state of affairs will not come about until we stop using our time reporting procedures as a tool for evaluating personnel performance.

When you, as a project leader, are estimating the time to do various tasks, you should keep in mind that your estimates are not only going to be used to determine schedules and project costs, they also set goals for people to meet. As C. Northcote Parkinson has observed, where people are concerned, work expands to fill the time allocated to it. Perhaps "at least" should be added. The moral is that if you make an estimate and it's overrun by a small amount, don't loosen up your estimating technique. Your estimate wasn't too tight, and the possibility exists that it's still too loose.

### EXERCISES

1. State four general rules of thumb for allocating personnel to tasks.
2. What kind of tasks should you, as a project leader, assign to yourself?
3. Give a couple of examples of tasks that are of the type you might assign to yourself.
4. In Appendix H are the internal specifications for program 2 of the payroll system. John Nazarevitz is assigned the responsibility for developing this program. (A resume for Nazarevitz appears in the case study in Appendix D.) Use the estimating standard in Appendix G to estimate the number of man-days it will take Nazarevitz to develop this program. The program is to be written in COBOL.

# MANPOWER PLANNING, PART THREE

## 9.1 DEVELOPING THE BAR CHART

As a result of completing the preceding steps in the development of a manpower plan, you now have available the following information:

1. A bubble chart showing:
   a. The tasks making up the job.
   b. The dependency between these tasks.
   c. The delivery dates on which these tasks depend.
2. A list of:
   a. Deadlines.
   b. Turnaround frequencies.
3. An indication of the skill requirements demanded by each task.
4. An estimate of how long it will take a person with the required skills to do each task.

It is now time to combine this information into a task plan.

An effective tool for organizing your manpower planning information into a task plan is the bar chart.

To give an example of a bar chart, suppose we have developed the following information with respect to the software system construction project.

1. Figure 9-1 is a bubble chart showing tasks, task dependency, and delivery dates.

2. The deadline for the software system is 30 weeks from now.

3. Computer X will first be available for testing purposes 17 weeks from now.

4. Unit test computer turnaround time is a maximum of one-half hour and is usually shorter. (Of course, here we are again simplifying for the sake of

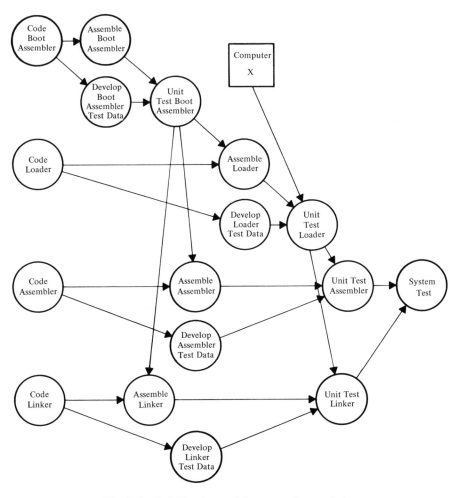

**Fig. 9-1  Bubble chart with external restraints.**

clarity. However, later in this chapter we'll remove this simplifying assumption to show the impact of a longer turnaround on a manpower plan.)

5. Blocks of system test computer time can be scheduled whenever required.

6. Abbott, Baker, Chisholm, and Delaney are available for assignment to the project. All have the skills required to do any of the tasks on the project. (This is, of course, also a gross simplification. However, for sake of exposition we'll persist in it and only note parenthetically that, generally speaking, skill requirements place significant limitations on your options as far as personnel assignment to tasks is concerned.)

7. The man-weeks required to do each task is estimated as follows:

| | |
|---|---|
| Code boot assembler | 8 |
| Code loader | 3 |
| Code assembler | 12 |
| Code linker | 12 |
| Assemble boot assembler | 1 |
| Assemble loader | 1 |
| Assemble assembler | 1 |
| Assembler linker | 1 |
| Develop boot assembler test | 2 |
| Develop loader test data | 1 |
| Develop assembler test data | 3 |
| Develop linker test data | 3 |
| Unit test boot assembler | 5 |
| Unit test loader | 1 |
| Unit test assembler | 8 |
| Unit test linker | 8 |
| System test | 8 |

(Obviously, in putting these estimates together we're once more simplifying by making certain that each task time estimate is an integral number of manweeks.)

A possible bar chart for this project is shown in Fig. 9-2.

A bar chart is basically a graph. Time is marked off on the x axis, and people are listed on the y axis. Tasks are then graphed in the body of the chart to show who is going to do what task, when they are going to start, and how long it is going to take them.

The bar chart in Fig. 9-2 was constructed in a completely mechanical way.

1. It was decided that two men would do the system test. (This wasn't an arbitrary decision. From the description of the job, it looks as if the two main parts of the system are the assembler and the linker and that one man should be assigned to each. Consequently, it was decided that both these men would

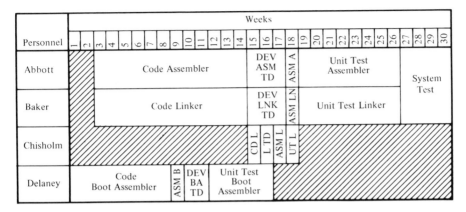

**Fig. 9-2   Bar chart.**

share in conducting the system test.) Since this task requires 8 man-weeks, it should take four weeks to complete. (This is an example of the difference between actual time [8 man-weeks] and elapsed time [4 weeks]. Having made this distinction, it becomes clear that what we were estimating in Chapter 8 was actual time, not elapsed time.) Abbott and Baker were assigned to do the system test.

2. According to the bubble chart, both the assembler and the linker must be unit tested before system testing can begin. The bar chart shows that we have scheduled system testing to begin in week 27. Therefore, the latest unit testing of the assembler and linker can be completed is in week 26. Consequently, to complete this project in a minimum amount of time, these tasks must be done in parallel. Therefore, one was assigned to Abbott and one to Baker.

3. It was decided that one man would do all tasks related to developing a program. Consequently, Abbott was assigned all tasks related to developing the assembler, and Baker all tasks related to developing the linker. These tasks were arranged in the order: code, develop test data, assemble, and unit test for the following reasons.

   a. According to the bubble chart, coding must come before assembling or developing test data, and both of these must come before unit testing.

   b. Developing test data has no other dependencies, so it was scheduled before assembling, which is also dependent on the boot assembler being unit tested.

4. The bubble chart indicates that the loader must be unit tested before the assembler or the linker can be unit tested. The bar chart shows that unit testing of the assembler and the linker are to begin in week 19. Therefore, the latest

the loader can be unit tested is week 18. Chisholm is assigned to this task, and the other tasks involved in developing the loader are also assigned to him and are scheduled in the same way as the assembler and linker tasks were scheduled for Abbott and Baker.

5. According to the bubble chart, before the loader, assembler, or linker can be assembled, the boot assembler must be unit tested. The bar chart shows that the loader is to be assembled before the assembler or linker and that the loader is to be assembled during week 17. Therefore, boot assembler unit testing must be complete at the end of week 16. This establishes the end point for the scheduling of the boot assembler development tasks, which are assigned to Delaney.

This mechanical method for developing the bar chart in Fig. 9-2 is called back-end loading. A bar chart developed by this method has two distinct features.

1. It is a task plan that will schedule a job to be done in a minimum amount of time. To use PERT-CPM terminology, it establishes overall job time as critical path time. As a matter of fact, you can read the critical path off such a bar chart. For the bar chart in Fig. 9-2, the critical path is all the boot assembler development tasks, the assembling and unit testing of the loader, the unit testing of either the assembler or the linker, and system testing. (It could be maintained that assembling the boot assembler isn't on the critical path, since it can be done in parallel with the development of the boot assembler test data, but it is probably impractical to assign these tasks to different people. As a consequence, both must be assigned to one person, which means they can't be done in parallel.)

2. A backend loaded bar chart shows the slack available. Slack is another PERT-CPM term and can be defined as follows. If everybody starts working as soon as possible (week 1 in our case), slack is the amount of time certain tasks can slip without postponing the completion date for the job. For example, in the bar chart in Fig. 9-2, Abbott and Baker each have two weeks of slack, Chisholm has 14 weeks, and Delaney none. As far as slack is concerned, the important thing about backend loading is that it squeezes all slack out of the schedule—personnel aren't brought on the job until they must do their tasks on schedule to avoid having the job miss its deadline.

Being a textbook example, all the task dependencies and delivery dates in the software development project as currently specified mesh perfectly to allow all tasks to be done just in time to meet the deadline. However, if the deadline had been any tighter, the project would have been impossible—30 weeks is the minimum amount of time in which this job can be done.

The importance of delivery dates cannot be overlooked either. For example, if computer $X$ was first available 18 weeks from now, backend loading produces the bar chart shown in Fig. 9-3, and the deadline must be relaxed by one week if

| Personnel | Weeks (1–31) |
|---|---|
| Abbott | Code Assembler → DEV ASM TD → ASM A → Unit Test Assembler → System Test |
| Baker | Code Linker → DEV LNK TD → ASM LN → Unit Test Linker → System Test |
| Chisholm | CD L / L TD / ASM L / UT L |
| Delaney | Code Boot Assembler → ASM B → DEV BA TD → Unit Test Boot Assembler |

**Fig. 9-3   Bar chart in which a delivery date results in a later completion date.**

the project is to remain possible. (The difference between the charts in Figs. 9-2 and 9-3 is that in Fig. 9-2 the loader can be unit tested in week 18, while in Fig. 9-3 it can't be unit tested until week 19.)

The bar chart in Fig. 9-3 indicates that there is little overlap between Chisholm's and Delaney's schedules. As a matter of fact, if completion of the loader could be delayed just one week, Chisholm could take on responsibility for the boot assembler, and Delaney could be released for other assignments. This reassignment of personnel has at least two advantages and one disadvantage. The advantages are:

1. Chisholm's work on the boot assembler should give him knowledge that he can apply in developing the loader.

2. There are only three, rather than four, people who have to communicate with each other on the project. This should reduce the intra-project communication time required on the project.

The disadvantage is that backup is reduced, so that personnel loss carries a greater potential impact.

However, these advantages and disadvantages are academic unless its possible to delay the project completion date by one more week. This is because of the dependency between tasks; if unit testing of the loader is delayed one week, then unit testing of the assembler and linker is delayed one week, which delays system testing by one week. A bar chart with this relaxed project deadline is shown in Fig. 9-4.

Rearrangement of tasks within a bar chart is a normal operation in developing a manpower plan. During this rearrangement you should keep your bubble chart available for ready reference so, when rearranging, you don't inadvertently violate a task dependency when scheduling tasks.

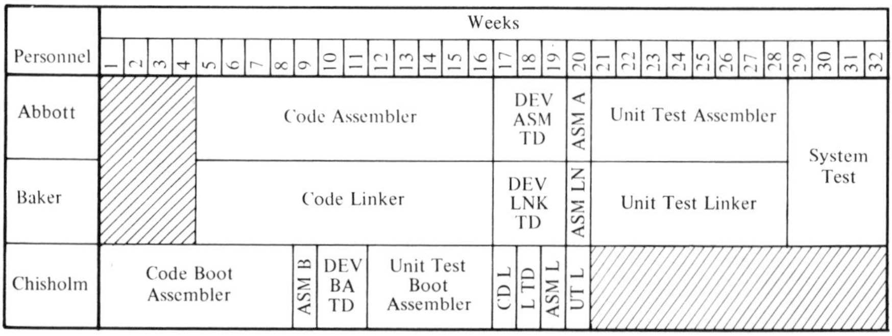

**Fig. 9-4   Bar chart with a relaxed project deadline.**

Now let's see what happens to our bar chart if unit test computer turnaround time deteriorates to the point where a person can productively spend only half of each day on assembly and unit test tasks. A backend loaded bar chart for this kind of external restraint is shown in Fig. 9-5.

In Fig. 9-5 we see the distinction between actual and elapsed time in another form. For example, it still takes Abbott 8 man-weeks to unit test the assembler, but now these 8 man-weeks are spread over 16 elapsed weeks. There are several typical results of such a situation.

1. People are assigned multiple tasks to be worked on in parallel. For example, Baker is expected to finish developing the linker test data at the same time as he is assembling the linker.

2. People are required to work on multiple projects in parallel. For example, during most of the period during which Chisholm is unit testing the boot assembler, he is able to devote only half his time productively to the software project.

3. The completion date is significantly delayed, because it is elapsed time, not actual time, that's meaningful as far as the critical path is concerned.

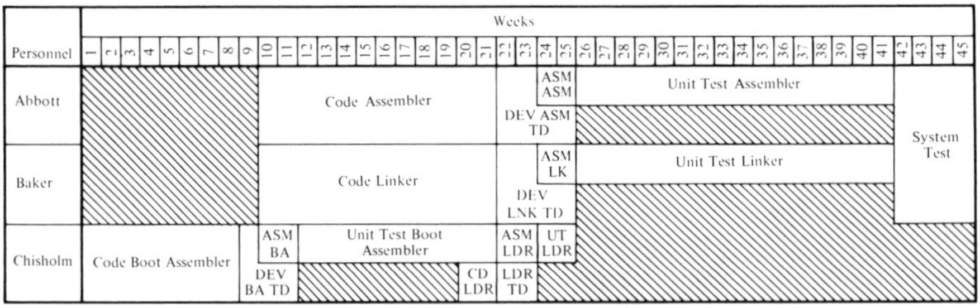

**Fig. 9-5   Bar chart with a reduced unit test computer time turnaround.**

Incidentally, it should never be necessary to assign a man more than two or, at the very maximum, three tasks, on the same or different projects, to be worked on in parallel. If this isn't the case, then working conditions at your installation are below the threshold necessary for maintaining motivated personnel.

## 9.2  ALLOWING FOR CONTINGENCIES

A task is a schedulable activity. For example, unit testing the linker is a task. Thus, if we adopt Fig. 9-4 as the bar chart for our software project, we can say that Baker will start unit testing the linker on week 21 and will work on this task for 8 weeks—we can talk about the activity in terms of a schedule. We may turn out to be wrong, but at least it makes sense to talk in terms of when a man is going to start a task and how long it will take him to complete the task.

However, people spend time on activities other than tasks. For example, in unit testing the linker, Baker may discover a bug in the boot assembler, and he may spend 2 days modifying the linker to get around the bug in the boot assembler. This is a legitimate activity, but it's not schedulable—it makes no sense to say, "On Tuesday of week 25 Baker will find a bug in the boot assembler, and it'll take him 2 days to modify the linker to work around the bug." We'll call such activities contingencies.

Some characteristic contingencies are as follows.

1. Temporary duty—A person on your project is required to temporarily give his attention to some special assignment. An example would be a person who is required to fix a previously undetected bug in a production program.

2. Inadequate personnel skill—The persons assigned to the project don't possess the skills required by the tasks to which they must be assigned.

3. Transfer—A person on your project is moved off your project, because he's needed on a higher priority project.

4. Late delivery—Resources don't arrive on the agreed upon delivery date. Examples of resources are personnel, hardware, software, and blocks of computer time.

5. Turnaround failure—Response time for repetitive services deteriorates below the level assumed when the work schedule was developed. Examples of such services are keypunching and running unit tests on the computer.

6. Inadequate operator skill—Functions aren't performed correctly because of operator misunderstanding. The operator may be a computer operator, a peripheral operator, a keypunch operator, etc.

7. Software failure—The project uses a program not developed by the project and discovers that this program doesn't perform according to specifications.

Time must then be spent:

a. Modifying project programs to get around the software bugs so work can go forward while the software is being corrected.

b. When the revised software is released, once more modifying the project programs to operate with the revised software.

8. Equipment failure—Equipment malfunctions. This could be the computer or other equipment, such as terminals or special purpose peripherals.

9. Lack of information—Certain information may be required before further progress can be made, and the information isn't forthcoming. Examples are decisions to be made and policies to be established.

10. Attrition—For some reason a person on your project leaves the company.

11. Absence—Sickness or excused time.

12. Company meeting—These are non-project-oriented meetings that the project personnel are required to attend. Examples are meetings on organizational changes and briefings on new employee benefits.

13. Promotion—A person on your project is moved off of your project because he has been promoted.

Perhaps we've now listed enough examples of contingencies to give a good idea of what contingencies are. Another way we can specify contingencies is by saying what they aren't. For example, holidays, vacations, and leaves of absence aren't contingencies. Why? Because they can be scheduled.

OK. So much for defining contingencies. Now, how do you provide for them in your plans? Since they can't be scheduled, and since they are statistical in nature (the most we can say about them is that there's some probability that they'll occur), the best we can do is make some kind of percentage allowance for them. For example, the bar chart in Fig. 9-4 calls for 76 man-weeks of effort to complete the job. If we decide that contingencies are going to occur at a level of about 10%, then one way to allow for contingencies would be to build another 7 or 8 man-weeks of time into the bar chart. One way of building this contingency allowance into the bar chart is shown in Fig. 9-6. Another way of building in this contingency is shown in Fig. 9-7.

We've just seen how, given a level at which you expect contingencies to occur, you can build an allowance for them in your bar chart. The question now is: How do you determine the level at which you expect contingencies to occur?

The fact that we can ask this question indicates that circumstances vary from project to project and that the expected contingency level varies with the circumstances. Consequently, the basic answer to the question must be that you have to rely on your knowledge of the circumstances to determine the expected contingency level.

However, there is a tool you can use to help you in evaluating the circum-

| Personnel | Weeks | | | | | | | | | | | | | | | | | | | | | | | | | | | | | | | | | | | |
|---|---|---|---|---|---|---|---|---|---|---|---|---|---|---|---|---|---|---|---|---|---|---|---|---|---|---|---|---|---|---|---|---|---|---|---|---|
| | 1 | 2 | 3 | 4 | 5 | 6 | 7 | 8 | 9 | 10 | 11 | 12 | 13 | 14 | 15 | 16 | 17 | 18 | 19 | 20 | 21 | 22 | 23 | 24 | 25 | 26 | 27 | 28 | 29 | 30 | 31 | 32 | 33 | 34 | 35 | 36 |
| Abbott | | | | | Code Assembler | | | | | | | | | | | | DEV ASM TD | | | ASM A | Unit Test Assembler | | | | | | | | | System Test | | | | Contingency | | |
| Baker | | | | | Code Linker | | | | | | | | | | | | DEV LNK TD | | | ASM LN | Unit Test Linker | | | | | | | | | | | | | | | |
| Chisholm | | | | Code Boot Assembler | | | | | ASM B | DEV BA TD | | Unit Test Boot Assembler | | | | | CD L | L TD | ASM L | UT L | | | | | | | | | | | | | | | | |

**Fig. 9-6  Bar chart with a block contingency allowance.**

stances of your particular situation. This tool is a checklist of commonly experienced contingencies that you can review item by item and ask yourself, "To what extent do I expect this type of contingency to occur?" The list of contingencies at the beginning of this section is a possible contingency checklist.

Typical questions you might ask yourself when determining the expected contingency level are as follows.

1. Temporary duty—How recently have programs written by this programmer gone into production? What is this person's experience in terms of programs that break down in production? How volatile is the applications area in which his programs have been written? To what extent is this person typically called on to perform special assignments, such as making presentations or evaluating system designs?

2. Inadequate personnel skill and transfers—How deep is the department's bench? What are the probabilities that you'll be assigned seasoned regulars rather than raw recruits? What has been the recent history of personnel assignments to projects in your department? How high is your project's priority?

| Personnel | Weeks | | | | | | | | | | | | | | | | | | | | | | | | | | | | | | | | | | | | |
|---|---|---|---|---|---|---|---|---|---|---|---|---|---|---|---|---|---|---|---|---|---|---|---|---|---|---|---|---|---|---|---|---|---|---|---|---|---|
| | 1 | 2 | 3 | 4 | 5 | 6 | 7 | 8 | 9 | 10 | 11 | 12 | 13 | 14 | 15 | 16 | 17 | 18 | 19 | 20 | 21 | 22 | 23 | 24 | 25 | 26 | 27 | 28 | 29 | 30 | 31 | 32 | 33 | 34 | 35 | 36 | 37 |
| Abbott | | | | | Code Assembler | | | | | | | | | | | | | CONT | DEV ASM TD | | ASM A | Unit Test Assembler | | | | | | | CONT | | System Test | | | | Contingency | |
| Baker | | | | | Code Linker | | | | | | | | | | | | | CONT | DEV LNK TD | | ASM LN | Unit Test Linker | | | | | | | CONT | | | | | | | |
| Chisholm | | | Code Boot Assembler | | | | | CONT | ASM B | DEV BA TD | | Unit Test Boot Assembler | | | | CONT | CD L | L TD | ASM L | UT L | CONT | | | | | | | | | | | | | | | | |

**Fig. 9-7  Bar chart with task-related contingency allowances.**

3. Late delivery—What has been the delivery history of your supplier? Is your delivery to be one of the first production models?

Similar questions can be raised for all the other types of contingencies on the checklist. As a matter of fact, you can easily come up with several more pertinent questions on those types of contingencies to which we just addressed ourselves above.

With respect to the range within which your expected contingency level might fall:

1. If your contingency experience remains at or below a level of 10%, you can consider yourself a master project leader.

2. There really is no upper limit to the degree to which contingency can occur, and if, for example, your assignment is to develop an application system for a computer system on which first delivery is yet to be made, an expected level of 50% for a construction phase project might be considered conservative.

There is much you, as a project leader, can do to keep down the occurrence of contingencies on your project. Doing so will require considerable time and effort on your part, but if you're not willing to make this investment, you shouldn't aspire to be a project leader. Consequently, any estimate you make of the expected level of contingency on your project must take into consideration a dedicated effort on your part to keep contingencies down.

As an indication of the general procedure you can use to keep down contingencies, consider an occurrence which we don't have on our contingency list, but which many people would include—that is, specifications change. We don't consider specifications change a contingency because either:

1. We're in the analysis phase, where the name of the game is to develop functional specifications (so a change to these not yet developed specifications makes little sense), or:

2. We're operating under a request for change procedure whereby, if the functional specifications change, we can change our plans accordingly. (As a consequence we don't have to make any allowance in our plans for such specifications change.)

In other words, by anticipating the need for specifications change and providing for it, we eliminate it as a contingency.

To all of which you may reply, "Come off it, Gildersleeve—you're just playing games. The fact that you adjust your plans for specifications changes doesn't alter the fact that the changes do introduce delay." We can hardly argue this point, but let us make several additional points.

1. The delay is tied directly to the specification change, and the user must explicitly approve the delay.

2. Users don't like delays—delays foul up their own plans.
3. Therefore, the user will try to avoid these delays. Specifically, he'll:
   a. Avoid making frivolous requests for change.
   b. Apply himself to getting the specifications firmed up in the analysis phase so changes aren't necessary.

So while we can't deny that, when a request for change occurs, delay is introduced independently of the existence of a request for change procedure, we'll maintain that the existence of the procedure will significantly reduce the number of requests.

Thus, the general procedure for keeping contingencies down is to anticipate them and make whatever provisions are necessary to minimize them. This approach frequently results in converting a contingency into an external restraint.

For example, take temporary duty. If one of Abbott's production programs unexpectedly blows up, there's nothing you, as his project leader, can do but grit your teeth and release him to temporary duty until he gets the problem cleared up. But if over any extended period of time, Abbott has a history, for whatever the reason, of spending about 20% of his time on temporary duty, then you should build this fact into your manpower plan, show on your bar chart that he's available for productive work on your project tasks only four days out of every five, and get your manager to approve your chart.

Again you can say, "But all this doesn't eliminate the delay. It just explicitly recognizes the delay in the plan." To which we can only reply, "And is that bad?" If a realistic plan shows an unacceptable completion date, adjustments are going to have to be made, and some of them are going to have to be made by your manager—perhaps he has to supply you with more manpower, perhaps something can be done to reduce Abbott's requirement for temporary duty. The basic point is that this approach requires you to both clearly define your expectations and get commitments from resource suppliers to deliver according to your expectations. Only if delivery deviates from expectation will contingency occur. This approach minimizes the possibility of such deviation, and that's what the game is all about.

Inadequate personnel skill? Your manpower plan should spell out the skill levels required. You should get your manager to approve your manpower plan. In doing so, what he's saying is that, if you don't get the skills you need, you can't meet your deadline. Then if you don't get those skills, you can legitimately campaign for a relaxation of deadline.

This general technique is sometimes known as covering your behind. The basic idea is: make clear what you need; get a commitment for delivery; and if delivery isn't made, put the blame where it belongs. But sticking someone else with the blame isn't the important point. What's important is that, if you do make your needs clear and get delivery commitments, you minimize the probability that anything will go wrong in the first place.

Transfer? The approach is really no different than the one for personnel skills —spell out in your manpower plan the skill levels you require and when you need them, and have your manager approve your manpower plan. If he assigns personnel to your project according to the plan and then subsequently transfers a man to another project, he does so only because the other project has higher priority than yours. A conscious part of his decision must be that, because of relative priorities, he has downgraded the skill level on your project, and consequently, he must relax your deadline.

Late delivery? Find our what realistic delivery dates are. Develop a plan that fits within these dates. And get commitments on delivery that'll allow you to carry out your plan.

Turnaround? Find out what a realistic turnaround is (not the nominal one, the real one) and get a commitment on it. Develop your plans to conform to this turnaround rate.

Inadequate operator skill? Define the skill level you need far enough in advance of your need so those in charge can upgrade their personnel appropriately. Communicate your need so that it's appreciated, and get a commitment on delivery.

Software failure? Hardware failure? These're tougher, but they're not immune to your expectations. Remember, both software and hardware failures are really people failures, and the performance of a person can be upgraded if he has a clear understanding of your expectations.

Lack of information? Spell out to the people, who must supply the information, what you need to know and when you need to know it. Anticipate your needs so the people have adequate time to develop the information on schedule.

Attrition? Minimizing this contingency is mostly a matter of motivation, which we'll take up later in this book. However, one other important consideration is as follows. The longer project duration, the greater the possibility of turnover. Consequently, on a long project the turnover should be built in to occur automatically and harmlessly. This is done by initially overstaffing the project by the addition of junior people. It's the job of the juniors to understudy the more senior people, and then, when the project is shaken out and well underway, the senior people, who're the most likely to become dissatisfied with being stuck on a project during a long construction phase, can be removed, hopefully for more productive work elsewhere, and can be replaced by the junior people who have been preparing for this takeover. Such an arrangement also allows junior people to obtain much needed experience.

Absence? Again, a matter of motivation.

Company meeting? I don't see much you can do in this area, but this shouldn't be a very significant contingency.

Promotion? This is the only kind of contingency you should encourage. Imagine the call on resources you could command if your reputation was that people who work on your project always get promoted.

## EXERCISES

1. What are the steps in the development of a manpower plan to do a given job?
2. For Exercise 4 at the end of Chapter 7, you developed a bubble chart to show the dependency between the tasks that must be done to take the payroll system, described in Appendix D, from its present design state to the point where the payroll department begins to use the system to generate the company's paychecks and to maintain its payroll records. One such possible bubble chart is shown in Fig. 9-8.

You are now going to complete the development of the manpower plan for the construction phase of this payroll system.

You are to choose a project staff from the personnel listed in the back of the case study in Appendix D. You may use as few or as many of these people as you want for as long as you want. Don't worry about what these people will do if you don't use them. We have lots of other work to which to assign them. It's just that the payroll

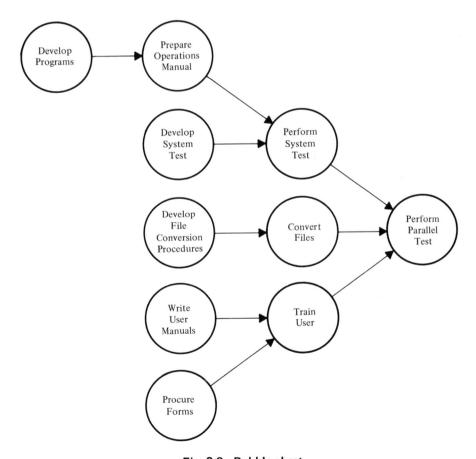

**Fig. 9-8  Bubble chart.**

project is high priority, and we want to give you as much opportunity as possible to select the project team you want.

When you develop your manpower plan, assign specific people to specific tasks. Don't talk about a senior programmer doing this and a programmer doing that. Say which senior programmer and which programmer. In other words, have reasons for your personnel assignments.

Also, when doing this exercise, we'd like you to use a kind of "doublethink." Obviously, when developing the manpower plan, you're playing the role of the project leader. However, at the same time, we'd like you to choose someone from the personnel available, appoint him as project leader, and tell us what tasks you'd assign to him.

This job must be done in 160 working days. That is, 160 working days from now the payroll department must be using the new system to generate the company's paychecks and to maintain its payroll records. Consequently, the acceptance test and all other tasks must be completed in 160 working days.

There are 20 working days in each month. Consequently, you have 8 months in which to complete this job. Incidentally, if you do a little calculation on the basis of this definition of a working day, you'll soon come to the conclusion that there are 48 weeks in a year. This, of course, is a misrepresentation, but for planning long-term projects, it does yield two advantages.

1. It standardizes months at 4 weeks each.
2. It automatically allows 4 weeks per year for holidays and vacations.

|  | Prepare | | Test | |
|---|---|---|---|---|
|  | Senior | Junior | Senior | Junior |
| 1.3.5.9.14. All Sorts | 5 | 7 | 5 | 7 |
| 2. Card to Tape Edit | 10 | 14 | 10 | 14 |
| 4. Reset and Update | 20 | 28 | 15 | 21 |
| 7. Detail Calculate | 30 | 42 | 20 | 28 |
| 8. Summary Calculate | 30 | 42 | 20 | 28 |
| 10. Print Transaction Trail | 15 | 21 | 5 | 7 |
| 11. Produce Vacation Report | 15 | 21 | 10 | 14 |
| 12. Tax Master Extract | 15 | 21 | 5 | 7 |
| 13. Produce FICA Report | 15 | 21 | 10 | 14 |
| 15. Produce State Unemployment and Disability Report | 15 | 21 | 5 | 7 |
| 16. Produce Reports and Checks Monitor | 35 | 49 | 30 | 42 |
| 17. Quarterly State Tax Report | 15 | 21 | 5 | 7 |
| 18. Produce 941 Forms | 15 | 21 | 5 | 7 |
| 25. Change CROF Code | 15 | 21 | 10 | 14 |

**Fig. 9-9. Man-Days Required per Task for Analysts and Senior Programmers (Senior) and Programmers and Programmer Trainees (Junior)**

To reduce the amount of time you'll need to work out this exercise, we're providing you with the task time estimates shown in Fig. 9-9. This chart is read as follows.

1. People are divided into two groups.
   a. Senior people (analysts and senior programmers).
   b. Junior people (programmers and programmer trainees).
2. Senior people do tasks faster than junior people. For example, it takes a senior person 10 days to prepare program 2 and another 10 days to test it, while it takes a junior person 14 days to prepare program 2 and another 14 days to test it.
3. The first entry isn't for one sort; it's for all 5 sorts—programs numbered 1, 3, 5, 9, and 14.

Please notice that these estimates are for only the "develop programs" bubble in the bubble chart. To work out this exercise, you'll have to estimate the time required to do the other tasks shown on the bubble chart yourself.

Analysts are paid $1100 a month, senior programmers $900 a month, programmers $700, and programmer trainees $650.

Computer unit test turnaround time is half an hour or less.

All programs are to be written in COBOL.

No unusual delays or interruptions are anticipated.

# COMPUTER TIME PLANNING

During the construction phase of the development of a data processing system, computer time is required for:

1. Acceptance testing.
2. File conversion.
3. System testing.
4. Unit testing.

## 10.1 ACCEPTANCE TESTING

The purpose of acceptance testing is to demonstrate to the user that the system is acceptable. As project leader, you shouldn't let the system enter acceptance testing unless system test results have convinced you that passage of the acceptance tests is practically a certainty. As a result, projecting the time required to run the acceptance tests should be no more than a matter of determining the data volumes to be processed in the acceptance testing and then extending these volumes by the performance rates of the system. However, running the acceptance testing may require blocks of time. As a consequence, the need must be anticipated, so arrangements for scheduling the time can be cleared with the computer center.

## 10.2   FILE CONVERSION

File conversion is a two-step process. First file conversion procedures are developed. Then the procedures are used to convert the files.

File conversion procedures frequently involve the use of special programs, in which case computer time to unit test these programs must be projected. In any case, time to system test the conversion procedures must be scheduled.

Like acceptance testing, file conversion is something that shouldn't be started unless system testing of the conversion procedures demonstrates beyond the shadow of a doubt that they are going to work. As a consequence, projecting file conversion time is a matter of determining volumes and extending them by conversion system running rates.

File conversion often involves extensive validity checking of the data being converted, and the reject rate is frequently high. Consequently, one file conversion volume that is sometimes underestimated is the amount of data which is initially rejected and which must, consequently, be recycled before it can be incorporated into the new file.

Once a file is converted, it is sometimes necessary to periodically process the file to keep it up to date until the new system is installed. Time for this updating operation must also be projected.

Like acceptance testing, various aspects of file conversion involve blocks of computer time and must be scheduled far enough in advance to allow the computer center to fit your requirements into their routine.

## 10.3   SYSTEM TESTING

The amount of time required to do system testing appears to vary widely. One of the variables seems to be that some systems have been subjected to more thorough unit testing before entering system testing than have others. However, if systematic, thorough unit testing has been conducted, then the amount of system testing required should be purely a function of the number of interfaces between program modules that must be tested in a system environment. Interestingly enough, the number of interfaces in a system seems to be more a function of system type than it is of number of program modules.

One system type is batch sequential. The prototype of a batch sequential system is shown in Fig. 10-1. The modules are programs, and each program accepts input and produces output, which becomes input to another program. As a re-

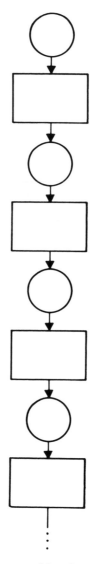

**Fig. 10-1  Prototype of batch sequential system.**

sult, there are about as many interfaces as there are modules, and both modules and interfaces increase in an arithmetic progression. As a result, the number of interfaces never becomes particularly high, and four to six cycles of system testing should always be enough to check out most of the interfaces.

The other type of system is what might be called "transaction responsive." Realtime systems, such as airline and hotel reservation systems, and control systems, such as operating systems, are examples of transaction responsive systems. The modules in a transaction responsive system are subroutines, and theoretically, each subroutine is independent of all others. In fact, however, all the subroutines tend to interface with each other through the common use of memory, computer time, operating system services, and table storage. As a consequence, for a system with $n$ modules, there tends to be about $(n - 1) + (n - 2) + (n - 3) + \ldots$ interfaces, and if another module is added, $n$ more interfaces are added. Therefore, you don't have to get involved in a very complicated system to begin contending with a lot of interfaces. Thus, it stands to reason that a transaction responsive system is going to require much more system test time than a batch sequential system.

Like acceptance testing and file conversion, system testing involves blocks of time and must be scheduled in advance with the computer center.

## 10.4 UNIT TESTING

From a scheduling point of view, there is no projection problem when it comes to unit test time. Instead, the problem is to arrive at an agreement as to what kind of turnaround you are going to experience. This turnaround rate then becomes an external restraint within which you develop your manpower plan.

However, you will be required to project your unit test time costs. The computer center charges your project will incur in this regard are going to be a function of the extent to which your project members use the center's facilities for unit testing. This utilization is, in turn, a function of:

1. The complexity of the programs being unit tested.
2. The capability of the persons doing the unit testing.

But these are the same two factors on which programming time was projected. As a consequence, it seems reasonable to propose that unit test costs could be projected directly from the manpower costs for developing the programs, and this approach is used with apparent satisfaction at several installations.

At present, there appears to be little requirement for project leaders to project the demand that their project unit testing is going to make on the computer center. However, installations are once more beginning to become sensitive to equipment capacity and utilization, and it is probably fair to predict that projections of unit test time demands on computer center facilities will once more become a project leader responsibility in the near future.

There appears to be universal agreement that unit test time is projected in terms of number of computer test shots required to unit test a program. Once this number is arrived at, it can be extended into a time demand by multiplying it by some "average time per test shot." This "average time per shot" will be expressed in terms of the way computer time is measured at your installation—it may be as simple as wall clock time; it may be as complicated as some combination of central processor unit time plus number of channel accesses and so on.

The question may be raised as to whether the concept "average time per shot" is meaningful, or whether time per shot varies so widely as to make the concept meaningless. Although this isn't the place to get into the subject, it does seem to us that there are good unit testing practices, and very briefly, at least two of these practices are as follows.

1. If a program exceeds a certain minimum size, then it should be divided into subprograms, so when the program is modified, only those subprograms in which the modifications occur need be recompiled.
2. Unit test data should be tailored to the tests that are to be run.

Adherence to these practices tends to minimize variations in time per test shot, and consequently, we would maintain that, in a well run shop, the concept of an average time per shot is quite meaningful.

The question then becomes: How do you estimate the number of shots required to unit test a program? Again, number of shots required should be a function of the complexity of the program being unit tested and the capability of the person doing the unit testing.

Since these are the same factors we used to project the man-days required to unit test the program, it seems reasonable to suppose that we could project number of test shots directly from our manpower plan. This would be done as follows.

Reproduced in Fig. 10-2 is the manpower plan we developed for our software project. This manpower plan indicates that Abbott is going to spend 8 weeks unit testing the assembler. If we can now come up with some concept of the number of shots per day that a person will use while unit testing a program, we

| Personnel | Weeks (1–36) | | | | | |
|---|---|---|---|---|---|---|
| Abbott | | Code Assembler | DEV ASM TD | ASM A | Unit Test Assembler | System Test / Contingency |
| Baker | | Code Linker | DEV LNK TD | ASM LN | Unit Test Linker | System Test / Contingency |
| Chisholm | Code Boot Assembler | ASM B / DEV BA TD | Unit Test Boot Assembler | CD L / L TD / ASM L / UT L | | |

Fig. 10-2  Bar chart.

can project the number of shots Abbott will use to unit test the assembler from the 8 week manpower estimate. For the sake of argument, say we decide that 2 shots a day is a good estimate. Then Abbott will need 80 shots to debug the assembler (8 X 5 X 2).

How frequently can a person effectively use a computer test shot when he is in a unit test mode? Obviously, your answer to this question is going to depend to some extent on the amount of computer time available at your installation for test purposes. The less there is available, the more your unit testing practices are going to rely on desk checking, and the less frequently programmers are going to be able to use test shots.

However, as the years pass, the cost per unit of production on computers continues to drop, the cost per unit of production from people continues to rise, and the less and less justification there is for restricting the use of computer time for effective testing purposes. Consequently, suppose there is no physical limit on the amount of computer time available for test purposes, and ask the question: How frequently can a person effectively use unit test computer time?

We would maintain that the only efficient way to run a computer center is with remote unit testing. Under these circumstances, the programmer's normal mode of operation is to submit a set of tests to the computer center and, at some later time, to receive the results of these tests. If the results conform to predictions, the program has passed the tests, and the programmer is ready to submit the program for the next set of tests. However, if the results don't check out, the programmer must inspect the results in the attempt to find out what's wrong, so he can modify his program and resubmit it for a repeated attempt to pass the tests.

We would maintain that, if after studying his test results for a couple of hours, the programmer has still not figured out what is wrong with his program, he would be better off applying himself to the development of further tests to help isolate the difficulty rather than to continue to study test results which are apparently ambiguous. As a result, we would propose that a programmer who knows what he's doing can effectively use a test shot on the average of at least every 4 man-hours of unit testing.

Given standards concerning average time per shot and number of shots per man-day when unit testing, a computer time schedule can be projected directly from a manpower plan. For example, given the following standards:

1. During assembly and unit test, a programmer will use two test shots per man-day.
2. Average time per shot is as follows.
   a. Assembly—$7\frac{1}{2}$ minutes.
   b. Unit test—15 minutes.

Assuming that these standards hold true for both computer X and computer Y (a prodigious oversimplification), then the projection of a computer time histo-

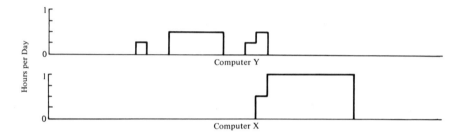

**Fig. 10-3   Unit test computer time projection.**

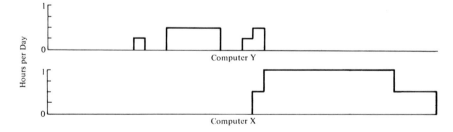

**Fig. 10-4   Computer time projection.**

gram can be made directly from the manpower plan for our example software project, as is shown in Fig. 10-3.

After the unit test computer time histogram has been constructed, time for system testing, file conversion, and acceptance testing can be added to it. For example, if we had determined that an hour of computer time per day would be used during system testing of our software package, a complete histogram of our computer time projection would be as shown in Fig. 10-4. This histogram also shows a contingency allowance of half an hour of computer time per day during the 4-week contingency period.

## EXERCISES

1. What aspects of the construction phase require computer time?
2. What is the major factor influencing the amount of system test computer time required?
3. As far as amount of system test computer time is concerned, what system types are there?
4. For Exercise 2 at the end of Chapter 9 you developed a manpower plan to take the payroll system, described in Appendix D, from its present design state to the point where the payroll department begins to use the system to generate the company's paychecks and to maintain its payroll records. One such possible manpower plan is shown in Fig. 10-5.

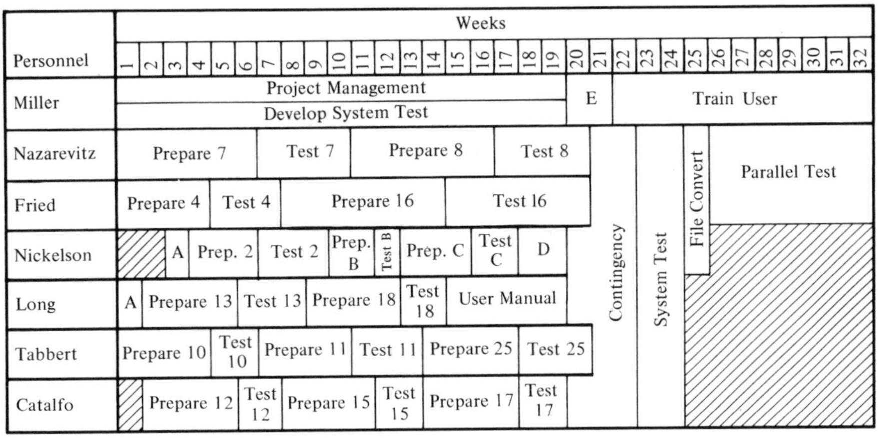

Fig. 10-5 **Payroll system construction phase manpower plan.**
**A—COBOL training.**
**B—Sorts.**
**C—File conversion procedures.**
**D—Operations manual.**
**E—Develop training program.**

You now should develop a projection of the computer time you'll need to support your manpower plan.

A computer shot in which a compile, a linkedit, and a test are done takes 10 minutes for a small program and 15 minutes for a large one. Programs 4, 7, 8, and 16 are large programs; all the others are small.

Cycle time is 2 hours. That is, given a master file containing records for all Omega employees, it takes 2 hours to pass this file from program 1 right on through program 25.

# PROJECTING SCHEDULES AND COSTS

You have now spent some considerable amount of time learning how to develop plans for the use of various resources—namely, manpower and computer time. It is now time to investigate the relationship between plans, schedules, and cost estimates.

In Fig. 11-1 is shown a manpower and computer time plan for constructing a software system consisting of a loader, an assembler, and a linker for the new computer $X$.

Once we have such a plan, establishing a schedule is child's play. For example, if anyone is interested in using the boot assembler, a glance at our plan is sufficient to establish that the earliest the boot assembler will be available for use is in week 17. Similarly, if anyone is interested in using the loader, assembler, or linker before they've been system tested, earliest use dates are week 21 for the loader and week 29 for the assembler and linker. The earliest the loader, assembler, and linker are available as a tested system is week 33, and we're not making any commitments to deliver such a system until week 37.

The important point is that, if you don't have a plan, you can't provide anyone with a schedule.

Much the same is true in the case of cost estimates, although somewhat more

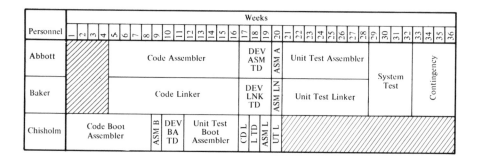

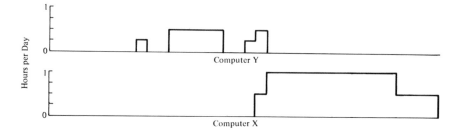

**Fig. 11-1    Manpower and computer time plan.**

work is required to convert a plan into a cost estimate. A form that can be used to develop a cost estimate is shown in Fig. 11-2.

For example, the plan in Fig. 11-1 shows that 84 man-weeks of manpower are going to be required. If Abbott, Baker, and Chisholm are each paid $275 a week, salary costs for our software project are going to be $23,100, as shown in Fig. 11-3.

But salary costs are only one part of manpower costs. Also included in manpower costs are the costs to supply such personnel supporting services as working space, furniture, filing facilities, stationery supplies, clerical support, reproduction facilities, employee benefits, management, and administration. These costs are called overhead costs, and they're applied to manpower as a percentage of salary costs. Most commonly, the rate structure used to extend man-weeks into dollars includes both salary and an overhead factor. Overhead costs typically range around 100% of manpower costs. For example, if, in the company in which we're doing our software project, overhead is 100% of salary, manpower costs for the project would be $23,100 for salary costs plus another $23,100 for overhead costs, which yields a total of $46,200, as shown in Fig. 11-3.

Computer time costs can be developed in a similar fashion. The computer time plan indicates the amount of the resource to be used, which is extended by a rate structure to yield a dollar cost. For example, Fig. 11-1 indicates that our

COST ESTIMATE

| PROJECT NO. | PROJECT PHASE | |
|---|---|---|
| PREPARED BY | | DATE |

SALARY

| NAME | WEEKS | SALARY | COST |
|---|---|---|---|
| | | | |
| | | | |
| | | | |
| | | | |
| | | | |
| | | | |
| | | | |
| | | | |

TOTAL [          ]

OVERHEAD _____  [          ]

COMPUTER TIME

HOURS [          ]    RATE [          ]    COST [          ]

TRAVEL AND LIVING EXPENSES _____  [          ]

SUPPORT SERVICES                    COST

| | |
|---|---|
| | |
| | |
| | |

TOTAL [          ]

GRAND TOTAL [          ]

**Fig. 11-2  Cost estimate form.**

COST ESTIMATE

| PROJECT NO. 12345 | PROJECT PHASE Construction | |
|---|---|---|
| PREPARED BY Tom Gildersleeve | | DATE 8/1/84 |

SALARY

| NAME | WEEKS | SALARY | COST |
|---|---|---|---|
| Albat | 32 | $275.00 | $8800.00 |
| Boker | 32 | 275.00 | 8800.00 |
| Chisholm | 20 | 275.00 | 5500.00 |
| | | | |
| | | | |
| | | | |
| | | | |
| | | | |
| | | TOTAL | $23,100.00 |

OVERHEAD _____ 23,100.00

COMPUTER TIME

HOURS 90    RATE $100.00    COST $9000.00

TRAVEL AND LIVING EXPENSES _____ —

SUPPORT SERVICES                           COST

| | |
|---|---|
| | |
| | |
| | |
| TOTAL | — |

GRAND TOTAL $55,200.00

**Fig. 11-3  Cost estimate.**

software project is going to use 17.5 hours of computer $Y$ time and 72.5 hours of computer $X$ time. If all computer time is $100 an hour, computer time costs for the software project would be $9000, as shown in Fig. 11-3.

The point we're developing here is that a cost estimate is a plan extended by a rate structure.

A third category of cost is travel and living. Members of projects developing systems for geographically dispersed offices or plants may be required to do some traveling, which then becomes a project cost. Here the rate structure is evident enough. Airline rates are regulated by the government. Car rental rates are published and well known. Company policy dictates an allowance for automobile mileage. Even if people charge actual living expenses, reliable per diem rates can be developed for the various locations to be visited. To arrive at a cost estimate for travel and living it's necessary to develop a travel plan—who's going to go where, how often are they going to go, how long are they going to stay, and are they going to have to rent a car? Once the travel plan has been determined, development of the cost estimate is a rote procedure of applying the rates to the plan.

A fourth and final category of cost is the residual category, called support services. In this category fall all the services that a project might conceivably contract for with some outside organization—another department of the company or an independent vendor. Some examples of support services are consultant services, proprietary software, and publication of manuals.

The cost estimate for a support service is typically obtained from the supplier of the service. The nature of the applicable rate structure isn't always apparent in the case of a support service, but the existence of one is evident from the fact that a supplier won't provide you with a quotation until you tell him what service you want. The consultant wants to know what you expect him to do, the software house wants to know what configuration you want of the various software options it offers, and the publisher wants to know how many copies of the manual you want printed and how many pages and illustrations there will be in the manual. In other words, the supplier wants you to make a plan, he then applies his rate structure to the plan, and he thus arrives at a cost estimate with which he supplies you.

Thus, for all categories of cost, developing a cost estimate is a matter of applying a rate structure to a plan. As a result, a cost estimate can't be reliable unless it's backed up by a plan. Therefore, if as a project leader, you're presented by your manager with a budget, it's proper for you to ask for the plan on which it's based, for only if you can follow this plan do you stand a chance of staying within budget. You must review the plan closely to see if you can follow it, for if you can't, then both the plan and the cost estimate derived from the plan are unrealistic, and it's your obligation to make your manager aware of this fact.

If you're presented with a budget unsupported by a plan, this doesn't mean the budget is inadequate, but it does make it suspect. What you must then do is consider the budget an external restraint and see if you can develop a realistic plan that fits within the budget. If you can, then you're on solid ground. If you can't, then you, your manager, and everyone else involved in the project are in potential trouble, for actions are being based on an unrealistic cost estimate, and once more, it's your obligation to make your manager aware of this fact.

The worst thing a project leader can do when given a job to be done with inadequate resources or within an unrealistic time frame is to merely say, "I'll try." As Robert Townsend, in his book *Up The Organization*, so aptly quotes Napoleon:

> A commander in chief cannot take as an excuse for his mistakes in warfare an order given by his minister or his sovereign, when the person giving the order is absent from the field of operations and is imperfectly aware or wholly unaware of the latest state of affairs. It follows that any commander in chief who undertakes to carry out a plan which he considers defective is at fault; he must put forward his reasons, insist on the plan being changed, and finally tender his resignation rather than be the instrument of his army's downfall.

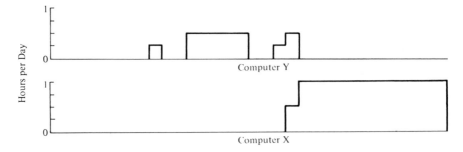

**Fig. 11-4 Manpower and computer time plan with no contingency allowance.**

COST ESTIMATE

| PROJECT NO. 12345 | PROJECT PHASE Construction |
| PREPARED BY Tom Gildersleeve | DATE 8/1/84 |

SALARY

| NAME | WEEKS | SALARY | COST |
|------|-------|--------|------|
| Abbot | 28 | $275.00 | $7700.00 |
| Baker | 28 | 275.00 | 7700.00 |
| Chisholm | 20 | 275.00 | 5500.00 |
| | | | |
| | | | |
| | | | |
| | | | |
| | | | |
| | | TOTAL | $20,900.00 |

OVERHEAD _____ 20,900.00

COMPUTER TIME

HOURS 80    RATE $100.00    COST 8000.00

TRAVEL AND LIVING EXPENSES _____ —

| SUPPORT SERVICES | COST |
|------------------|------|
| | |
| | |
| | |
| TOTAL | |

CONTINGENCY ALLOWANCE    SUBTOTAL 49,800.00

PERCENTAGE 20%    AMOUNT 9960.00

GRAND TOTAL $59,760.00

**Fig. 11-5  Cost estimate with contingency allowance.**

With the exception of the fact that Napoleon neglects to mention the possibility that the sovereign may be able to demonstrate to the commander in chief that the plan is, in fact, sound, Napoleon's advice is certainly to the point.

While we're on the subject of cost estimates, it would be appropriate to cover a method of allowing for contingencies that's an alternative to building the allowance into the manpower and computer time plans.

In Fig. 11-4 is shown a manpower and computer time plan identical to the one shown in Fig. 11-1, except that the plan in Fig. 11-4 has no allowance for contingencies.

The plan in Fig. 11-4 is costed out on the form shown in Fig. 11-5.

As you can see from Fig. 11-5, the contingency allowance that wasn't present in the manpower or the computer time plan is instead built into the cost estimate.

The theory behind this kind of contingency allowance is that the schedule isn't going to be allowed to slip, and if the project gets into difficulty, the dollars in the contingency allowance are going to be used to buy additional resources, not initially planned on, to bail out the project. Possible resources purchased in this

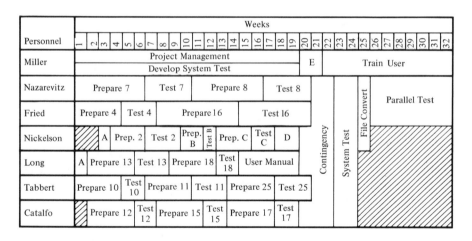

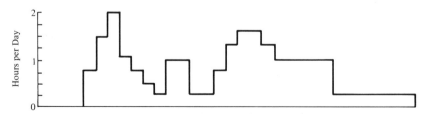

**Fig. 11-6   Manpower and computer time plan.**

COST ESTIMATE

| PROJECT NO. | PROJECT PHASE | |
|---|---|---|
| PREPARED BY | | DATE |

SALARY

| NAME | WEEKS | SALARY | COST |
|---|---|---|---|
| | | | |
| | | | |
| | | | |
| | | | |
| | | | |
| | | | |
| | | | |
| | | | |

TOTAL [ ]

OVERHEAD _____ [ ]

COMPUTER TIME

HOURS [ ]    RATE [ ]    COST [ ]

TRAVEL AND LIVING EXPENSES _____ [ ]

SUPPORT SERVICES                    COST

| | |
|---|---|
| | |
| | |
| | |

TOTAL [ ]

GRAND TOTAL [ ]

**Fig. 11-7   Cost estimate form.**

way might be added manpower, additional computer time, and perhaps some support services.

However, because of other factors, such as unavailability of more computer time or lack of knowledge on the part of new manpower, the convertibility of dollars into resources often turns out to be more sticky than anticipated. As a consequence, we recommend that:

1. If you've a choice, build your contingency allowance into your plan rather than into your cost estimate.
2. If you must build your contingency allowance into your cost estimate, increase your percentage allowance to compensate for the degree to which you anticipate a lack of convertibility from dollars to resources.

### EXERCISES

1. Should you commit to a fixed price and completion date on a project:
   a. To do the analysis phase of a data processing system development?
   b. With incomplete definition?
2. Develop a checklist of cost categories to be taken into consideration in estimating the cost of a project.
3. For Exercise 2 at the end of Chapter 9 you developed a manpower plan to take the payroll system, described in Appendix D, from its present design state to the point where the payroll department begins to use the system to generate the company's paychecks and to maintain its payroll records. For Exercise 4 at the end of Chapter 10 you developed a computer time plan to support your manpower plan. One such possible manpower and computer time plan is shown in Fig. 11-6.

   You're now to develop a cost estimate for this construction phase of the payroll system. For your convenience, a blank cost estimate form is supplied in Fig. 11-7.

   Analysts are paid $1100 a month, senior programmers $900 a month, programmers $700, and programmer trainees $650.

   Overhead is 100% of salary.

   Computer time is $100 an hour.

   There's no travel requirement, nor are any support services planned.

# THE USE OF PLANS

This is the conclusion of section III of this book, which addresses itself to the planning of a project phase. We'd like to use an example to both summarize this section and to serve as a lead into section IV.

Suppose you're located in New York and want to drive to Boston. The first thing you'd probably do is get your road map and decide what route you're going to take. You might decide on a route as is shown in Fig. 12-1. Here your route is to take Route 95 to New Haven, Route 91 to Hartford, Route 84 (which inexplicably and abruptly changes into Route 86) to Sturbridge, and Route 90 to Boston.

Obviously, this route map is a plan for getting from New York to Boston. And in passing we might make two observations.

1. Once you have your plan, you can quote a schedule—you can tell anyone who's interested when you'll arrive in New Haven, Hartford, Sturbridge, and ultimately, Boston.

2. You can also provide anyone who wants it with a cost estimate—you can measure off the miles on your route and extend this figure by 15 cents a mile or whatever other rate you consider appropriate.

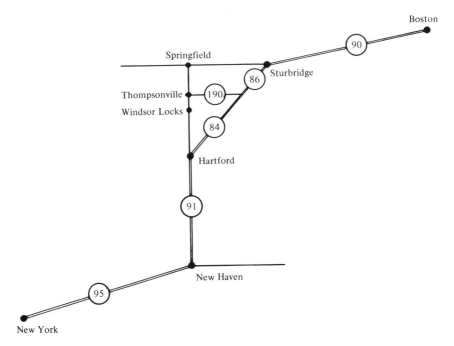

**Fig. 12-1  Route map.**

However, you use your plan for a third purpose, also. You use it to direct your progress as you move from your origin to your destination. Reflect for a moment on the fact that, if you hadn't made your plan before you started on your trip, when you drove your car out of your driveway you wouldn't even know which way to turn!

Our analogy between a car trip and a project has one other moral, which is that planning isn't a one-time thing. As you progress toward your destination you often find that progress begins to deviate from plan. It then becomes necessary to modify your plan to maintain your best posture toward your goal.

For example, suppose that it's about an hour now since you left New Haven, and you're still on Route 91—you haven't found the exit to Route 84. All of a sudden, you see an exit marked "Windsor Locks," and this strikes you as strange. So you pull over to the side of the road and look at your road map. Sure enough, Windsor Locks is north of Hartford—you've missed the exit to Route 84. Now you must decide what you're going to do—are you going to go back to Hartford and pick up Route 84, are you going to continue north on 91 until you hit Route 90, or are you going to go to Thompsonville and cut across Route 190 to get back on your original plan? Regardless of your ultimate decision, please notice two things.

1. Without a plan, you can't tell whether you're on course or not.
2. Once you determine that you're off course, your plan provides the context in which you decide what you're going to do next.

As a consequence, always keep in mind when you're developing a plan that you aren't only developing a mechanism with which to project schedules and costs, you're also developing the basic tool you'll be using and modifying to guide your project's progress toward its goal.

Planning is one of the project leader's coordination responsibilities—the other two are monitoring progress and controlling performance. In section IV we will take up these other two coordination responsibilities.

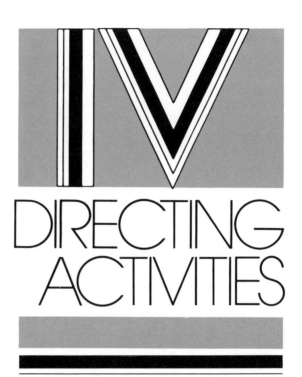

# IV

# DIRECTING
# ACTIVITIES

# 13
# MONITORING
# THE SCHEDULE

In Section IV we are going to be concerned with the project leader's responsibilities with respect to the ongoing activities in which the project members engage in their collective effort to reach the project goal. We're going to analyze these responsibilities into two subject areas: (1) monitoring the schedule, and (2) controlling performance.

When the project leader is monitoring a project member's schedule, he's trying to determine the answer to the question, "Is the project member on time?"

When the project leader is controlling a project member's performance, he's trying to answer the question, "Is the project member doing what he's supposed to be doing?" Perhaps an example will clarify this question. Suppose that, as project leader, you've assigned Fried to develop program 16 in the payroll system. If our estimate turns out to be correct, then for 7 weeks, Fried is going to be sitting at his desk, first filling large sheets of paper with flowchart symbols and then recording line after line of code on COBOL coding sheets. And day after day, as the sheets of coding paper accumulate on Fried's desk, the question that's going to keep rumbling around in the back of your mind is, "When this guy gets all through writing the code for program 16, is the program he has written going to do anything like what the design specifications say program 16 should do?" This question is the problem of control in a nutshell.

We don't maintain that the question of whether a project member is on time is independent of the question of control. On the contrary, they're closely related. For example, if at the end of 7 weeks, Fried tells you he has the code for program 16 complete, then presumably he's on time. However, if subsequent unit testing of his code demonstrates that it has severe logical problems and great chunks of it have to be ripped out and replaced, then not only was Fried's performance not controlled, but he didn't really have the code done on time either.

Nevertheless, we'd maintain that the tools a project leader uses to monitor a project member's schedule are different from the tools he uses to control the project member's performance. Consequently, we're going to analytically separate these two functions and discuss them one at a time. Thus, in Chapters 13 and 14 we'll concern ourselves exclusively with monitoring the schedule and will postpone consideration of controlling performance until Chapters 15–17.

Let's represent the problem of monitoring a project member's schedule graphically, as shown in Fig. 13-1. The horizontal axis of the graph in Fig. 13-1 represents the passage of time. The vertical axis represents the amount of effort a person puts in during the course of one day.

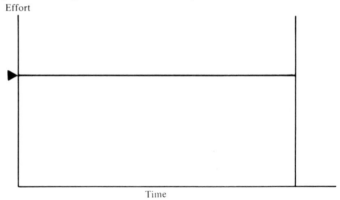

Fig. 13-1   The amount of effort needed to do a task.

Now, let's suppose we have a task to be done; for example, let's suppose there is a program we want developed. Let's also suppose we give this task to Charlie Brown.

We can mark off on our graph when we expect Charlie Brown to be finished with the task. The upright bar on the right of the graph in Fig. 13-1 can represent Charlie's deadline. Then the origin of our graph represents where we are today, and the baseline between the origin and the deadline represents the number of days we expect to pass before Charlie finishes his task.

We've marked off with an arrowhead on the vertical axis of our graph the point that represents the amount of effort we expect from a person putting in a normal workday.

Suppose we expect Charlie to start today and work full-time on his task to get finished in time to meet his deadline. Then the area under the horizontal line, across the top of our graph from the point of a normal workday's effort to Charlie's deadline, represents the amount of effort we think Charlie will have to expend to get his task done. Thus, if we've done a good job of planning, Charlie ought to be able to put in a normal amount of effort each workday and meet his deadline with no difficulty.

But what does Charlie's effort curve really look like? If Charlie is typical, his effort curve is going to look something like the curve in Fig. 13-2. As a result, Charlie may, in the early days of his task, dig himself such a hole that, even though, as his deadline nears, he puts out more and more effort, to the point where he's working considerable amounts of overtime on his own, he finds it impossible to completely recover in the short span of time left, and he misses his deadline.

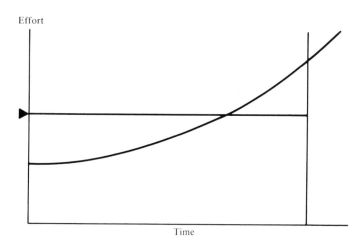

**Fig. 13-2 Typical effort curve.**

So Charlie overran his deadline. This is precisely the situation we want to avoid, and it's what monitoring the schedule is all about. But before we try to figure out what we can do to keep Charlie on schedule, let's first try to determine why he fell behind schedule in the first place.

First of all, it's important to say that the chances are very low that Charlie was late because he's a malingerer or because he deliberately set out to miss his deadline. The fact that he was willing to put in so much extra effort toward the end of his task in an attempt to recover lost time argues overwhelmingly against such a contention. No, the situation that led to Charlie's downfall is a much more common and prosaic one.

At any given point in time, there are a number of activities contending for

Charlie's attention. Not only is there the task we've given Charlie, there're other work related goals.

1. There may be correspondence, brochures, and periodicals to be read.
2. There may be meetings, seminars, and classes he'd like to attend.
3. There may be subjects he'd like to discuss with his fellow workers.
4. And there may be some research he'd like to do.

In addition to these work-related goals, Charlie has personal goals that are also contending for his attention.

1. He may need a haircut.
2. He may have to buy an anniversary present for his wife.
3. He may have some legal problems to work out with his lawyer.
4. And the football pool for this week hasn't been worked up yet.

To allocate his time among these contending goals with a minimum of anxiety, Charlie must assign them relative priorities. One of the dimensions on which Charlie is going to rank goals is the relative importance they take on in his eyes. Thus, he might consider getting an anniversary present for his wife the single most important thing he has to do. Doing his task might rank second, and so on.

However, another dimension on which Charlie will, in all probability, rank his goals is the immediacy with which each goal can be or must be achieved. As a result, although Charlie is quite willing to concede that getting his task done is much more important than reading the brochures which come in the mail or working out the football pool, the fact that it only takes a few minutes a day to read the brochures and the fact that the football pool must be worked out before the end of the week may well cause him to assign a higher priority to reading brochures and working out the football pool than he assigns to getting his task assignment completed. As a consequence, Charlie will continue to spend portions of his time pursuing short-term goals until his task deadline itself begins to assume the proportions of a short-term goal. But by then it may well be too late.

If this pursuit of short-term goals is the main reason why people miss deadlines, and such appears to be the case, then the solution to the problem is to, instead of having one long-term deadline for the task, have a series of short-term goals for a series of subtasks that, taken together, make up the task. We'll call these short-term goals *checkpoints*.

The chances are Charlie will behave toward these checkpoints the same as he did toward his task deadline, but when he misses a checkpoint, all isn't lost—the deadline hasn't yet been breached, and there's still a long period of time in which a recovery can be made. Thus, such a checkpoint structure acts as an early warning system to give you an opportunity to provide aid and assistance before a deadline is missed.

But more importantly, a checkpoint structure acts as a self-pacing device for the man doing the task. When he misses a checkpoint, he himself knows he's behind schedule, and he can henceforth maintain a high level of effort until he does get back on schedule.

To perform their functions, checkpoints must have certain characteristics. First of all, it must be easy to determine whether the checkpoint has been reached. This means that a checkpoint should be tied either to the production of a product or the occurrence of an event.

A second characteristic of good checkpoints is that the person who is to meet them must consider them realistic. This means he should participate in setting them up.

A third characteristic of good checkpoints is that they should be separated by relatively short periods of time, so that the person doing the task doesn't have time enough to really get into a jam before a checkpoint comes up against which to measure his progress.

## EXERCISES

1. What's the relation between a plan, a cost estimate, and checkpoints?
2. What are the characteristics of good checkpoints?
3. In Exercise 2 at the end of Chapter 9 you developed a manpower plan to take the payroll system, described in Appendix D, from its present design state to the point where the payroll department begins to use the system to generate the company's paychecks and to maintain its payroll records. One such possible manpower plan is shown in Fig. 13-3. You're now going to develop a checkpoint plan designed to monitor the progress of each project member as he works on his assigned tasks. For each checkpoint, describe the product or event that signifies attainment of the checkpoint.

| Personnel | Weeks |
|---|---|
| | 1 2 3 4 5 6 7 8 9 10 11 12 13 14 15 16 17 18 19 20 21 22 23 24 25 26 27 28 29 30 31 32 |
| Miller | Project Management / Develop System Test ... E ... Train User |
| Nazarevitz | Prepare 7 \| Test 7 \| Prepare 8 \| Test 8 ... File Convert ... Parallel Test |
| Fried | Prepare 4 \| Test 4 \| Prepare 16 \| Test 16 |
| Nickelson | A \| Prep. 2 \| Test 2 \| Prep. B \| Test B \| Prep. C \| Test C \| D ... Contingency ... System Test |
| Long | A \| Prepare 13 \| Test 13 \| Prepare 18 \| Test 18 \| User Manual |
| Tabbert | Prepare 10 \| Test 10 \| Prepare 11 \| Test 11 \| Prepare 25 \| Test 25 |
| Catalfo | Prepare 12 \| Test 12 \| Prepare 15 \| Test 15 \| Prepare 17 \| Test 17 |

**Fig. 13-3  Payroll system construction phase manpower plan.**
A—COBOL training.          C—File conversion procedures.
B—Sorts.                   D—Operations manual.
E—Develop training program.

# 14.
# MEETING
# CHECKPOINTS

At the end of Chapter 13 you set up a series of checkpoints to monitor the progress of each project member working on the payroll system. Now, presuming that you're the project leader on the payroll project, what can you do to maximize the probability that the project members will meet their checkpoints? Please write your answer in the space at the bottom of this page.

A suggested approach to the solution of this exercise is to write down a list of the reasons you've heard given for missing checkpoints. Inspection of this list might then give you some clue as to how to improve the probability of meeting checkpoints.

1.

2.

3.

4.

5.

6.

7.

8.

9.

10.

A partial list of reasons often given for missing checkpoints might go as follows.

1. I had to fix a bug in one of my other programs.
2. It took 2 days for me to get my test shot back.
3. Charlie hasn't generated the information I need to finish coding.
4. There's a bug in the data management system.

There is probably little point in continuing with this list. It is apparent from the above partial list that what we are generating is a list of contingencies. The fact of the matter is that it is contingencies which are cited as reasons for missing checkpoints.

Therefore, it stands to reason that, to maximize the probability that project personnel will meet their checkpoints, you should minimize the occurrence of contingency. In Chapter 9 we emphasized the importance of a sincere dedication on the part of the project leader to keeping contingencies down. The significance of this dedication to the project leader's success can perhaps now be more fully appreciated. Again, as Robert Townsend so succinctly puts it:

> When you get right down to it, one of the most important tasks of a manager is to eliminate his people's excuses for failure. But if you're a paper manager, hiding in your office, they may not tell you about the problems only you can solve. So get out and ask them if there's anything you can do to help. Pretty soon they're standing right out there in the open with nobody but themselves to blame. Then they get to work, then they turn on to success, and then they have the strength of ten. (*Up the Organization*, Fawcett Publications, 1971, p. 41.)

Despite your best efforts, checkpoints will be missed. When a checkpoint is missed, there are several things you must do.

1. You must determine the underlying cause of the failure. This is important for several reasons.
   a. The cause may be of a general nature that will cause other people on your project to miss their checkpoints, also.
   b. Even if the cause is peculiar to this individual, it may cause him to miss other checkpoints, too.

   Obviously, once you determine the underlying cause, you must take steps to eliminate it. Determining the underlying cause is an exercise in problem solving, which we can't get into in this book, but one thing of which you should be aware is that the reason the person gives for missing the checkpoint may not be the underlying cause. For example, he may complain of poor computer turnaround, but the real cause may be something he's doing to offend the computer center scheduler.

2. You must determine what has to be done to recover from the missed checkpoint in time to meet the deadline for the person's job assignment. Perhaps a

little extra effort on the person's part will get him back on schedule; perhaps he needs some help, either from you or from someone that you can get temporarily assigned to such duty.

3. If the checkpoint has been missed badly and no recovery procedure available to you is going to prevent overrunning the deadline, then you must inform those people, who are depending on delivery at deadline time, of the slippage *right away*. The sooner they're told, the more chance they'll have to adjust their activities to the slippage.

### EXERCISE

What do you do when a checkpoint is missed?

# CONTROLLING PERFORMANCE

We're now ready to address the question of controlling performance. Remember, the problem of controlling performance is the attempt to answer the question, "Is the project member doing what he's supposed to be doing?"

## 15.1 THE DISTINCTION BETWEEN PERFORMANCE AND QUALITY OF PERFORMANCE

When people talk about performance they tend to talk about two related but different things. We might call one the performance itself and the other the quality of the performance. For example, let's take the case of assigning Fried the task of developing program 16 in the payroll system. First of all, Fried must write a program that will function in the manner called for by the design specifications of the payroll system—this is the *performance* we're looking for from Fried. But in addition, Fried is expected to write program 16 in accordance with certain standards called for by the installation: there are flow-charting standards he must follow, there are standards as to how he's to organize his program, there are standards as to how he's to insert notes in his code, and so on—all this we could call the *quality* of the performance we expect of Fried.

Of course, as project leader, you must be concerned with the quality of the performance of the people on your project, and if the quality of a person's performance isn't up to the level of his job description, then you must see that the person is either upgraded or replaced. But your initial assumption should be that a man does possess the professional skills called for by his job description, and it's primarily the responsibility of the functional supervisor to see that this is so. On the other hand, the responsibility of seeing that the project member performs, in such a manner that his activity contributes to the attainment of the overall project goal, is completely your responsibility.

## 15.2  THE RELATION BETWEEN PERFORMANCE AND PROJECT PHASES

Perhaps the best way to fit the subject of performance and its control into the context of the phases in the development of a data processing system is to review the book up to here from this point of view.

In Chapter 3 we determined that the development of a data processing system goes through basically three phases.

1. Analysis—What the system is going to do is determined.
2. Design—How the system is going to be constructed is determined.
3. Construction—The system is constructed.

In Chapters 7, 8, and 9 we were concerned with the procedure for developing a manpower plan. The steps in this procedure are as follows.

1. Enumerate the tasks making up the job.
2. Determine the dependency between tasks.
3. Determine the external restraints.
4. Allocate personnel to tasks.
5. Estimate the time required to do each task.
6. Allow for contingencies.

Whether you're developing a manpower plan to analyze a system, design a system, or construct a system, the same procedure is followed—it is a general technique.

In Chapter 10 we addressed ourselves to the development of computer time plans. At the moment, the vast majority of data processing projects use computer time in the construction phase of system development only, and we confined ourselves to a consideration of computer time estimating for this phase only.

In Chapters 13 and 14 we discussed the use of checkpoints as the fundamental technique for monitoring the schedule of project members. Making sure project members are on time in the completion of their tasks is of concern to the project leader in the analysis, design, and construction phases, and the checkpoint is a general tool for monitoring schedules in all three phases.

Now we're addressing ourselves to the subject of controlling performance. Controlling the performance of the project members is something that you, as a project leader, want to do in all three phases—analysis, design, and construction. Yet the basic purpose of each phase is different, and consequently, the performance in each phase is different. These facts lead to the idea that the method for controlling performance in each phase may be different, and such is, indeed, the case. As a consequence, when we address ourselves to the subject of controlling performance, we're going to have to do it one phase at a time. We're going to have to discuss the techniques for controlling performance in the analysis phase, the techniques for controlling performance in the design phase, and the techniques for controlling performance in the construction phase.

We have just finished saying that the techniques you, as a project leader, use to control the performance of project members varies depending on which phase in the development of a data processing system your project is in. We also said that this variation occurs because the performance which goes on in each phase is different, and we said that the performance differs by phase because the purpose of each phase is different. As a consequence, we might get a better understanding of these varying control techniques if we have a clear understanding of what we're trying to do in each phase of system development.

Therefore, before reading any further, write as an exercise the purpose of each phase in the development of a data processing system. What is the purpose of the construction phase? Of the design phase? Of the analysis phase.

When you've completed this exercise, please look at the following page to get our viewpoint.

The purpose of the construction phase is to construct a data processing system that conforms to the specifications laid down in the design and analysis phases. The operative words here are "that conform to the specifications laid down in the design and analysis phases." The object isn't to construct just any system, but to construct one that conforms to specifications.

The input to the design phase is the functional specifications, which specify what the system is going to do. The purpose of the design phase is to decide how to construct the system so that it will function as specified in the functional specifications. In a word, the purpose of the design phase is to decide on the design of the system. However, there is generally more than one way to construct the system so it functions as specified, and these various designs are considered better or worse than their alternatives in a variety of ways depending on the point of view that is taken—the computer center considers the design from the point of view of how smoothly the specified system will fit into its operating environment; the maintenance department considers the design from the point of view of how easy the system will be to maintain; the auditors consider the design from the point of view of how amenable the system is to audit; and the system designers consider the system from the point of view of how efficiently it uses available data processing facilities. To some extent, these points of view conflict, and the purpose of the design phase is to settle on a design that effects the optimum compromise between all conflicting interests. Such a design would be considered the "best" of the alternatives.

The purpose of the analysis phase is to come to an agreement with the user as to what the proposed system is going to do.

We can summarize the purpose of the three phases in the development of a data processing system as follows:

Analysis—Come to an agreement with the user as to what the system is going to do.

Design—Determine the best design for the system.

Construction—Construct the system according to specifications.

We have now determined the purpose of each phase in the development of a data processing system. In doing so we have also specified the performance that you, as a project leader, are looking for from the project members in each one of the phases. Thus:

1. In the analysis phase, you're looking for performance that will result in agreement with the user as to what the system is going to do.

2. In the design phase, you're looking for performance that will result in the best design for the system.

3. In the construction phase, you're looking for performance that will result in a system constructed according to specifications.

It is now time to turn our attention to the techniques you, as a project leader, use to control the performance of the project members in the construction, design, and analysis phases so their performance produces the results appropriate to the purpose of each phase.

Let's start by asking: What techniques should a project leader use to control the performance of project members in the construction phase so their performance produces a system constructed according to specifications?

Perhaps the first answer that comes to mind is testing—that is, preparing data and predetermined results on the basis of the functional and design specifications, and then seeing if the system produces the predetermined results when fed the prepared data. Certainly testing is an essential control technique; without it there's no way to unequivocally demonstrate that the system operates as specified.

However, the drawback to testing as a control technique is that it doesn't become effective until the system is built. It would be desirable to have some technique that becomes operative earlier in the construction phase.

One such control technique is the use of internal specifications. Let us explain what we mean by this.

Most data processing systems are subdivided into parts, called modules. A module may be a program or a subroutine. Associated with each module is a document that describes what the functions of the module are and how it goes about performing its functions. This document is variously called the program narrative, the program specifications, and so on. We'll call this document the internal specifications for the module.

The ultimate justification for internal specifications is that it's necessary to make the module maintainable, and the practice of first developing the module and then writing the internal specifications isn't unknown. However, it's now fairly well recognized that, if the internal specifications are written as the first step in the development of the module, then the internal specifications operate as a control on the programmer's performance. His job is to develop a module that conforms to the internal specifications; if he deliberately departs from the internal specifications in developing the module, then his job should be explained to him; it should be necessary to make this explanation only once.

In some instances, the internal specifications are prepared in advance and given to the programmer when he's assigned the module to develop. As far as controlling the programmer's performance is concerned, the problem with this approach is whether the programmer understands what the internal specifications call for. The suggested solution to this problem is to let the programmer absorb the internal specifications and then discuss the internal specifications with him and see if he sounds like he understands them.

However, we suggest the opposite approach. First discuss the what and the how of the module with the programmer, and then let him write the internal specifications for your review. Presumably this review will result in revisions, which require review, and so on, but when the programmer has prepared a revised set of internal specifications of which you approve, the chances are excellent that you and the programmer have a common understanding of the module he's to develop.

A third control technique that can be used in the construction phase is conventions. For example, of the 18 programs in the payroll system for which you developed construction plans, five are sorts. Of the remaining 13, nine pass the master file. You can have a standard data description made for the master file, put it on the library, and require that every program passing the master file use the library description for the file. In so doing, you've conventionalized that part of the data division of those programs passing the master file, which means that, for that part of those programs, your control is absolute.

Now, what control techniques should you use in the design phase so the project member's performance produces the best system design?

First of all, we must remember that "best" means the optimum compromise between the conflicting desires of the interested parties. Therefore, one control technique is to be certain every one of the interested parties has an opportunity to review the proposed design and discuss it with all other interested parties before they collectively approve the design. All this is, of course, the idea and purpose of the design review committee, which constitutes the essential design control technique.

Of course, many of the viewpoints of the interested parties can be anticipated—to such an extent, in fact, that many of them are documented and standardized. Thus, the computer center has design standards as to what characteristics will and won't make a system acceptable from an operating point of view; the maintenance department has standards as to what will and won't make a system acceptable from a maintenance point of view; and the design department has standards as to what will and won't utilize present data processing facilities efficiently. The job description of every system designer should call for him to either conform to these standards when designing systems or to justify and get clearance from the interested party for any deviation from standard. As a consequence, specification of these standards becomes a second design control technique.

Another thing that must be recognized about system design is that there's no way to know when you've developed the best design. The most you can hope for is to recognize the best design among conceivable alternatives. Therefore, a third control technique is to require that system designers develop alternative designs and have reasons why one design was selected over the alternatives.

Finally, what control techniques should you use in the analysis phase so the project members' performance produces agreement with the user as to what the system is going to do?

User approval of the functional specifications is the final demonstration that such agreement has been reached. The need to get approval operates as a control on the project members during the development of the functional specifications and will encourage them to adhere to all aspects of good system analysis practice during the analysis phase. However, the ultimate requirement for assuring that the user's approval of the functional specifications is meaningful, and not perfunctory, is to have the user participate actively at a high level during the development of the functional specifications.

There is one control technique appropriate to all three phases: communication between the project members. When more than one person works on a project, there is always the problem of whether the products of the various individual efforts will fit together into a smoothly operating system. If the people talk to each other about their work, this problem is minimized.

One way to get project members to communicate is to hold periodic project meetings, at each of which one project member makes a presentation on what he's doing on the project. In particular, if two project members aren't getting together to resolve an interface definition problem, a meeting between them that you call and attend as an interested observer may break the ice.

However, the best way to get people to talk to one another is to keep them physically close to one another. Analysts, designers, and programmers shouldn't be encouraged to identify their work habitat in terms of a particular location. Instead, they should be encouraged to identify with their furniture. Then, when a person is assigned to a project, he and his furniture are moved to where all the people working on the project are located.

## EXERCISE

Make a list of the techniques you'd use to control performance in the analysis, design, and construction phases.

# THE TICKLER FILE

In Chapter 15, our procedure for determining the control techniques appropriate to a particular phase was to determine the purpose of a phase, determine what performance would lead to achieving that purpose, and to then develop techniques which would encourage the performance we were looking for. It might be useful to apply this procedure to at least some aspects of the project leader's job.

Twice now (once in Chapter 9 and once in Chapter 14) we've emphasized that one main aspect of your job as project leader is to be forward looking. You must anticipate the problems the project could run into in the future, make plans to avoid these problems, communicate these plans to the people who are in a position to deliver the resources required to avoid the problems, and obtain commitments from these people concerning delivery of these resources. At the same time, you make commitments concerning deliveries you and the project are to make. In a word, a good bit of your activity is future oriented. You obtain commitments from other people, and you make commitments as to what's going to happen in the future.

As a human, you're not going to remember all these commitments. Yet it is crucial that you do so.

1. Your reputation depends on your ability to deliver on your commitments.

2. Your ability to avoid problems for your project depends on seeing that the commitments made to you are met.

The one way to be sure to remember a commitment is to enter it into a file that will remind you of the commitment when the time for you to act on the commitment has come. We'll call such a file a tickler file. It is also commonly known as a followup file or a suspense file.

A tickler file is organized by date. It may be an actual file of papers, or it may be a desk calendar, or a month at a glance calendar. It is used as follows.

For example, suppose you've agreed to make a presentation to a number of user personnel on Friday the 19th. Then you make note of this fact and file it under Tuesday the 16th or Wednesday the 17th, so you'll get the reminder far enough in advance to give yourself time to prepare the presentation.

Or suppose you've received a commitment from someone concerning delivery of information, equipment, manpower, supplies, what have you. Place an entry, which will remind you to remind the person of his commitment, into your tickler file far enough in advance so that when you do remind the person, he still has time enough to deliver on schedule. Reminding people of their commitments is known as followup, and unfortunately, all too often, it's an essential part of obtaining delivery. Thus, getting delivery is typically a two-step process: (1) getting a commitment from a person to make the delivery; (2) following up with the person so he'll take the steps necessary to make delivery.

A tickler file will work if you do two things.

1. Make an entry in it each time you make a commitment or have a commitment made to you.
2. Look at it every day so it can remind you of the actions to be taken that day.

### EXERCISES

1. Why should you have a tickler file?
2. What two things must you do to make a tickler file work?

# DOCUMENTATION

At almost every step in this book we've had something to say about documentation. However, our comments about documentation have always been in the context of concern with some other subject. Nevertheless, documentation is an important topic in itself, and at this point in the book we'd like to address it exclusively.

The first document produced in the development of a data processing system is the functional specifications. A set of standards for functional specifications is given in Appendix B.

As we said in Chapter 3, user approval of the functional specifications marks the end of the analysis phase in the development of a data processing system. Consequently, system development can't get past the analysis phase until the functional specifications have been developed and approved.

The next document produced during the development of a data processing system is the design specifications. A set of standards for design specifications is given in Appendix A.

As we said in Chapter 3, design review committee approval of the design specifications marks the end of the design phase in system development. Consequently, system development can't get past the design phase until the design specifications have been developed and approved.

System development then enters the construction phase. During the construction phase many computer-program modules are developed, and several documents are prepared for each one of these modules.

The first document produced in the development of a program module is the internal specifications. An example of internal specifications for a program is given in Appendix H. An example of internal specifications for a subroutine is given in Appendix I. Together, these examples demonstrate that, regardless of whether the internal specifications are for a program or a subroutine, the specifications have a common format, which is depicted in outline form in Fig. 17-1.

As we said in Chapter 15, no other steps in the development of a module should be taken until the internal specifications have been written and approved. Consequently, the computer-program part of system construction cannot be completed until the internal specifications for all modules have been written and approved.

In Chapter 15 we proposed that the optimum way of developing the internal specifications is to have the programmer write them for your review and approval. The objection is sometimes raised that this is asking too much from the programmer in terms of creativity. To determine the validity of this objection, let's take Fig. 17-1 and review it item by item to see just how much creativity is involved.

1. Input
   a. Medium
   b. Format
   c. Sequence or Organization and Access Method
   d. Content
   e. Restrictions
2. Output
   a. Medium
   b. Format
   c. Sequence or Organization and Access Method
   d. Content
   e. Restrictions
3. Tables
   a. Format
   b. Content
   c. Use
4. Processing
   a. Tests on Input Fields
   b. Output Field Source
5. Error Handling
6. Notes

**Fig. 17-1  Internal Specification Contents.**

The first two items in the internal specifications contents are descriptions of the input to and the output from the module. There's no creativity involved here. All this information was developed during the design phase. All that is required to put together these two parts of the internal specifications is to find the information in the applicable design documents.

The third item on the internal specifications table of contents is a description of the tables used by this module. How much creativity is involved here is a matter of whether the tables to be described are used exclusively by this module or are used in common by several modules. If a table is used in common by several modules, then its format, content, and use will have been specified in the design phase, and all that is required to incorporate the table's description in the internal specifications is to find the applicable information in the design documents. If the table is unique to the module, the programmer will have to determine its format, content and use, but this is, in no sense, the imposition of a special requirement on the programmer—this is just part of his normal job assignment. All we're asking him to do is to design the table at the time he writes the internal specifications, rather than wait until he writes the code. All this is well within the programmer's ability and can hardly be considered an extension of his responsibilities.

The fourth item on the table of contents is a description of the processing done by the module. It is possible that some of this information may have to be rewritten to cast it into a context appropriate to internal specifications, but we would deny that there is any basic creativity involved here. All the processing done by the system is specified in the functional specifications, and writing the processing section of the internal specifications for a given module is a matter of locating, in the functional specifications, descriptions appropriate to this module.

Perhaps we have now gone far enough to demonstrate that the writing of the internal specifications is not an exercise in creativity, but instead, is primarily a matter of collecting and organizing information. And if a person can't collect and organize information, we have serious doubts as to his qualifications as a programmer. As a result, we see little reason to not ask programmers to write internal specifications. Just the opposite, there seems to be every reason why programmers should write internal specifications.

One approach to the development of internal specifications that might significantly reduce the programmer's writing burden is as follows. Since so much of the information in internal specifications is material taken from design and functional specifications, instead of reproducing the information in the internal specifications, the internal specifications can be written to simply refer to the appropriate sections of the other documents for the pertinent information. This approach has the added advantage of having each unit of information appearing in one document only, which makes specification changes easier to control.

A second document produced in the development of a program module is the logical analysis. The need for a logical analysis document can be met by either a decision table or a flow chart.

The validity of a flow chart as a type of documentation is clouded by the fact that it is also used as an aid in analysis while coding. In this latter function, it may take almost any form and be done on any level. But the function of a flow chart as a document is to aid someone who is interested in isolating, in a program, the code that performs a particular logical function; it is a kind of roadmap for the coding. As such, it serves this function only if it is made at a logical function level. Detailed flow charts may aid in coding, but they are not a form of documentation. A schematic of the level of flow charting that serves as a form of module documentation is shown in Fig. 17-2.

A flow chart at this documentation level serves its purpose if it shows how the program module is to be organized into a main chain and a number of subroutines. Such module organization is a necessity for ease of debugging and maintenance. Therefore, there is every reason why a programmer should be required to produce such a logical analysis document before he is allowed to begin writing code.

A third document produced in the development of a program module is the program listing. Program listings are produced as an automatic by-product of the compilation process. The only question with respect to program listings is: Are they documents? That is: Are they readable? The answer is: They will be if the programmer comments his code appropriately as he writes it. You should expect this from him as a matter of course, since his job description should call for him to comment his code according to installation standards. These standards should require at least the following:

1. Use of meaningful datanames. You can enforce this use by conventionalizing the data descriptions used.
2. Organization of the code as specified in the logical analysis.
3. A descriptive note before each routine or other functionally identifiable block of code.

Beside program-module documentation, several other documents are produced during the construction phase. One of these documents is what we'll call the regression test. This test consists of a test plan, test data, and predetermined results for the system. The regression test is prepared for use when the system goes into production. A production system is always subject to maintenance changes, and one of the dangers with such changes is that, when a change is made, the change may not only alter the system as desired, it may also alter the system in unanticipated and undesirable ways. The regression test is used to detect such undesirable alterations. After a maintenance modification has been made to a system, the system is then run against the regression test, to make sure the rest of the system still performs as desired, before putting the modified system into production.

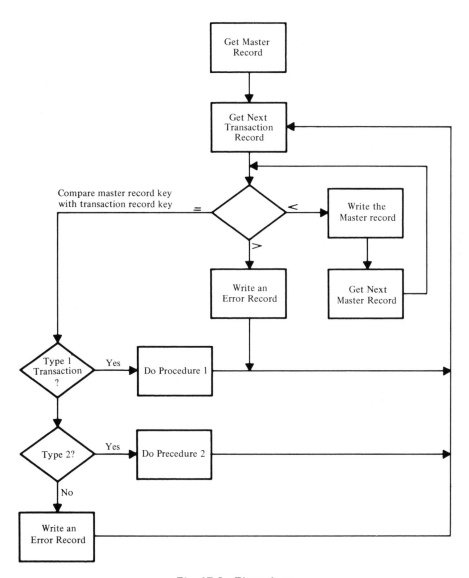

**Fig. 17-2 Flow chart.**

Development of a regression test is a project responsibility and should be a requirement for the maintenance department to accept the system as maintainable. If you, as a project leader, anticipate the need to develop a regression test as you should, the economical time to develop the regression test is as a subset of the system test.

As we said in Chapter 7, the system test must be developed before it can be performed, and as we said in Chapter 10, you shouldn't allow a system to enter acceptance testing until system test results have convinced you that passage of the acceptance test is practically a certainty. Consequently, system construction can't be completed before system test development is completed. And if the regression test is developed as a subset of the system test, the construction phase can't be completed until the regression test has been developed.

Another document produced during the construction phase is the operations manual. The operations manual is developed according to the standards specified by the computer center.

As we said in Chapter 7, the operations manual must be prepared before the system test can be considered complete. Consequently, the construction phase can't be completed until the operations manual has been prepared.

A third document produced during construction is the user manual. As seen in Chapter 4, the user manual must be prepared before user training takes place, which in turn must start before acceptance testing can begin. Consequently, the construction phase can't be completed until the user manual has been prepared.

We've now discussed the following documents.

1. Functional specifications.
2. Design specifications.
3. Internal specifications.
4. Logical analysis.
5. Program listing.
6. Regression test.
7. Operations manual.
8. User manual.

Our contention is that if you have all these documents for a system, you have a well-documented system. The important point is that every one of the documents in the above list is developed as a by-product of the efforts of the project to put the system into production. In other words, if you run your project as we agree you should, there should be no great effort toward the end of the project to develop the system documentation. Instead, it should all have been developed as a matter of course in the normal development activities engaged in during project life.

An example of functional specifications is given in Appendix J. This example is a small part of the functional specifications for the payroll system described in Appendix D—specifically, that part which describes the personnel action form, one of the two transaction inputs to the system.

If you look at the last page of Appendix J, you'll see that we're deceiving you. For on this last page is reproduced a copy of the final personnel action form.

This form would never be developed to this final state for the functional specifications. Appendix J is actually a part of the user manual for the payroll system.

However, we don't feel bad about this deception, since it emphasizes the point we want to make about functional specifications. We maintain that:

1. By the time the functional specifications are complete, you should know in detail what is going to be on the personnel action form, and in general, you should have decided on its layout.
2. The functional specifications should be written in user manual form, which is the ideal way to describe the user's interface with the system to the user in the user's words.

As we pointed out in Chapter 9, writing the user manual should be primarily a matter of modifying the functional specifications. If we were to engage in specious quantification, we'd say that, when the functional specifications are complete, 90% of the user manual has been written. The other 10% represents modifications and a description of the detection and handling of error situations, which may become clearer in the construction phase.

Documentation not only means developing documents. It also means revising the documents to keep them up to date.

When documents are developed, they're then typically distributed. When a document is revised, the already distributed copies must also be revised, and the recipients of previous distributions must be encouraged to update themselves by reading the revisions. This is best accomplished by making it easy for the recipient to both revise his copy of the document and update himself. Thus, the recipient should never be required to write anything to revise his documents. Either the whole document should be reissued, or if the revision is less wholesale, revised replacement pages should be issued. This latter approach, of course, requires that the document originally be issued in looseleaf form.

Also, there should be, in a revision document, a clear indication of what was revised, so the recipient need read only the revised information. This can be done with the use of a revision bar, a narrow vertical black line in the left margin to indicate content changes and additions—clerical changes need not be so marked.

The original document and each revision should carry a date so a record can be kept of what the latest version of a document is.

Finally, when a document is issued, a list of recipients should be established and then maintained, so when a revision is made, it can be distributed to all current document holders.

## EXERCISES

1. Does a special effort have to be made to develop the documentation for a data processing system?

2. Why doesn't a special effort have to be made to develop the documentation for a data processing system?

3. During the analysis, design, and construction phases of a project, a number of documents are produced in the normal course of system development work. Collectively, these documents make up the documentation of the system. Suppose you're going to collect all these documents in one volume. Please write the table of contents for this volume.

4. To whose specifications is the operations manual written?

5. Is preparing the user manual a major effort? If so, why? If not, why not?

6. What is a regression test? What is its purpose?

# COMMUNICATION

# COMMUNICATION

Throughout this book we've placed ourselves in the position of the project leader. In sections III and IV our perspective has been to look down into the project. Our concern has been with planning, monitoring, and controlling the project members' activities. These might be called the project leader's coordination responsibilities.

In this chapter we're going to look at things somewhat differently. We recognize that a project doesn't exist in a vacuum, but in a living, changing environment. Maintaining our position as project leader, we're going to change our perspective and start looking out into the project's environment. Our concern is now going to be with the project leader's communication responsibilities.

Typical inhabitants of a data processing project's environment are:

1. The user.
2. Your manager.
3. The computer center.
4. Service organizations, both within and without the company, that may be supplying your project with various required services.

To gain insight into the meaning and function of your communication responsibilities, it may be useful to look at the group-leader relationship in general. The first question we might ask is why, when there's a group, is there always a leader? For a better understanding of this question, it might be pertinent to ask a more fundamental question: Why are there groups in the first place?

The answer appears to be that, deliberately or by chance, people recognize that they can, as a group, attain goals beyond their reach as individuals. They collectively attain these goals by specializing their activities according to their skills and aptitudes. Thus, in the proverbial Indian tribe, the fat men do the fishing, the lean men do the hunting, and the wise men make the medicine.

If the specialized activities of the group members are to mesh in the drive for their common goal, the activities must be coordinated. This coordination function is performed by the leader. Thus, the leader is the group member whose specialty is coordination. The leader may acquire his position by hereditary succession; democratic process; naked force; appointment; or as in many social groups, the process by which the leader is chosen may be much less formal and obvious. However, every group has a leader, whose particular specialty is coordination.

The next interesting thing we might notice about groups and leaders is that, not only does the leader of a group take the responsibility for coordinating the group's activities, he's also the chief communicator between the group and its environment. Thus, the President of the United States coordinates domestic policy; he also happens to be the chief foreign officer of the country. The coach of a little league ball club decides who'll play where and what the club's strategy and tactics will be; he also negotiates with the coaches of other teams concerning the possibilities, locations, and times of games between their teams. The pattern is ubiquitous. And the question is: Why?

One factor is the "little green man syndrome." When the flying saucer settles to the ground and the little green man steps out, he says, "Take me to your leader." The outsider who wants to know something about a group's activities doesn't want to talk to just any group member. He wants to talk to the coordinator, since he assumes the coordinator is the group member with the overall perspective of the group's activities. Thus, there are forces in a group's environment that draw the coordinator into communication.

But there are also forces within a group that push the coordinator into communication. Within a group the members' specialized activities impinge on one another, and it's in these areas of potential conflict that the members look to their leader to coordinate their activities. From time to time the specialized activities of a group member will also impinge on the group's environment, and just as the group member looks to his leader to coordinate his activities with his fellow group members, he expects his leader to give him direction so he can optimize his activities with respect to the environment also. In other words, the group members not only expect their leader to know what's going on in the group, they also expect him to know what's going on in the environment. Despite the force and authority a leader wields, to some extent he also maintains his position through the consent of the governed. If the group members don't feel their leader is in adequate communication with the group's environment—so his knowledge of circumstances is limited—a credibility gap arises between the leader and the group, and the group may well withhold their willingness to accept the leader's coordination. President Johnson's unprecedented decision to not seek a second term is a dramatic example of how a group can turn its leader out.

The moral of this investigation into group-leader relationships is that if you want to do an effective job of coordinating, you must pay attention to your communication responsibilities, for the two are mutually dependent, and you can't neglect one without degrading the other.

As a project leader, you must maintain a balance between your communication and coordination responsibilities. If you concentrate on your coordination responsibilities to the exclusion of your communication responsibilities, you'll become progressively more out of touch with what's going on in your project's environment, and ultimately, your coordination will become unreal and ineffective. On the other hand, if you concentrate on your communication responsibilities to the exclusion of your coordination responsibilities, you'll become progressively more out of touch with what's going on in your project, and ultimately, you'll cease to have anything about which to communicate.

Most of us with a programming and design background don't have a problem appreciating the importance of coordination, but the initial reaction of many of us to the idea of communication is that it's an interruption, a distraction, and a waste of time. Given our background, this attitude isn't difficult to understand. When we were programmers we were given well-bounded problems to solve, and their solution required long periods of intense concentration. When we became designers, the size of the problems with which we wrestled became significantly larger, but the nature of the work didn't change—it was still a matter of solving the problem within the boundaries set for the problem, and it still required long periods of intense concentration. Now, when we become project leaders and are given a project goal to achieve, our reaction is frequently, "O.K., you've given me a job to do. Now leave me alone so I can get it done."

Unfortunately, the attitude that served us so well as programmers and designers is no longer functional for us as project leaders. From now on, when we receive an invitation to communicate, we must stifle our initial negative reaction, and instead, consider the invitation as an opportunity to deepen our understanding of the context in which our project is operating.

All this doesn't mean you automatically accept every invitation to communicate that is offered. You must maintain a balance between your communication and coordination activities; you have plenty of coordination responsibilities; and therefore, the amount of time you can devote to communication is limited. What you want to do is participate in those communications that are productive, both for you and the people with whom you're communicating, and turn down the invitations to communication which are going to be unproductive, particularly for you. (By *productive* we mean communication that furthers your understanding of the environment in which your project is operating and that, consequently, increases your ability to be an effective coordinator.)

You don't have to worry about getting invitations to communicate. If you show yourself to be a cooperative communicator willing to dispense meaningful information, the "little green man syndrome" will guarantee that you'll get the invitations you need and then some. The basic problem is: How do you tell which invitations to accept, and which ones to decline, at the time the invitation is offered?

## 18.1   AVOIDING UNPRODUCTIVE MEETINGS

One type of communication that chews up prodigious amounts of time is meetings. If you could only tell beforehend which meetings to attend and which can be safely avoided, you'd save yourself a tremendous amount of time. Fortunately, there are a couple of tests you can apply to distinguish the gold from the dross.

There is only one legitimate reason for calling a meeting: to get those attending to agree on the next step to be taken toward the solution of a problem the attendees face in common. This is called the purpose of the meeting.

Unfortunately, not every meeting that is called has a purpose. For example, sometimes a meeting is called just because "we haven't had a meeting for a while."

Of course, the invitation to a meeting should state the meeting's purpose, so the attendees can prepare themselves to participate fully in the meeting. If an invitation doesn't state the meeting's purpose, you can hardly be faulted for getting in touch with the person who has called the meeting and saying, "Charlie, I got your invitation to the meeting next Tuesday. Thank you very much. I'd like to contribute to your meeting as much as possible, and I'm wondering if you can tell me the meeting's purpose, so I can prepare myself." It's amazing how frequently this question is an absolute conversation stopper. If the person who called the meeting doesn't know its purpose, we suggest that you discover you've a previous engagement for next Tuesday.

Once you've ascertained the meeting's purpose, you should decide whether you can contribute to the meeting. If you can, then by all means, you should attend the meeting. It is an opportunity for you to help the other attendees, and such meetings are the ones most likely to produce information you can use in doing your job.

People are sometimes invited to meetings that do have a purpose, but to which they can't contribute. For example, technical people are often invited to meetings on the off chance that some technical question may arise. This isn't sufficient justification for tying such people down for the length of the meeting.

If after you've determined the purpose of the meeting, you can't see how you can contribute to the meeting, you can hardly be condemned for saying, "O.K., Charlie, that certainly is a good reason for having a meeting, but frankly, I don't quite see how I fit in. In what way can I contribute?" If Charlie's reason for your attendance doesn't sound compelling to you, once more suggest a "previous engagement." For example, if the only reason you've been invited is because Charlie feels there's some remote chance that, sometime during the meeting, someone might raise a question only you can answer, then you might reply, "Charlie, I can see how I might be of assistance to you in that regard. Unfortunately, I'm all tied up next Tuesday, but I'll be here in the office, and if a question does arise, please call me. I'd be glad to take time out to give you the answer."

Later on in this chapter, after we've established some groundwork by discussing certain other aspects of communications, we'll return to the subject of how to avoid unnecessary communications. For now, let's turn our attention to what are, perhaps, some of the more characteristic types of communications that flow between you, as the project leader, and some of the inhabitants of your project's environment.

We've identified four typical inhabitants of a data processing project's environment.

1. The user.
2. Your manager.
3. The computer center.
4. Service organizations.

One type of communication between you and the user that we have already discussed quite thoroughly is requests for change. (See Chapter 3.)

## 18.2  HANDLING POTENTIALLY DISRUPTIVE COMMUNICATIONS

Requests for change are an example of a potentially disruptive form of communication. By *disruptive* we mean disruptive to your ability to carry out your coordination responsibilities.

A request for change is disruptive when it's communicated directly to a project member and he agrees on his own to make the change. As a consequence, the specifications as this particular project member sees them and the specifications as they appear to you and the other project members now, to some extent, differ, and this difference in specifications creates a coordination problem for you.

One way you control the potentially disruptive effects of requests for change is to channel them. You tell the user all requests for change are to be submitted to you. And you tell the project members that, if any member of the user organization makes a request for change to any one of them, he is to:

1. Listen politely.
2. Not make any commitments.
3. After the member of the user organization has left, come to you and describe what has happened, and you'll take it from there.

Another way you control the potentially disruptive effects of requests for change is to formalize them. You design a form on which they are to be submitted, and you establish a procedure for processing the form.

We appreciate that, in giving this advice, we're encouraging you to establish some paperwork. As long as that paperwork is performing a positive function, fine. The trouble with most paperwork is that it hangs on long after the need for it has disappeared. So, when you formalize a communication, do a favor for those who come after you—make clear why you formalized it, and if the need for it goes away, do away with the paperwork.

## 18.3  STATUS REPORTS

Another type of communication between you and both the user and your manager is status reports. A status report is a written report on the status of your project that is submitted to the user and your manager on a periodic basis.

Unquestionably, the status report performs the function of supplying the recipient with status information, although it has been truly said that a status report should contain no surprises. That is to say, if a development occurs on your project which either the user or your manager would consider significant, you don't wait until status report time to communicate with respect to that development—instead, you tell the interested parties about it right away.

A more important function of a status report is that its preparation forces you to review the progress of your project to date, assess that progress in terms of your overall goals and plans, and adjust your plans appropriately to maintain your best posture toward your long-term goals. Let's take a look at status reports from this point of view, and in doing so, we may be able to come up with an outline of what a status report should cover.

In preparing a status report, the first thing you're going to have to do is develop a comprehensive list of all the accomplishments, or lack thereof, that have occurred since submission of your last status report. This list consists of all checkpoints and deadlines met by the project members during the last report period, and represents your progress during the last report period.

Next, you must evaluate your progress during the last report period against the goals you set for that report period, which in turn, gives you a picture of where you now stand in terms of your long-term goals and plans.

In making this evaluation you'll pinpoint problems (contingencies) of various types.

1. Problems that have occurred and which have set you back, but which have subsequently been solved.
2. Problems that have occurred and which are setting you back, but for which you now have a solution, which is presently being applied.
3. Problems that have occurred, which are setting you back, which are beyond your control, and for which you've suggested a solution which hasn't yet been implemented.
4. Problems that have occurred, which are setting you back, which are beyond your control, and for which you can't suggest a solution. (Entries in this category should be rare, but we don't want to completely eliminate the possibility.)

Once you've enumerated your accomplishments, evaluated your progress toward your long-term goals, and identified your problems, you're ready to develop your short-term plans for maintaining your best posture toward your long-term goals. These plans will take the form of short-term goals you set for yourself to reach during the next report period.

While you're formulating your goals for the next report period, you'll anticipate problems that may arise in attaining these goals. These will all be problems that are beyond your control and will be some form of delivery failure.

When you've taken all the steps described above, you'll have done a thorough job of reviewing your project; in all probability, you will have discovered things about your project that you were previously either completely unaware of or unwilling to admit; and you'll have collected a comprehensive amount of status information in the following categories.

1. Accomplishments in the last report period.
2. Overall progress toward long-term goals.
3. Problems.
4. Goals for the next report period.

In putting this information together, you'll have collected all the information a user or manager could conceivably want in a status report. As a matter of fact, you have exactly the opposite problem—too much information. The user will find the great bulk of this information irrelevant to his concerns, and even your manager will be interested in only selected portions of this information.

But of course, this is nothing more than the classic problem of report writing. Writing reports is always a two-step procedure: (1) collect the pertinent information; (2) organize the information so the recipient will read it.

Organizing the information will require some work on your part, and it's fair for you to ask: Am I really interested in having the user and my manager read my status reports, or am I preparing and submitting status reports as a perfunctory exercise in keeping the natives quiet? We think you're interested in having the user and your manager read your status reports, for two reasons.

1. If your status reports keep the recipients informed in a meaningful way, this can only increase their desire to aid you when you need their help, which you do almost constantly.
2. Status report time is an ideal time to remind the user and your manager of those problems of yours whose solutions lie in their hands. They won't get reminded unless they read your report.

So how should a status report be organized? We believe that all the information you have collected should be incorporated into the status report as a series of appendices. The cover report to these appendices should be not more than a page, or two at the most, that highlights the information detailed in the appendices.

The cover report to the user should be different than the cover report to your manager, since the user and your manager have different concerns. The cover report by itself is probably sufficient as a status report to the user, but the appendices should be attached to the cover report for your manager, for even though he'll probably never look at them all, after having read the cover report, he may want to selectively review the appendices.

The next question is: How frequently should a status report be prepared? If you're leading a project such as the payroll project we've been using in this book as a case study exercise, and if you do everything we've described above to collect the information on which your status report is to be based, it wouldn't be surprising if it took you a day or two to do the collecting. You obviously can't do this kind of review too frequently, or you aren't going to have time to competently handle all your other project leader responsibilities.

We recommend that you prepare a status report, in the manner described, once a month. If company procedures require you to submit a status report more frequently, you can submit interim, exception reports as updates to your comprehensive monthly report.

If you're going to prepare a status report only once a month, and if that report is to be comprehensive, we recommend that you take notes during the month, because at the end of the month you aren't going to remember everything significant which has happened during the month. We aren't suggesting anything fancy. A manila folder in which you drop notes when significant things happen is sufficient. Many significant events come accompanied by documents, and in this case, you don't have to make any notes at all—just drop a copy of the accompanying document in your folder. If it's necessary to write a note, the note doesn't have to be comprehensive—just a few words to remind you of the event is sufficient. The object isn't to develop some well-organized, easily readable historical document, but simply to assemble a collection of notes which will assure that you do incorporate all the pertinent information in your next status report.

We might call the folder in which you're collecting your historical notes a log, except that the word "log" implies a permanent historical record. We conceive of the notes in the folder as being quite temporary—when you've used them all to remind you of the various items that should be included in your status report, they can be disposed of.

As a matter of fact, we'd maintain that, if you prepare your status reports as described, a file of your status reports over the life of your project constitutes an excellent project history, and no other record keeping for historical purposes should be necessary.

This raises the question: Is there any reason why a project history should be kept? In the course of your work as project leader, you'll find that, on occasion, you'll want to reconstruct what happened at some prior point in the life of your project. Without a project history, your reconstruction abilities are going to be partial at best. This need alone would appear to be sufficient justification for keeping a project history. But there's another reason, also, and this reason leads us back to the topic of avoiding unnecessary communications.

## 18.4  AVOIDING UNNECESSARY REPORT WRITING

From time to time, perhaps more frequently than we like to think, project leaders are asked to prepare reports on special subjects. For example, the data processing manager may have given one of his staff the assignment to investigate the extent to which the systems and programming group meets its deadlines. Consequently, as part of his information collecting operation, the staff man asks you to prepare a report on the deadlines set up on your project; the extent to which they are met; and where deadlines have been missed, by how much they have been missed, and why.

Now, there is every reason why the data processing manager should want to conduct such an investigation, and every reason why his staff man should come to you to collect information for the investigation. As a consequence, if you don't have this information available in a documented form, you've no alternative but to grit your teeth and prepare the special report.

But, if you've been preparing status reports as we've recommended and are collecting them in a historical file, you already have all the information the staff man wants in a documented form. Now all you have to do is make a copy of your historical file, present the staff man with the copy, and your obligation has been met. You've provided the information. Now it's up to the staff man to organize the information in the best way he sees fit.

## 18.5  COMMUNICATING WITH SERVICE ORGANIZATIONS

The term *service organizations* covers a wide spectrum of organizations from consultants and proprietary software houses to publishers. The one thing they have in common is that they're all in the same position with respect to you as you are with respect to the user. Therefore, if you run into any problem in dealing with one of these organizations and you don't know quite how to handle the problem, a general approach would be to think of the most similar situation the user could be in with relation to you and ask yourself how the user would approach the problem. Thus, you contract for the services of service organizations; you define what your needs are; if necessary, you enter a phased development procedure with them; you request status reports; you set deadlines; you keep them notified of all your changes of plans; and so on. And in dealing with service organizations, always remember the major complaint you have of users—they don't get involved enough at a high level. Don't be a poor user.

## 18.6  COMMUNICATING WITH THE COMPUTER CENTER

Communication with the computer center occurs in two different contexts.

1. Ultimately, the computer center will run the system you're developing on a production basis. Here your communication must be concerned with seeing that the system is installed in the computer center as smoothly as possible—that the operations manual is in good order and does its job; that the system will fit into the center's overall schedule; that the center has been informed with sufficient lead time of the supplies and facilities which must be available to run the system; that center personnel have the skills required to run the system, and so on.
2. With respect to test time, the computer center is one more instance of a service organization and should be communicated with accordingly.

### EXERCISES

1. What points should a status report cover?
2. What's the purpose of a status report?
   a. For the recipient?
   b. For the sender?

3. What are the mechanics of constructing a project history?
4. People operate in groups by specializing their activities. What is the group leader's specialty?
5. What two forces push a group leader into communication with the group's environment?
6. What two questions should you ask to determine if it's worthwhile for you to attend a meeting?
7. What are two general techniques for handling potentially disruptive communications?
8. How frequently should you prepare a comprehensive status report?
9. How do you make sure all the significant things that happened this month get into this month's status report?
10. What do you represent to a service organization?

# VII
# GENERAL PROJECT CONSIDERATIONS

# TIME REPORTING

In the context of project management, one topic that almost always arises, and about which the greatest anxiety is frequently shown, is time estimating. The message that seems to be coming across on this topic goes something like this: "If I could only figure out some way of reliably estimating the time required to get my jobs done, my biggest management problems would be solved."

The anxiety associated with this topic might be interpreted as genuine concern for repeated failure to solve a vexing problem. But other evidence suggests a more cynical explanation. Suppose it was possible to come up with a simple, foolproof way of telling just how long it should take to do various systems and programming jobs—then what would people use as an excuse for not getting done on time?

The first discrepancy between the facts and this missionary zeal to find the time-estimating touchstone takes the following shape. Since time estimating has to do with what's going to happen in the future, it is, by nature, an "iffy" business. As a result, nobody gets very upset if actual time varies from estimated by some small amount. What gets people's dander is the consistency with which we in data processing overrun our estimates by the hundreds of percents. And of those instances we've investigated, little of the overrun can be attributed to poor estimates. Instead, we find that one or more of these holds true:

1. The user wasn't firmly identified.
2. Research was confused with production.
3. Firm commitments were made on the basis of inadequate specifications.
4. An adequate set of functional specifications wasn't developed.
5. User approval of the functional specifications wasn't required.
6. A request for change procedure wasn't enforced.
7. Design review committee approval of the design specifications wasn't required.
8. User agreement as to what constituted system acceptance wasn't obtained before acceptance testing.
9. Necessary tasks were overlooked.
10. Task dependencies were overlooked.
11. Clearance was not obtained on the delivery dates and turnaround rates on which planning was based.
12. The project leader was overburdened with detailed tasks.
13. Plans made no allowance for contingencies.
14. Checkpoints weren't used to monitor progress.
15. Performance wasn't adequately controlled.
16. Communications broke down.

Some combination of these failures in management occurred. Of course, management is damned hard work even when you know what you're doing, and as long as nobody has come up with any good estimating techniques . . . well, rationalization is a universal human condition.

A second discrepancy is that, wherever progress in time estimating has occurred—as a matter of fact, wherever any progress in human knowledge and the ability to predict is concerned—the first feeble step has always been to start developing models. In time-estimating circles, these models are called time-estimating standards, and with all this concern about the ability to project time requirements, you'd expect to find an effort to establish and refine time-estimating standards in almost every installation, wouldn't you? We know how many we've found. How many can you count?

Of course, to be effective in model building, one needs a history of experience. (You might even call it a data base.) Then one can study this accumulated experience, find patterns, build models, make projections, and compare predicted with actual. Any good data processor knows that.

On the surface, at least, we do seem to be collecting this data. The majority of installations do have their people fill out a timecard of one sort or another. And under these circumstances, it seems legitimate to ask: Why isn't this data base being used for developing estimating standards? Unfortunately, we think we know the answer—the data being collected is so distorted that it's not worth working with.

The time reporting systems with which we're familiar are one of two types.

1. They feed the payroll system. The primary rule here seems to be: You can put anything you want on your timecard, but be sure it adds up to 40 hours.
2. They feed so-called "project management" systems. We have several things we'd like to say about such systems.
   a. They're misnamed. They're not project management systems—that is, they aren't systems which manage projects. They are, in fact, time reporting systems that have the ability to generate variance reports. (Some also have the ability to keep track of personnel availability and make time estimates, which are nice planning tools, but that still doesn't make them management systems. If you don't agree with us, ask yourself this question: Of the 16 management problems listed above, how many do these systems solve?)
   b. We can understand why they're misnamed. If we were selling such a package, we'd call it a project management system, too. After all, how many prospects think they have a time reporting problem? (Notice that this is a different question than, "How many installations have a time reporting problem?" to which the answer must be, "Most or all.")
   c. The problem arises when management tries to use their system according to its name. Thus, instead of using variance reports to try to refine their estimating techniques, they use them to evaluate personnel performance. It's sad to see that, of all the ways to evaluate performance, management chooses the least effective—the time report.
   d. The inevitable consequence is that personnel see their timecards as a pawn in the game of getting ahead (or staying even). As a result, the data collected on a timecard tends to be more a reflection of the employee's ingenuity than of how he used his time.

Arg! Is it any wonder that, when someone starts talking to us about the problems he has with time estimating, our mind begins to cloud over with a thin film of depression? When we start to use time reports exclusively to find out how people use their time, we may start to improve our estimating techniques.

As a project leader, you should review the time reports completed by your project members. But remember, the only purpose of your review is to help your project members complete their time reports as accurately as possible. You don't use this review to evaluate their performance. Checkpoints, job definitions, and adequacy of task performance are the proper tools for performance evaluation.

An example of a time report is given in Appendix K.

# MOTIVATION

A major resource used in all phases of system development is personnel. As a project leader, you attain your goal by getting your project members to complete their tasks successfully. People do perform differently depending on the environment in which they work. Creating and maintaining an environment that encourages people to complete their tasks successfully is the goal of motivation, and, consequently, you can't divorce yourself from the need to motivate.

We've all been dealing with people all our lives. We know they react better in some situations than in others, and we've some idea how to bring about those situations. The purpose of this chapter is to clarify these concepts and encourage you to use them.

It takes a lot of enjoyable and successful cooperative activity to build a good relationship with a person, but it takes only one harsh word or thoughtless act to establish a bad relationship. No one expects you to be perfect, and if you've demonstrated a consistently sincere attempt to get along with people, your gaffs will tend to be forgiven and forgotten. Nevertheless, in every human relations situation, there's something that can be done to improve the relationship and something that can be done to harm it. Loosely speaking, these can be referred to as the right and wrong things to do. Although it's often easier to do the wrong thing, you must exercise the self-control to take the trouble to do the right thing.

Perhaps the most general thing which can be said about motivation is that if you give people the opportunity, they typically provide their own motivation for doing their tasks. Different people bring different interests to their jobs—some look for increasing responsibility, some for the opportunity to learn new skills, some for the challenge of a previously unsolved problem, some for security, and so on. If you allow the person to shape his tasks to his interests, one important aspect of your motivation problem is solved. Part of this shaping involves assigning tasks that fit people's interests. But many tasks can be approached in a variety of ways, and it's important to not overspecify a task assignment, so the person to whom the task is assigned can see it from his own point of view. For example, given the chance, a person may interpret a maintenance task as an opportunity to learn how a particular data processing problem is solved. Or for example, when assigned a task highly similar to a task just completed, if allowed to, a person may consider it an opportunity to refine skills learned on the previous task. A striking illustration of this type of motivation is as follows.

An installation had converted from one computer to another. It had about 200 Fortran programs that were instrumental to installation operation. The Fortran language specifications for the newly installed computer varied somewhat from those for the replaced computer. Consequently, each Fortran program had to be inspected and modified for the replacement computer. One person was assigned this job.

Here was a prime example of an apparently boring job assignment. Having modified one program, the programmer had only 199 more programs for which to make similar modifications. But this programmer had systems programming interests. Consequently, his approach to the job was to study the two sets of language specifications and build a translator that would automatically modify the 200 programs. By not having his job assignment overspecified, the programmer was able to cast it into a frame that was interesting to him, and a potentially deadening assignment was transformed into a stimulating and educational experience.

Another reason for not overspecifying a task assignment is that, within their interests, skills, and capabilities, most people want to work on assignments they consider their own. They want a sense of accomplishment. As a project leader, you must retain some control over what's done. But if you not only tell a person what he's to do, but also how he's to do it, he can't think of himself as a person using his skills and capabilities to carry out an assignment—he can only consider himself a tool you're using to reach your goal.

Most of us have little difficulty passing out responsibility at the time task assignments are made, since we recognize that delegation of these responsibilities is the only way to achieve our goal. But as work progresses and we discover that project members are carrying out their assignments in ways different from the way we'd have approached them, it's difficult to refrain from suggesting our approach. Yet we must. For any suggestion on our part assumes some aspect of an order, due to its source. And making such suggestions demonstrates that we didn't give the project members responsibility for their assignments after all—we're really retaining it ourselves.

A paradigm for making suggestions might go as follows.

1. A project member is carrying out an assignment differently than you would, but it looks as if his approach will work. Under these circumstances you should keep your peace and let the project member pursue his own approach.

2. The project member is making some mistakes, but they're of such a nature that he'll eventually recognize them and be able to recover from them. Once more you should keep your peace. The project member will learn more and get a greater sense of accomplishment from his work if he finds and corrects his errors himself. Remember: The right to make decisions is the right to make mistakes.

3. The project member is making major mistakes that will mire both him and the project in significant difficulties if he's allowed to continue unchecked. This is a situation you can't allow to go on. Your approach should be as follows.

   a. By means of a discussion you get the project member to recognize the problem. Your part in the discussion should be to ask questions such as "What happens if . . . ?" By answering these questions, the project member is allowed to discover the problem.

   b. Once the project member has recognized the problem, it's time for you to be quiet. The object is to get the project member to suggest a solution to the problem. If you've been successful in convincing the project member that the task is his responsibility, he won't hesitate to start proposing solutions.

   c. Proposed solutions that don't solve the problem are handled the same way as the original problem. That is, if the proposed solution involves difficulties, ask the project member questions which cause him to find the difficulties.

   d. Eventually, the project member will suggest a solution that's as good as, or better than, any solution you could've proposed. But the real benefit of this approach is that, throughout the discussion, it's clear that it's the project member who's making the decisions (all you've done is ask questions), and he has every right to continue to consider his assignment as his responsibility.

The technique described above is called participative decision making, and it can be used in all situations in which a person isn't prepared to be given full responsibility for a task. For example, you can never let a project member set up his checkpoints completely by himself. Nevertheless, when it's time to set up checkpoints, all you have to do initially is invite the project member to set up his checkpoints. When he proposes his checkpoints to you, there are two possible situations.

1. The proposed checkpoints appear reasonable to you. In this case, you've only to accept the proposed checkpoints.

2. The checkpoints appear unreasonable to you. Either they're too tight or too loose. In either case, the project member must have arrived at his set of checkpoints from a different set of assumptions than you used. Consequently, in this situation, the first step is to ask the project member how he arrived at his set of checkpoints. If he can demonstrate that his reasoning is sound, then once more, you've only to accept his set of checkpoints. (Of course, you must then go back and modify your own plans accordingly.) If, on the other hand, you find his reasoning deficient at some point, there's a question you can ask him. (For example, if it appears the project member has overlooked something which has to be done to complete his task, you can say, "And you've included the time to generate the test data [or whatever the something is] in your estimate?") In so doing, you should be able to get the project member to arrive at an acceptable set of checkpoints without once suggesting what the set should be. You now have a reasonable set of checkpoints for the task, but they were established by the project member, and he should be encouraged to think of them as "his."

This project member should emerge from a participative decision making session with the feeling that he has made all the decisions. However, running such a session isn't easy work. You must be knowledgeable in the area in which the decision is going to be made; otherwise, you aren't going to be able to intelligently guide the discussion. Ideally, you should already have a solution in mind when the discussion begins. At the same time, you must be flexible enough to adjust if the project member takes an approach different from yours.

The concept of having the project member consider his assignment as his responsibility isn't a game you play only until the project member completes his assignment. The delegation must be forever. Thus, any credit for a task well done must always go completely to the project member. If not, he's going to justifiably feel duped, and your credibility will suffer.

We've been emphasizing that most people want to feel a sense of accomplishment. Up to now, we've been concentrating on a project member's accomplishments with respect to his task assignments. But a job involves more than completing tasks, and most people want to feel they've performed on the job in the most general sense. To do this, they must know what good performance is.

The first step in this direction is to make your performance expectations clear to the project members. Task assignments and checkpoints are two aspects of performance we've already discussed. Others are:

1. When the working day starts.
2. What dress code is practiced.
3. What procedures are to be followed. Examples of procedures are:
   a. When and how interviews are to be documented.
   b. What constitutes a logical analysis of a program and how it's to be documented.
   c. What a unit test plan consists of and when it's to be prepared.

Of help in this area are installation standards. However, the lack of such standards doesn't relieve you of the responsibility to articulate your expectations and make them clear to the project members.

One aspect of making your expectations clear is to adhere to them personally. Project members can hardly consider adherence to a procedure important if you don't follow it.

A second aspect of making your expectations clear is to give credit when they're met. Most of us are too sparing with our credit. We tend to reserve it for outstanding achievements. If a person just does his job, we ask, "Why is that deserving of any particular credit? After all, he only did what he was supposed to." But then, isn't this what we want, and, therefore, isn't credit due?

Another thing with which you should be concerned with respect to giving credit is whether your accolades are being apportioned so the performance you want is being encouraged. The classic example of a misallocation of credit is as follows. On the day the payroll is to be calculated, a bug is discovered in the calculation program. Charlie Brown, who wrote the program, dives in to find the bug and fix it. He works all day, eats supper at his desk, and labors far into the night. Finally, at 2 a.m., Charlie finds the bug, the program is fixed, the system is run, and the paychecks are printed just in time for payday. There's no question that Charlie deserves credit for his dedication. But how about the three other programmers who also worked on the payroll system and who used testing techniques that precluded a breakdown in production? Did they receive proper credit for their performance, or were they just doing their job? And which kind of performance is more desirable, anyhow?

A third aspect of making your expectations clear is to help people improve their performance when it fails to meet expectations. This brings up the subject of performance review. Performance review isn't a periodic responsibility of yours; it's a continuous one. The time to talk to a project member about his performance failure is at the time you notice that it tends to be habitual. An occasional failure isn't generally grounds for reviewing a project member's performance with him. He frequently recognizes the failure himself, and his own efforts to improve himself will have better results than anything you can do. However, repeated failure usually indicates that the project member doesn't recognize his performance as substandard.

Some general rules for conducting performance reviews are as follows.

1. Hold the review in private. The project member may not be aware that his performance isn't satisfactory. His shortcomings should be pointed out to him in private so he can improve without having been subjected to public embarrassment.

2. Schedule the review so there's plenty of time to hold it. The review shouldn't be rushed.

3. Make arrangements so nothing interrupts the review. The project member's performance is of prime importance to him, and you should demonstrate that it's of prime importance to you, too.

4. Use the "sandwich" technique—that is, sandwich unfavorable remarks between favorable ones. Compliment the project member at the beginning and end of the review.

5. Be objective. Cite specific instances of performance failure.

6. Allow the project member to express his reaction to your evaluation. He should have the opportunity to state what obstacles stand in the way of his doing a good job. Here you may find the underlying cause of unsatisfactory performance. If you're asked for advice, don't be too quick to give your opinion. Let the project member talk. Ask him questions. Often the first problem mentioned by the project member isn't the basic problem. He might be more concerned about something else.

7. Don't show anger or hostility, regardless of the remarks the project member makes. Nobody says you can't be human and lose your temper now and then, but do it at some time other than when you're conducting a performance review.

8. Don't be too determined to prove the project member wrong. Help him save face and leave his self-respect intact. Confidence in you will be increased if the project member realizes that you aren't arbitrary and that incorrect evaluations are subject to change.

9. Take your time. Acceptance of your criticisms and suggestions may not come immediately. It may be quite a while before the project member will admit his errors. As a matter of fact, it's unlikely that the project member will agree with your criticisms during the review. When criticized, most people rise to their own defense. Don't let this bother you. Make your

points and listen to what the project member has to say. Then conclude the review session and see if the project member's performance improves. After a review session, a person will often take your advice even though he denied everything you said in the review. And this change in performance is what you're interested in. Whether the person agrees with you in the review session is immaterial.

10. If the project member wants to talk, let him go. Don't interrupt.

11. If you feel it's necessary to bring up a personality shortcoming, be specific. If you can't pinpoint how an alleged personality fault causes a performance failure, it's better not to venture into this touchy area.

A performance review has one of several possible outcomes.

1. Performance improves.

2. Performance doesn't improve. Under such circumstances, another performance review must be held.

   a. If the project member is interested in improving his performance, a series of performance reviews may succeed where one has failed.

   b. If the project member isn't interested in improving his performance, a series of performance reviews generally convinces him that he isn't going to get ahead working on your project. Usually, such people eventually quit to look for greener pastures. Departure of such a person may cause a temporary inconvenience, but in the long run, both your project and your company are better off.

One area in which your performance expectations must be particularly clear has to do with contingency allowances. As we concluded when discussing manpower planning, any realistic time estimate for a task includes an allowance for contingency. Every project member must understand that his performance evaluation in terms of his ability to get his work done on schedule is based on a time estimate that does *not* include a contingency allowance. Only if the project member actually experiences contingency can his work run over into the contingency allowance period and still be considered satisfactory, and then, the runover must be only to the extent contingency has occurred. Even though the project hasn't missed any deadlines, the performance of a project member who hasn't experienced contingency but who still doesn't complete his task until the end of his contingency allowance period is unsatisfactory and must be evaluated as such.

In every organization there is a system of rewards involving raises, promotions, and opportunities. Not only do most people want the self-satisfaction of accomplishment, they also want to know that their performance is recognized. Such will be the case only if the reward system passes out raises, promotions, and opportunities in rough proportion to level of performance. As a project leader, it isn't your prerogative to distribute these rewards; this is done by your manager. However, you're the person who's most knowledgeable with respect to the performance of your project members, and your manager makes his reward decisions largely on the basis of the appraisals you make of your project members' performance. These appraisals should be written, and if the reward system is to consistently reflect performance, it's essential that they be honest. They must describe both the project members' achievements and failings.

For the project members to have confidence in the reward system, each project member should be privy to his performance appraisal. This is the reason the appraisal should be written. Then he sees the same appraisal as does your manager.

Another reason for writing a project member's performance appraisal and then letting the project member read it is that, under such circumstances, you're going to exercise maximum care when you choose the words which are going to become part of the project member's permanent personnel record. Nothing in a project member's performance appraisal should come as a surprise to him. If there's anything negative in the appraisal, he should have already heard about it several times in the performance reviews you've previously held with him.

The assignment of tasks according to project members' interests; a clear broadcast of your performance expectations; the giving of credit; the conduct of timely, constructive performance reviews; and the submission of honest performance appraisals represents one major area of motivation having to do with the creation of a work environment in which each project member's self-motivation has an opportunity to experience maximum sway. Another major area of motivation has to do with the development of a team.

There is so little question that a team of people accomplishes more than the same individuals working on separate tasks that, in this book, we'll accept the statement as fact. Instead, we'll concentrate on ways you can promote a feeling of team membership in your project members.

A member of a group recognizes himself as such because he has more in common with the other group members than he has with people who aren't members—his attitudes are more like theirs, he knows more about them, he talks with them more, he does more things with them, and he's physically nearer to them. All these commonalities are ways you can engender a team feeling.

1. One of the less frequently cited advantages of project organization is the built-in opportunity to use the project goal to generate among the project members the attitude of a team working toward a common goal.

2. One way of generating this attitude is to keep everyone on the project informed as to what's going on in the project as a whole. Thus, the orientation of each project member includes, not only what he's doing on the project, but also what the overall goal of the project is and what the role of each

project member is in the attainment of that goal. It's not necessary for each project member to have his personal copy of all the project documentation, but a complete set of this documentation should be available to him if he wants to refer to it. A copy of each status report you prepare for your manager should be circulated among the project members so each member can keep abreast of the progress of the project as a whole. A specifications change may affect the work of only some project members, but all should be made aware of the change so no one feels left out. Every question a project member asks you about the project deserves a thorough answer, even if the answer has no bearing on the work of the project member asking the question; the fact that the project member asked the question indicates that he's identifying with the project rather than with his personal assignment—such identification should be encouraged.

3. One way to disseminate information to the project members is to hold project meetings. A good agenda for a meeting is to have one project member report on his work. But also, holding the meeting brings the project members close to each other physically.

4. An even better way to establish this feeling of physical identity is to seat the project members next to each other in their work environment.

5. Such a seating arrangement also encourages the project members to talk with each other.

A third major area of motivation is concerned with working conditions. Any part of the project members' work environment that helps them do their work is motivating; any part that introduces interruption and delay is demotivating. Thus, you should see that office facilities are adequate—that there are enough desks, chairs, wastepaper baskets, filing cabinets, bookcases, phones, and calendars; that there're adequate stationery supplies—tablets of lined paper, coding paper, pencils, pens, and templates; that there's adequate clerical support—typing and keypunching; that adequate computer time is available on an adequately maintained machine; that the software is usable; that operators are competent; that distractions are minimized; and so on. Once more, what we're talking about is your responsibility for keeping contingencies from occurring. A person who's expected to meet a deadline under a continuous barrage of interruptions and delays will continue to struggle for just so long. After that his attitude will degenerate into one of, "Oh, well. What's the use of trying?" which is the antithesis of being motivated.

The final area of motivation with which we'll deal here is concerned with your role as leader. As we agreed when we were discussing your communication responsibilities, every project member is, to some extent, a specialist in some aspect of the project, and the project members leave it to you as leader to coordinate their special activities to arrive at the overall project goal. As a consequence, whenever a project member confronts a problem that extends beyond his range of specialization, he'll come to you for guidance. If direction isn't forthcoming, the project member is left in an ambiguous situation, in which motivation tends to wane. These facts have several implications as far as the way you carry out your role as project leader.

1. You must be available, both physically and in terms of attitude, so project members can bring their problems to you.

2. You must be sure that the requests for direction which project members bring to you lie outside their individual areas of responsibility. Some people will bring to you problems that are completely within the bounds of their own assignments and which they should resolve themselves. Rather than give direction in these areas, you must return such problems to your people unsolved and with the understanding that they have the right, privilege, and responsibility to resolve these problems.

3. However, when a problem is beyond a given project member's task assignment, you must render a decision promptly. This doesn't mean you must make snap decisions—it does mean that, after a reasonable amount of time for reflection (usually a day or two, at most), direction must be forthcoming.

The need for direction from you often arises at conflict points in system development—what a project member wants to do conflicts with the desires of the user, the computer center, or some other outside group; or it conflicts with what some other project member is doing. The need to give direction at these conflict points presents you with both a benefit and a danger. The benefit is that, by becoming involved in the resolution of these conflicts, you get an opportunity to remain abreast of what are probably the most important aspects of the system development going on in your project.

The danger is that, because the conflict is between the needs and desires of two or more parties, any resolution of the conflict may result in personal disappointment for someone. The best way to minimize this danger appears to be to get the conflicting parties to participate with you in resolving the problem. Your main role in the ensuing discussion is to keep everyone's attention focused on the overall goals of the project, and if you've been successful in generating a team approach to system development, you should be able to get the conflicting parties to resolve their difficulties with a minimum of disappointment.

The most important thing you can do when a project member comes to you with a problem is listen. Often the only thing the project member needs is a sounding board. As a consequence, with only a few questions on your part, or sometimes nothing more than respectful attention, the project member will go on to solve his problem right in the middle of his presentation.

## EXERCISE

List some of the ways to motivate project members.

# CONSTRUCTION CONSIDERATIONS

Some people reach the position of project leader via an analyst or user route that bypasses the opportunity to gain experience in the construction of data processing systems. Such people sometimes express anxiety about not knowing more about the nuts and bolts of this system development phase. The purpose of this chapter is to present enough information concerning construction activities to allay these fears.

## 21.1 PROGRAM PREPARATION

Programming consists of taking the plans developed for the computer data processing system during system design and implementing them in the form of programs to be run on the computer. The point at which programming begins is significant. Until now months of time and effort have been invested in system analysis and design. Nevertheless, any change, any fact previously neglected, generally doesn't cause delay or jeopardize work already done. Usually all that's required to rectify the matter is to add a note in some document, change a notation on a system flow chart, or delete a line on a record layout. However, once programming begins, the picture changes.

The situation is analogous to building a house. As long as the house is on the drawing board, a change is inexpensive. It requires little more than a rub with the architect's eraser and a few new lines with a pencil. But when the building is started, each change is an "extra" whose cost is directly related to the degree of completion of the house. Each program instruction written for the system is another brick laid and mortared in the construction of the system. A change or addition that would have been innocent during system design may be costly in terms of revisions to programs already written. Each step taken during construction more firmly imbeds the steps previously taken in the erection of the structure and increases the difficulty of change. Moreover, changes have ramifications beyond the alteration of already written programs. With the step into programming, documentation proliferates. There's now a team of programmers, each of whom possesses documentation of the system to the extent to which it's applicable to the programs he's been assigned to prepare. Each change involves an administrative problem in keeping this documentation up to date.

The development of the programs for a system is done by programmers. Each programmer is assigned to prepare several programs in the system, but the programs assigned to a programmer bear no necessary relationship, one to another, as far as the system is concerned.

As a result, the programming of the system is a program-by-program affair. A programmer is assigned a program, he's told what input is fed into the program and what output the program is to produce, he's given some idea of the procedures to be accomplished in the program, and he's then allowed to prepare the program.

## 21.2   PROGRAM TESTING

One of the programmer's responsibilities is to test the program to which he has been assigned. That is, after he has written the coding that constitutes his program he must run the program on the computer to ascertain whether it performs as expected. The programmer prepares test data he believes conforms to the description of the input given him. The analyst may cooperate in the construction of this data. The programmer runs his program against this test data to perform the unit test. This test session reveals inadequacies in the program—inadequacies created by misunderstandings and inadvertent slips on the programmer's part. The programmer corrects and improves his program on the basis of the results of the test session and once more submits the program for test running. When by repetitions of this testing and correcting cycle the programmer becomes satisfied with his program's performance, it's turned over as a unit tested program.

Unit testing really begins concurrently with the preparation of the program.

The program should be organized into a main chain and a number of relatively independent subroutines. Then unit testing becomes a more manageable, two-step process: (1) test each subroutine to see that it performs as expected; (2) test to see that the subroutines hang together in a functioning whole.

The purpose of testing is to demonstrate that the program will correctly process any data fed to it. Most programs place limits on the data they're designed to process. For example, a program may require that a file be in sequential order by key or that an amount never exceed $9999.99. Programs should be designed to specifically exclude what they aren't prepared to process. Thus, if a file must be in sequence, its sequence should be tested; if an amount can't exceed a given limit, there should be a test to see that the limit isn't exceeded. Only when a program is so constructed is there a chance to demonstrate through testing that it'll run properly.

The programmer should plan his testing. The basic structure of a unit test plan is always the same—in a phrase, from simple to complex. First a test is run to see if the program will correctly process one standard transaction. When this test runs, then another transaction path is tested, and so on, one path at a time, until all paths have been tested. Small volume data is used. After each of the individual paths has been tested, the testing of the processing of combinations of data is begun. Again, the combinations are tested one at a time until all significant combinations have been checked out. The various program initiation and termination possibilities are checked out. Again, small volume data is used. End of volume situations can be tested by introducing artificially short files. Finally, the error paths are checked out one by one and in any likely combination with a minimum of test data. Effective unit testing is a skill that can be learned. A useful tool in this learning process is a set of installation testing procedures. In sum, a unit test plan is a checklist of all the program possibilities that are to be tested. This checklist should cause every path through the program to be checked at least once.

On this simple frame a wide variety of tests can be developed depending on the program being tested. Each kind of test requires preparation. For commercial applications some amount of ingenuity may be required to construct a variety of tests with a minimum of data. For scientific applications a series of hand calculations may be needed. For assemblers and compilers, source programs to be processed must be written. For subroutines, special programs may have to be created to drive the subroutine through the tests. For complex programs, testing techniques may be built directly into the program to be tested. Special steps may have to be taken to print out for inspection or otherwise test the output produced on tape or disk. Development of test data involves, not only the input data to be fed into the test, but also a predetermination of the output to be expected from the test.

## 21.3   PREPARING COMPUTER CENTER OPERATING PROCEDURES

When a programmer unit tests a program, he prepares a set of test operating instructions for this purpose. Consequently, when all programs in a system have been unit tested, there are operating instructions for each program. However, the system isn't run in the computer center as a sequence of programs but as a system. Moreover, it's generally necessary to modify the instructions to some extent to convert them from test to production status. Thus, the writing of system operating instructions is a distinct construction task. They're written according to standards set by the computer center.

## 21.4   SYSTEM TESTING

When programming is complete, there are a set of programs, each of which is attested to by the programmer assigned to it as being correct in terms of the manner in which he understands the program's requirements. It must now be determined whether these programs fit together as a functioning system. Perhaps because of faulty communication when the programmer was told what a program is to do, the program doesn't meet system design requirements. Perhaps the individually prepared programs are inconsistent one with another and consequently, as a whole, don't make up a functioning system. It must be ascertained that the programs don't have these faults and do, as a result, constitute an acceptable data processing system. This aim is accomplished by the system test.

In the system test the sequence of programs making up the system is run as it would be in the functioning system. In this way inconsistencies between programs and inadequacies of the computer system are pinpointed in much the same way as errors in each program were isolated during unit testing. Test data is used to perform the system test except that now the test data is the same for the whole system, instead of being made especially for each program.

In preparing test data for a system test, make it as exhaustive as possible. That is, have it incorporate as many of the situations which could arise in operations as possible to test the system from every angle.

If the system is large, schedule the system test in parts. The first time the system is run it probably won't run to completion anyhow. Later when the major errors have been weeded out of the subsystems into which the system has been divided for testing purposes, the system can be run as a whole. Check out the file establishment and file maintenance programs first so they can be used for their purposes while the rest of the system is being tested.

Begin the test with a low volume of data, just enough to test major controls and the integration between programs. When the errors have been eliminated from these areas, more extensive data can be used to test the finer details of the system. Start at the beginning of the system and work through it so the gross errors are eliminated first. When the system more or less hangs together, the finer errors can be weeded out.

A computer system usually generates several intermediary files, output of one program that constitutes input to a subsequent one. Print these intermediary files. Such printouts constitute an aid in error location. They can be checked out for conformance with expectations just as are final outputs. In checking output, pay particular attention to the first and last records of a file. They're the most likely to be in error. Normal procedure may be performing well when initial and windup procedures still contain errors.

Programmers should be on hand for system test. They may be able to spot the reason for some errors more readily than the analyst. Be sure to check out the system for recycled data such as corrections to errors as well as normally introduced data. For a system to be operating correctly all parts of it must perform equally well.

The ideal situation is for a team, independent of the programming team, to do system testing; in many cases, the extent of the work required to prepare and perform the system test justifies the existence of such a team. It's desirable to have at least one person on this test team who is user oriented. Such a team would be provided with functional specifications and then would prepare to use the system with no further knowledge of it. In this way they perform a true quality control function, and the product that passes their tests stands a better chance of standing up in a live situation than does one tested only by the programmers who built it. One advantage of such an approach is that the test team may find deficiencies in the functional specifications as well as in the system.

System test must be exhaustive. When changes are made to correct detected errors, the tests that have been passed previously become suspect, since the changes may create a situation in which these tests no longer run correctly. Before the system is released from system test, it must pass all tests without the need for modification.

System test is the optimum time for checking out operating procedures. Until the system hangs together fairly well, the project may want to retain responsibility for running the system. However, once this point has passed, it becomes advantageous to turn operation of the system over to the computer center for the following reasons.

1. Computer center personnel are given the opportunity to become familiar with system operation.
2. Testing of the operating procedures, as well as the system, is effected.

## 21.5  DEVELOPING FILE CONVERSION PROCEDURES

The majority of the permanent records, accumulations, and other information maintained in a computer data processing system is stored on magnetic tape, drums, disks, and so forth. Examples of such information are the employee data of a payroll application, the inventory information of a stock control system, and the vendor information of an accounts payable system. Before the introduction of the computing system this information is usually kept in a variety of punched card files, index card files, visible files, ledger cards, and binders of various types.

Another distinction between computer master files and these files in other data processing systems is the greater degree of consolidation of information in the former. For example, employee information might be stored in four or five card files in a punched card application. Another example of information consolidation is in the insurance field. For ordinary life insurance an insurance company may have four departments to handle premium billing and accounting, policyholder dividends, policy loans, and valuation. In a noncomputer data processing system each of these departments would maintain its own records. In a computer system these records are consolidated into one policyholder file.

The collection of this master information from a number of sources varying in type as well as in location and the organization and coordination of this data into a single stream of information is quite an undertaking. The record design of the master file was fixed during system design. This record design specifies what information the master file is to contain and the format in which the data is to appear. What must be done to collect, organize, and convert the master file to the form specified by the record design is to set up a procedure for this purpose.

File conversion boils down to a system design problem. It's an exercise for the analyst; he knows what output he wants; he knows the sources for his information; he must design a system that produces the output from the input. But the analyst can't create and implement this procedure independent of the user. He must be certain that his filemaking system doesn't access the current records in a way which would disrupt current procedures. He must be apprised of the quantity and quality of the clerical force that will be available to him for implementation of the procedures. For the answer to these and other questions the analyst must turn to the user. With cooperation similar to that involved in their work during analysis, the analyst and user can work out a procedure for creating the master file.

Since the end product of filemaking is a magnetic file, file conversion involves one or more computer programs to accept the file information and record it in the format specified by the master file record design. One part of these conversion programs is the audit of the information being converted. This audit consists of a validity check of all information submitted for incorporation in the master file. Its purpose is to catch errors introduced into the master file because of mistakes made during filemaking. However, the audit delivers an added benefit. When master records are converted, the audit unearths inconsistencies and other mistakes in the existing records which were previously undetected.

There's one alternative to an independent filemaking operation that's feasible under certain circumstances. For example, in a sales statistics application the master file may consist of an accumulation of information on sales experience as it occurs. In such a situation it's possible for the computer application to start out with no master file and have the computer data processing system build the master file over a period of time on the basis of the transactions that occur.

In some cases the master file may be created by the method just described, even though an existing master file must be in evidence when the computer data processing system is inaugurated. The way this approach is implemented is to introduce, immediately before the cutover to the computer system, bogus transactions that cause the system to create a master file which duplicates the records required to be carried into the new system from the old.

## 21.6   VOLUME TESTING

After the system has passed the quality control tests prepared by the test team, it's subjected to volume testing. Generally, the only practical way to perform this kind of test is with live data.

The major new task in volume testing with live data is to provide the files with which the tests are to be run. In some way the files used in the old system must be converted to the medium and format required by the new. Generally, the procedures developed to convert the files at the time of system cutover can also be used to generate volume test data.

## 21.7   FILE CONVERSION

Once the conversion of the master file is complete some procedure must be instituted to keep the master file up to date. Because the master file has been converted doesn't mean the company operation associated with that file, whether it's payroll or accounts receivable, is going to cease to operate. The company operation will continue. Moreover, it's unlikely that the computer procedures associated with the master file go operational at the same instant the master file conversion is completed. The current data processing procedure, whether it's punched card, manual, or other, must continue to keep records up to date with respect to the company operation. The master file no sooner gets converted than it's threatened with going out of date. To prevent this situation a procedure for keeping the master file up to date must be prepared. One technique is to use the conversion system each time an updated copy of the files is desired. This technique works well when the files in the old system are already in a fairly consolidated form. If, on the other hand, this information is scattered and the collection of this data is a significant undertaking, it may be more desirable to maintain the files in their new form as well as their old once the conversion is complete. Special maintenance programs can be written for this purpose, or the file maintenance phase of the new system might be pushed through system test first to be ready for this purpose.

## 21.8  FORM DESIGN

A computer data processing system, like any other data processing system, requires some data collection mechanism and some method of reporting its findings. Consequently, input forms, cards, output forms, and all other types of man/machine interface mediums must be designed.

It's the analyst's responsibility to determine form layout and to fix the number of copies and quantities of forms required. He then must coordinate with a form design expert, who determines the physical nature of the form—the quality of paper to be used, the type of reproduction to be employed, etc. This expert may be a representative of a forms manufacturer.

When a system is in production, forms control, reordering, and such are handled by production personnel. However, for test running it's up to the project leader to determine the required lead time and order the forms in time to have them on hand for training and testing purposes.

## 21.9  PREPARING USER MANUALS

Computerization of a data processing operation generally changes the clerical procedure associated with the operation. Preparation must be made for a smooth transition to these changed procedures. One area in which preparation is necessary is documentation of procedure in the form of a user manual.

There are two types of documents that must be prepared for the user manual. One is the work aid, which is any document a clerk uses in his work. For example, the encoding directory to which a clerk refers to decide what code should be assigned to a sales account or city is a work aid.

The other type of documentation necessary in the development of a clerical procedure is the procedure manual which specifies what the procedure is. This type of documentation is important for several reasons.

1. Development of a procedure manual forces decisions on policy and procedural details that otherwise might never be considered until the situation arises in the performance of the procedure.

2. A procedure manual facilitates the training of personnel. The time required for training decreases when training is done with documentation, and training effectiveness increases.

3. A procedure manual promotes uniformity of performance. More people perform a procedure the same way if they have a model of the procedure for reference.

4. A procedure manual establishes a basis for control. It states what the proper procedure is and allows resolution of the question of whether a particular method is acceptable.

5. A procedure manual preserves experience. If a procedure is documented, the loss of a man never means loss of procedure details.

6. A procedure manual, as an objective document, facilitates the examination and revision of procedures.

For these reasons it's important that procedure manuals be prepared. Also, when the procedure is instituted, mechanics for keeping the procedure manual up to date should be set up to handle the inevitable changes in procedure when they occur.

Publication of manuals is time consuming. Therefore, this lead time must be taken into consideration in setting up the deadline for completion of the user manual draft.

If the functional specifications have been properly prepared, writing the user manual shouldn't be a major effort. Mostly it should consist of a modification of the functional specifications.

## 21.10  USER TRAINING

Besides documentation, orientation and training are essential to a successful clerical operation. New forms must be filled out and new procedures followed, and clerks must be trained for these jobs.

## 21.11  PARALLEL TESTING

Once the new system has demonstrated in volume test that it can handle large volumes of data, it's put into parallel test. At this point the new system is instituted, but the old system isn't dispensed with. Instead, continued reliance is put on the old system to produce the required results, and the two are run in parallel to see if they produce equivalent results.

Parallel running provides the ideal occasion for a dry run of procedures for the clerical force that will service the computer system. During parallel running as much of the computer system as possible should be put into operation to see if it hangs together. Parallel running is the first opportunity for the error detection, correction, and reinsertion procedures to be tested in their entirety. All error printouts from the computer system should be routed to correction points as called for by the system setup, the errors should be investigated and corrected, and the corrections should be sent back for reinsertion into the computer system. These procedures should be followed to determine whether they're adequate for their purpose, whether control is being maintained over this avenue of transaction movement, and whether the procedure fits within the established time schedule. Parallel running is the time to revise timing estimates originally made for the system to a more realistic level.

## 21.12 PROVIDING FOR MAINTENANCE

A good test plan reduces the number of errors in an accepted system to a minimum. Too often both the data processing department and the user are willing to accept inadequate testing and then invest in an extensive period of maintenance that's really a continuation of the construction phase.

Despite the existence of a significant amount of this correct-the-errors kind of job, the bulk of the work referred to as maintenance is concerned with modification and extension of the system after it has been accepted. Provision must be made for this job.

Two important steps in preparing for maintenance are:

1. Preparation of good documentation.
2. Development of well organized programs.

Both of the above expedite the determination of what should be done where to implement a change, and a well-organized program is easier to change, since it consists of many small, functional subroutines with as little interdependence as possible. This statement certainly holds in the case of maintenance done by a programmer with no previous familiarity with the system. And when it's conceded that man's memory is short, it can be recognized that the programmer with previous exposure to the system is only somewhat better off than the one with no previous familiarity, and that consequently, good documentation and well-organized programs are generally useful maintenance tools.

Based on the studies he has made, Mr. Dick Brandon estimates that, for every dollar spent to put a system on the air, 25 cents is spent each year to maintain the system. In other words, every four years the original cost of the system is expended to keep the system running! Willingness to accept poor test procedures, inadequate documentation, and badly organized programs are major contributors to this expense.

Another provision for maintenance is the development of a regression test. The purpose of a regression test is to combat the following situation.

Because of a previously undetected error or because of a needed change, it becomes necessary to modify the system. In making the modification, previously nonexistent errors are introduced into the system.

A regression test is a standard testing procedure designed to prove a system. After modifications are made to a system, it should be run against its regression test before being put back into production. The purpose of the test run is to protect against gratuitous error in the maintenance procedure.

### EXERCISES

1. Who decides on the proper weight for forms paper?
2. What's the programmer's role in preparing system test data? Why?
3. a.  List three steps that should be taken to prepare for maintenance.
   b.  How do these steps ease the maintenance job?

(The material in this chapter is taken, in part, from Chapters 15–18 of the book *System Design for Computer Applications* by H. N. Laden and T. R. Gildersleeve, published in 1963 by John Wiley & Sons, Inc.)

# FOR YOUR MANAGER

As we've said in many places in this book, the existence of good installation standards and procedures that are both documented and enforced is of great aid to you in carrying out your project leader responsibilities. This chapter describes what these standards and procedures should be. It's written for your manager. Therefore, in the following, the word "you" refers to your manager, not you. If you want, you can, starting with the next page, lift this chapter right out of this book and present it to your manager as an aid for his planning.

# PROJECT CONTROL FOR MANAGERS

## 1 INTRODUCTION

Management means accomplishing objectives by establishing an environment favorable to performance by people operating in organized groups.

A systems and programming manager typically has three responsibilities.

1. Development of data processing systems.
2. Maintenance of data processing systems.
3. Research into new data processing uses and methods.

Consequently, managing a systems and programming group is a matter of establishing an environment favorable to the development and maintenance of, and research into data processing systems.

This paper is based on the conviction that all development of data processing systems and much of the maintenance of such systems is most effectively handled by a systems and programming group organized on a project basis. The essence of project organization is that, for each specific system development goal, a single individual, known as the project leader, is given total responsibility for reaching the goal. As a result, managing a systems and programming group becomes largely a matter of establishing an environment in which project leaders can be as productive as possible.

This paper is divided into three parts.

1. What is the environment most favorable to project leader performance?
2. How do you handle those maintenance responsibilities not done on a project basis?
3. How do you handle research?

## 2 PROJECTS

### 2.1 The User

The project leader is successful only if he satisfies his user, which he can do only if he knows who his user is. Consequently, for each project:

1. The user should be identified by the company. (A data processing steering committee is the best way to get this done.)
2. All project costs should be billed back to the user.

A useful tool for identifying users is the request for services form.

## 2.2  Development Phases

Data processing systems are developed in three phases.

1. Analysis—determining what the system is going to do.
2. Design—determining how the system is going to be constructed.
3. Construction—building and installing the system.

The point is that these are three distinct, chronological steps—you can't decide how to do something until you know what you want to do, and you can't do something until you know how to do it. Moreover, projections can't be reliable until design is complete.

You can keep projects from getting out of control by requiring that:

1. Each phase be completed before the next is started.
2. The user re-evaluate feasibility at the end of each phase.

### ANALYSIS

The goal of analysis is to come to an agreement with the user on what the system is going to do. You can maximize the probability that this will occur by:

1. Requiring that at least one upper level operating manager from the user organization participate full-time in the analysis phase.
2. Maintaining an education program to teach users:
   a. What to expect from data processing.
   b. What the user's system development responsibilities are.
   c. How the user is to carry out his responsibilities.
3. Establishing a policy that analysis isn't complete (that is, that design can't start) until the user signs off on the system functional specifications.
4. Establishing and enforcing a request for change procedure as the only avenue through which the user can institute change in signed off fucntional specifications.

Useful tools with which you can provide the project leader are:

1. Functional specifications standards.
2. A request for change form.

### DESIGN

The goal of design is to come up with a good one. You can maximize the probability that this will occur by:

1. Establishing and maintaining design standards.
2. Requiring that at least one alternative design be considered.
3. Establishing a policy that design isn't complete (that is, that construction

can't start) until a design review committee signs off on the system design specifications. Represented on this committee must be at least:

a. The senior system design cadre.
b. The computer center.
c. The system maintenance operation.
d. The internal auditors.

A useful tool with which you can provide the project leader is design specification standards.

## CONSTRUCTION

The goal of construction is to build the system according to the functional and design specifications. You can maximize the probability that this will occur by:

1. Requiring that the project leader and the user agree on what will demonstrate system acceptability. (The optimum time to develop these acceptance test specifications is as part of the functional specifications.)

2. Establishing a policy that:
   a. Program module internal specifications be approved by the project leader before module logical analysis can begin.
   b. After internal specifications have been approved, module changes can be made only by modifying the internal specifications and having the project leader approve the modification.
   c. Module logical analysis be done before coding can begin.
   d. Logical analysis be on a logical level and organize the module into a main chain and subroutines.
   e. Modules be coded the way they've been logically analyzed.
   f. Coding be annotated.
   g. A unit test plan be developed before unit testing can begin.
   h. The programmer custom develop his own unit test data.
   i. System test data be developed by others than those who have developed the programs making up the system.
   j. The operations manual be written according to computer center standards.
   k. Computer center personnel run the system test from the operations manual.
   l. The user manual be written before training of user personnel can begin.
   m. User personnel be trained before the acceptance test can begin.
   n. User personnel provide the input and handle the output of the acceptance test.

Useful tools with which you can provide the project leader are standards for:

1. Internal specifications.
2. Logical analysis.
3. Programming language.
4. Annotation of coding.
5. Unit testing.
6. System testing.
7. Operations manuals.
8. User manuals.
9. Acceptance testing.

## 2.3  Planning

To allow the user to evaluate system feasibility at the end of each development phase, and to control development, the project leader must, at the end of each phase, develop two plans.

1. One for the rest of system development.
2. One for the next phase of system development.

Consequently, you should supply the project leader with resources to accomplish the next development phase only after:

1. He has submitted acceptable plans.
2. The user reaffirms system feasibility.

You must require that a plan consist of:

1. A bubble chart.
2. A list of external restraints.
3. A manpower plan (a bar chart) incorporating an explicit contingency allowance.
4. If appropriate:
   a. A computer time plan.
   b. A travel plan.
   c. A specification of required support services.
5. A cost estimate.

You must evaluate a project leader's performance on the basis of his ability to meet his projections within the following error ranges.

1. Plans made at the end of the initiation phase—100%
2. Plans made at the end of the analysis phase—50%
3. Plans made at the end of the design phase—10%

Useful tools with which you can provide the project leader are:

1. Specifications for:
   a. Bubble charts.
   b. Bar charts.
   c. Computer time scheduling.
   d. Cost estimates.
2. Standards for:
   a. Manpower task time estimating.
   b. Contingency allowance.
   d. Manpower costs (including overhead).
   e. Computer time costs.
   f. Travel and living costs.
3. Checklists for:
   a. Systems and programming activities.
   b. External restraints.
   c. Contingencies.

Manpower task time estimating standards can be improved if a time reporting system that contributes to the accumulation of a meaningful data base is instituted.


## 2.4  Staying on Schedule

Things you can do to help the project leader stay on schedule are:

1. See that commitments made to the data processing department, such as equipment and software delivery, are kept.
2. Minimize contingencies—for example, see that the computer center honors commitments on test time and keypunching turnaround.
3. Don't allow the project leader to assign detailed tasks to himself.
4. Require the use of checkpoints.

A useful tool with which you can provide the project leader is a definition of standard checkpoints.


## 2.5  Communication

Things you can do to help the project leader carry out his communication responsibilities are:

1. Require immediate notification when attainment of the project deadline becomes threatened.

2. Require a comprehensive status report once a month (but then don't pester him for other reports).
3. Provide a method for distributing documentation.
4. Establish and enforce a procedure for keeping distributed documentation up to date.
5. Allow the project leader to report status to the user.
6. Don't invite the project leader to meetings unless he has a significant contribution to make.
7. Require the project leader to approve expense reports and support service invoices (but then don't burden him with other paperwork).

Useful tools with which you can provide the project leader are:

1. Status report standards.
2. Guidelines for expense report approval.

## 2.6  Motivation

Things you can do to help the project leader motivate his project members are:

1. Avoid a crisis atmosphere; instead, establish an atmosphere of business as usual.
2. Require the project leader to make task assignments that develop personnel.
3. Require the project leader to counsel his project members on their performance.
4. Require the project leader to submit written performance appraisals.
5. Require that the project leader review each written performance appraisal with the person appraised.
6. Allow the project leader to relocate the project members to a common work area.
7. Establish standards for:
   a. Working hours.
   b. Personal conduct and appearance.

## 2.7  Skills

When a person is assigned to a project, the project leader should be able to tell from the person's job title what the person's minimum skills are. Only in this way can the project leader establish what activities he has a right to assume the person can handle. Without this information, the project leader won't be able to make meaningful performance evaluations, and he won't be able to assign tasks designed to develop personnel.

Consequently, each position in your organization should be defined in terms of a list of skills (activities which a person can perform) that a person must possess at a minimum to qualify for the position. Moreover, your personnel must be assigned job titles on the basis of their ability to meet the minimum performance standards defined by these skill lists.

Once these position definition and personnel classification steps have been taken, to maintain a motivated staff, you're going to have to provide an education program that'll allow people to upgrade their skills and thus qualify for promotion. The skill lists that define the job positions also determine the content of the education program.

## 3  MAINTENANCE

Many system enhancements can be handled on a project basis. Maintenance work that doesn't justify establishing a project falls into two categories.

1. Rapid—The change must be made as soon as possible.
2. Deliberate—A change is desirable, but its timetable for implementation isn't crucial.

If maintenance is rapid, the original developers generally retain responsibility for maintaining the system, or in their absence, other senior people are assigned this job. In this kind of situation, maintenance work is given highest priority, and the work is known as "fire fighting." The idea is to make rapid maintenance a high prestige activity.

Deliberate maintenance must be handled a different way. The easiest way to provide for deliberate maintenance is to let the original developers retain this responsibility. However, it's doubtful that this method is the most economical. It leaves experienced people on a job that less experienced personnel can handle.

A better technique is to bring trainees onto the project early enough to get them acquainted with the system before the project is complete. During system development certain changes and enhancements to the system are usually generated and tabled until the initial system is installed. The trainee programmers can be given the job of implementing these changes and enhancements, and use the original developers as consultants. If such changes and enhancements aren't present, the programmers can be given an earlier version of the system they're to maintain. This earlier version will have bugs in it that the trainee programmers are required to find and correct. When the system is accepted, the trainees take over the maintenance responsibility. In this way, the trainees get the opportunity to get in-depth, on-the-job training in the design and construction of the system they're maintaining.

To make such an approach to deliberate maintenance possible, the system developed must meet certain requirements.

1. It must conform to good design and programming practices. Otherwise, it won't perform its function of developing the trainees.
2. It must be well documented, so the trainees can find their way around in the system.
3. There must be a regression test to protect against degradation of a production system because of errors made by trainee personnel.

The trainees are also going to need direction in terms of what modifications and enhancements to make, and the priority in which these changes are to be made. This direction is given by someone who's assigned responsibility for supervising maintenance operations.

You can assure that a system is maintainable (that is, that it meets the requirements listed above), by setting up standards a project product must meet before a project can be considered concluded and ready to have its product pass into maintenance. In other words, you establish your own acceptance test in addition to the user's. These standards can be enforced by the maintenance operations supervisor, who's charged with the responsibility for passing on the adequacy of a project's test procedures, documentation, and program organization. Not until the maintenance operations supervisor gives his approval is a project considered complete and the project leader relieved of his responsibility.

Maintenance work can't be budgeted the same way as project work, but it can be handled on a request for services basis, and its costs can be billed back to users.

## 4  RESEARCH

The fundamental difference between project and research efforts is that analysis, design, and construction activities go on concurrently in research. The essence of research is that the goal to be reached is always, to some extent, unknown. As a consequence, the direction of research activity typically changes even while design and construction activities are going on.

There are at least two corollaries of this fundamental distinction.

1. Research efforts must be funded on hope rather than on the basis of a cost/benefit analysis. The justification for a research effort goes something like, "Here's what looks like a promising area. Let's fund a research effort of $x$ dollars and see what happens."
2. People assigned to a research effort must be highly self-motivating, because there's little way to tell whether people on a research effort are producing or not.

Systems and programming research seems to fall into two categories.

1. Research into new applications. Modeling would be an example of such research.

2. Research into new techniques. Investigation into programming languages or operating systems would be examples of this type of research.

You might well persuade a user to finance research into a new application, but the chances are you'll have to finance research into new techniques yourself and then build this cost into your rate structure as an overhead factor.

A basic question with respect to research is: When should a development effort be removed from research and placed into implementation? That is, when should it stop being viewed as development because it appears that there might be some payoffs (research); and start being viewed as development that's going to be applied to produce significant benefits (implementation).

Two factors appear to operate in making this decision.

1. The maturity of the product being developed. (How ready is it to go?)
2. The size of the payoff to be realized by using the product. (How badly do we need it?)

Of the two, the second factor seems to be prime. That is, as long as the need doesn't exist, the product doesn't come out of research. Another way of stating this might be: Before a product is taken out of research, its economic feasibility must be proven. (Repeated failure to make this demonstration might indicate that the research effort should be abandoned.)

Once the economic desirability of the product has been demonstrated, the maturity of the product then becomes the determining factor in the question of when the transfer is to occur. That is, after the economic feasibility of a product has been proven, it's taken out of research as soon as its technical and operational feasibility have been demonstrated. In two-cent words, before you try to implement a product, be sure it stands a good chance of working.

Possible questions to ask in the attempt to determine technical and operational feasibility are as follows.

1. Has a model been built?
2. Has the attempt been made to isolate and solve problems?
   a. On a theoretical level?
   b. By building components to see if they'll work?
   c. By recasting a substantial part of an existing system into a framework that uses the new product?
3. Suppose the remaining problems prove difficult to solve. Will this constitute no more than an irritation, or will it seriously jeopardize the realization of the desired economies?

# EXERCISE SOLUTIONS

## Chapter 2

1. Who the user is, is a good question. If you work with the Manufacturing Department to develop a system they can use to control their operations, you lay yourself open to the charge that you ignored management's needs for information. If you build a management information system, you can be accused of making a career out of a request for a simple manufacturing control system. You better get some clarification.

2. There's no question about it—the home office marketing department is your user. If there are aspects of the system the field doesn't like, you should see that their objections are brought to the marketing department's attention, but after the field has had their day in court, it's the marketing department that decides what the system is and is not going to do.

3. Your company is your user. It's customers are analogous to the branch offices in Exercise 2.

## Chapter 3

1. You're in the analysis phase. The fact that you're negotiating with your user as to what the system is going to do means the functional specifications aren't even written yet, let alone approved by the user. The fact that you're doing a lot of design work

has nothing to do with the question. "What phase are you in?" is code for "How much confidence can I have in your estimates?", and since functional specifications haven't been approved, your error range is at the 100% level.

2. There's insufficient information with which to answer this question. What work is being done has nothing to do with what phase you're in. To know what phase you're in (how confident you are of your estimates), you must know what level of specifications (functional or design) have been approved.

3. Your response is, "If the project is in the construction phase, then approved functional and design specifications must exist. May I see them, please?" If they can't be produced, then you must respectfully submit that your manager is wrong as to phase identification.

4. To be a purist, you must say that the payroll system is in the analysis phase, since the case study includes no approved functional specifications. Let's say that such specifications do exist, but that to save space, they weren't included in the case study. Then you must say that the system is in the design phase, since the design specifications in the case study are incomplete (to note just one deficiency, there are no file layouts), and design review committee approval isn't present. Again, let's say that some of the design specifications were left out of the case study just to save space, that complete design specifications do exist, and that they have been approved by the design review committee. We can then legitimately say the case study payroll system has just entered the construction phase, which is what we want to say.

5. The analysis phase ends when the functional specifications, which have been documented by the data processing department, are approved by the user. Provided that the feasibility decision, which the user makes at the end of the analysis phase, is positive, the design phase then begins.

6. You should require that the user make his request in writing and that he classify the change as postponable or not. If the change is postponable, you should table it until the currently specified system is installed. If the change isn't postponable, you should project the changes that will be required in costs and schedules to incorporate the specifications change, and inform the user of this price which he'll have to pay for the requested change. Only when the user accepts the price, should you make the change.

7. The user makes a feasibility decision at the end of each of the initiation, analysis, and design phases in the development of a data processing system.

8. The user makes a feasibility decision more than once beacuse, at the end of each successive phase in the development of a data processing system, more confidence can be placed in the development and operating cost projections for the system.

9. More confidence can be placed in the development and operating cost projections, for a data processing system, at the end of each successive phase in the development of the system, because with each passing phase, specifications for the system become more firm.

10. You know that, with each passing phase in the development of a data processing system, the specifications for the system become more firm because each successive phase is considered complete only when an increasingly specific set of written specifications have been signed off.

11. The design review committee signs off on the design specifications for a data processing system.

12. A responsible representative of each group, within the company, that's generally interested in data processing system design, sits on the design review committee.

13. Some typical groups represented on the design review committee are the system design group, the computer center, the system maintenance group, and the company auditors.

14. A good way to develop the examples to be included in the functional specifications of a data processing system is to simulate the operation of the system with the user of the system.

## Chapter 4

1. The end of the construction phase in the development of a data processing system is marked by the system passing the acceptance test.

2. Agreement must come before it's time to run the acceptance test. The ideal time is to develop the acceptance test specifications as part of the functional specifications.

3. The agreement must cover at least the following areas.

   a. The nature of the test. Will it be parallel, pilot, benchmark, or what?
   b. What constitutes successful operation. For example, in parallel operation, results are hardly ever completely commensurate; consequently, the degree to which coincidence of results is required must be spelled out.
   c. The ways in which satisfactory operation will be detected and demonstrated. For example, will people compare results or will some type of automated checking technique be developed?
   d. The degree of competence that user personnel must acquire in the use of the system.
   e. The user manuals that must be available.

4. During the acceptance test. The optimum training environment is one in which:

   a. Actual operating conditions are, as much as possible, duplicated.
   b. Mistakes aren't as costly as they would be in the actual operating environment.

   Acceptance test has both these characteristics.

## Chapter 6

Plans are used to project schedules and costs, and to direct activities.

## Chapter 7

1. Two bases on which to subdivide a job into tasks are:
   a. The functions performed by the system.
   b. The activities performed in getting the job done.

2. Three kinds of external restraints are:
   a. Deadlines.
   b. Delivery dates.
   c. Turnaround rates.

3. Delivery dates can be shown on a bubble chart.

4. A bubble chart showing the dependency between the tasks making up the construction phase of the payroll system project is shown in Fig. S-1. Some remarks concerning this bubble chart are appropriate.

   a. This bubble chart is certainly a high-level chart. The bubbles represent whole groups of tasks, and if the chart were constructed on the basis of a finer task distinction, a more intricate network of dependencies would be revealed. The bubbles on this chart basically represent the highest level of construction activities listed in Appendix E. The point we're trying to emphasize by developing the bubble chart at this high level is that there are many tasks other than developing programs which must be done to make the system operational. In reviewing your bubble chart the question you must ask yourself is: regardless of the level at which you enumerated tasks, did you give due consideration to all the tasks that must be done, or did you concentrate on the development of programs?

   b. There's nothing immutable about all the dependencies shown in this bubble chart.

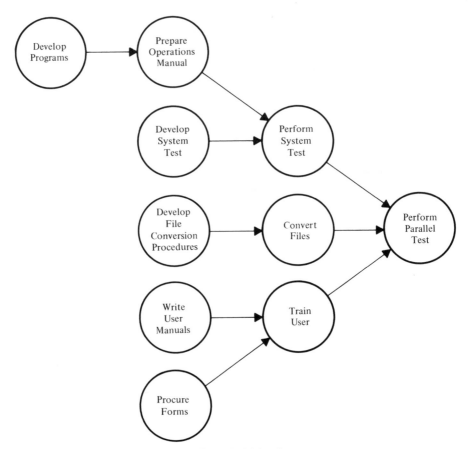

**Fig. S-1   Bubble chart.**

For example, if you decided that you'd use the file conversion procedures to develop unit test data, then the group of tasks concerned with program development are dependent on the development of these conversion procedures.

c. However, some of the dependencies on this bubble chart are quite necessary. For example:

1) Programs must be completely developed before preparation of the operations manual can be finished. Until program development is complete, there's always the possibility that some change in program construction will have ramifications as far as operations is concerned.

2) The system test can't be complete until it has been demonstrated that the computer center can run the system in their normal operations environment. Therefore, the operations manual must be completely prepared before system test can be completed.

3) Obviously, the system test must be developed before it can be performed.

# Chapter 8

1. Four general rules of thumb for allocating personnel to tasks are:

a. Assign tasks commensurate with a person's skills.

b. Assign tasks to broaden both the extent and range of skills.

c. Assign a person related tasks.

d. Assign the more critical tasks to the more responsible people.

2. You should assign to yourself tasks that keep you oriented to the system as a whole.

3. Two examples of the type of work you might assign to yourself are:

a. Writing the user manual.

b. Developing the system test.

4. A step-by-step application of the standard to the task might be as follows.

According to the program development time estimating standard, the estimate of the time Nazarevitz needs to develop program 2 is constructed by following a series of steps. The first step is to determine program complexity. This step is subdivided into two parts, weighting the program's input and output characteristics, and weighting the program's major processing functions.

In step 1A we're to weight the program's input and output characteristics. This weighting is done through the use of table 1.

There is card input with multiple formats. Table 1 tells us we should weight this input-output characteristic two points.

There is an output tape file, which is to be given a weight of one point.

There is printer output, although it can't be said to be a file in the normal sense of the word. Two different types of information (diagnostics and several counts) are printed, but neither requires any real formatting. Thus, it'd seem that the maximum weight that could be assigned to this output is one.

Thus, total input-output weighting is four.

In step 1B we're to weight program 2's major processing functions. This weighting is to be done through the use of Table 2.

Program 2 is written in COBOL. Therefore, it's the first five entries in Table 2 that are pertinent in the weighting of program 2's processing functions.

With respect to the restructuring of data, there are some restructure data operations in program 2, but they all appear to be related to the building of the output tape records. Therefore, this function doesn't seem to be done in program 2, and consequently, no weighting points are assigned for it.

With respect to condition checking, the validation checks to be performed by program 2 are simple, but there are a lot of them. Therefore, the condition checking function of program 2 should be considered complex, and should consequently be assigned four weighting points.

The data retrieval and presentation function apparently has to do with table and direct access file handling, neither of which is done in program 2. Therefore, no weighting points are assigned to it.

With respect to calculation, there are some arithmetic computations, but they're almost all done in connection with other operations. Therefore, this function can be assigned, at most, minimum weight. Let's give the calculate function a weight of one.

With respect to linkage, program 2 will probably not use overlays; the specifications don't call for any restart procedures or interface with other modules; and while all programs interface with an operating system, program 2 doesn't require other than the standard interfaces. Therefore, this function is considered inapplicable and isn't assigned any weight.

Thus, total processing functions weight is five, and as a consequence, program 2 is given a weighting of nine for program complexity.

The second step in estimating how long it'll take Nazarevitz to develop program 2 is to determine Nazarevitz's programming know-how. Table 3 is used to evaluate this programmer characteristic.

The case study and the standard don't have an identical complement of job titles. Where titles are common, the job definitions differ. Consequently, it is inadvisable to determine programming know-how from job title alone. Therefore, the determination will be made on the basis of job definition.

Nazarevitz has written and implemented programs of various complexities. He has experience with the particular programming system. However, he has no experience with the particular configuration. Thus, according to the job definitions, he's either a programmer or an apprentice. Since Omega considers Nazarevitz a senior man, let's call him a programmer but put him in the bottom of the programmer class, which allows one and one-half man-days per program weighting point.

The third step is to determine Nazarevitz's job knowledge, for which Table 4 is used.

The standard leaves the definition of job knowledge unclear. Since the job definitions in step 2 indicate that programming know-how is concerned with knowledge of programming skills, languages, and hardware, it seems likely that job knowledge refers to knowledge of the application for which the program is being developed. Therefore, we'll assume that what we're to evaluate here is Nazarevitz's knowledge of payroll.

It's unlikely that applications knowledge would ever not be useful in developing a program. Therefore, let's eliminate the "no job knowledge required" column.

However, detailed payroll knowledge wouldn't be necessary to develop an effective, efficient card to tape edit program. Consequently, let's agree that Nazarevitz requires only some knowledge of payroll.

There's no indication in Nazarevitz's resume that he has any detailed knowledge of payroll. However, few people are completely ignorant on the subject of payroll. So let's say that Nazarevitz has a fair general knowledge of payroll.

This determines a job knowledge factor of 0.75 man-days per weighting point.

Adding the weighting factors for programming know-how and job knowledge together gives a weight of 2.25 to Nazarevitz's skill level.

Multiplying the program complexity factor of nine by the personnel capability factor of 2.25 indicates that it'll take 20¼ man-days for Nazarevitz to develop program 2. The calculatoin is summarized below.

| Program Complexity | |
|---|---|
| Input Output | |
| Input | |
| Card-multiple formats | 2 |
| Output | |
| Tape file | 1 |
| Print | 1 |
| | 4 |
| | |
| Processing | |
| Restructure data | 0 |
| Condition checking | 4 |
| Data retrieval | 0 |
| Calculate | 1 |
| Linkage | 0 |
| | 5 |
| | 9 |
| | |
| Personnel Capability | |
| Programming Knowhow | 1.50 |
| Job Knowledge | 0.75 |
| | 2.25 |

$$9 \times 2.25 = 20.25 \text{ man-days}$$

If you've never used a standard for time estimating before, perhaps you were pleased to find that there's a methodical way of organizing your thinking in this area. In any case, despite the usefulness of the standard in Appendix G, you probably noticed that in some areas the standard was either ambiguous or downright inadequate. In other words, it could be improved significantly, just by refining it. Why not start using it and improving on it today?

Nevertheless, it must be admitted that in data processing, as in every other field of endeavor, no matter how refined estimating techniques become, time estimating will never become a precise science. Does this mean that it will remain impossible for us to avoid the situation where we experience a severe overrun of 100% or more? We don't think so. Even today, with estimating techniques as primitive as they are, the cause for severe overrun can seldom be identified as poor estimating—it is much more likely that the cause is *poor management.*

Let's put this discussion into context. This whole book is concerned with project management, yet only one section of one chapter of the book is concerned with time estimating. If you experience a large overrun, it's unlikely that you'll be able to trace all your problems back to faulty time-estimating techniques. More likely is that you'll have failed in one or more of your management responsibilities. For example:

1. You didn't get a firm user identification.
2. You didn't develop an adequate set of functional specifications.
3. You didn't require the user to approve the functional specifications before upgrading the confidence level of your estimates.
4. You didn't enforce a request for change procedure.
5. You didn't get design review committee approval of your design specifications before starting construction.
6. You didn't get agreement from the user on what constituted system acceptance before entering acceptance testing.
7. You overlooked necessary tasks.
8. You overlooked task dependencies.
9. You didn't get clearance for the delivery dates and turnaround rates on which you based your planning.
10. And so on.
11. And so on.
12. And so on.

In other words, inability to estimate precisely is too often used as a rationalization for ineffective management.

## Chapter 9

1. The steps in the development of a manpower plan are:
   a. Enumerate the tasks making up the job.
   b. Determine the dependency between tasks.
   c. Determine the external restraints.
   d. Allocate personnel to tasks.
   e. Estimate the time to do each task.
   f. Allow for contingencies.

2. Our plan is shown in Fig. S-2.

First of all, we must say that the plan shown in Fig. S-2 is only one of many feasible plans. Any plan development involves a series of choices among alternatives, and no one set of choices is necessarily right. We'll tell you why we made the choices we did, and in those areas where our plan differs from yours, you must decide who has the better reasons for the choices made.

Right at the outset, we can say that we operated under the principle of developing a "safe" plan. There seems to be a significant amount of concern with getting the payroll system in and operating smoothly. Therefore, we wanted to develop a plan that would allow us to absorb as many difficulties as possible and still meet our deadline. An indication of this perspective is the fact that, if everything goes as planned, we'll have the system completely built after only two thirds of the time allocated to system

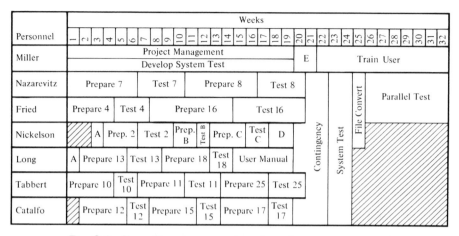

**Fig. S-2   Payroll system construction phase manpower plan.**
A—COBOL training.
B—Sorts.
C—File conversion procedures.
D—Operations manual.
E—Develop training program.

construction have elapsed. We've the remaining one third of the time to make sure the system hangs together, get the files converted, and get the user trained.

We started off by deciding we'd take a full two months to get the files converted and run the parallel test. As a consequence, we just blocked off the last eight weeks of time for this purpose.

The payroll system is a batch sequential system. Consequently, if we do thorough unit testing, system testing shouldn't be too demanding. Therefore, we allowed only two weeks for system testing, which would be blocked off just before entering the file conversion and parallel testing period.

This allowance for system testing, file conversion, and acceptance testing left 22 weeks for constructing the system. Although the exercise statement says no unusual delays or interruptions are anticipated, so a contingency level of 10% might be reasonable, we decided to follow our conservative bent and allow for a contingency level of about 15%. Consequently, we blocked off the three weeks preceding the system test for contingencies.

All this left any individual working on the project 19 weeks, or 95 days, to devote to individual tasks.

Our next decision was to appoint Miller project leader. We chose Miller because of his seniority at Omega and his experience with the current payroll system.

We then inspected the programs making up the system and determined that programs 2, 4, 7, 8, and 16 are critical—that is, if any of them don't run, the whole system is down. We decided that, if possible, we'd assign our senior men to these critical programs.

According to the time estimates given in the exercise, it'll take senior personnel 220 man-days to develop these critical programs.

| Critical Programs | Senior Man-days |
|:---:|:---:|
| 2 | 20 |
| 4 | 35 |
| 7 | 50 |
| 8 | 50 |
| 16 | 65 |
| | 220 |

If we assign senior people to all these critical programs, we'll then need three senior people. But unless we have Miller develop one or more of these programs, we've only two senior people (Fried and Nazarevitz) available. Our prejudice was to not use Miller for such tasks, so for the time being at least, we assumed that a junior person was going to develop one or more of these critical programs.

Programs 7 and 8 appear to be somewhat closely related, and it might make sense to assign them both to one person. It's estimated that it'll take a senior man 100 days to develop these programs, so if we cut our contingency period a little short, we could assign them both to one person. They both involve calculations, and program 8 involves summaries, both of which Nazarevitz has experience with. Therefore, we assigned these programs to Nazarevitz.

Programs 4 and 16 also require 100 senior man-days to develop. Therefore, we decided to assign these programs to Fried.

This task assignment left us with junior people to handle all the other program development tasks. These tasks require a total of 287 junior man-days.

| Programs | Junior Man-days |
|:---:|:---:|
| 1, 3, 5, 9, 14 | 14 |
| 2 | 28 |
| 10 | 28 |
| 11 | 35 |
| 12 | 28 |
| 13 | 35 |
| 15 | 28 |
| 17 | 28 |
| 18 | 28 |
| 25 | 35 |
| | 287 |

Dividing this total by 95 indicated that we must assign at least three junior people to the project.

We were now beginning to get some idea of the size of the project, and consequently, we were ready to make some decisions concerning task assignments for the project leader. First of all, we decided that, during the acceptance test period, we'd cut project size to the project leader and the two senior people. This made for a relatively small project during this period, and we decided that Miller could assume full responsibility for user training, which would be going on during this period. Of course, this meant he'd also have to take the responsibility for some user training before entering the acceptance period, and he'd also have to develop the training program, which would consume most of his time during the system test and contingency periods, but we did want Miller to take the responsibility for this training (so he'd maintain, as much as possible, a user attitude toward the system), and therefore, we went ahead and assigned these training tasks to him.

Our calculations indicated that, during the first five months of the project, there'd be five or six people on the project. Therefore, we knew we had to keep Miller's task assignments to a minimum during this period. It might have been reasonable to not give him any more assignments at all, but we finally decided to give him one more. Logical possibilities were development of the system test and writing the user manual. Remembering that Charlene Long was an English major at college, and might, therefore, be suited to the writing of the user manual, we decided to have Miller develop the system test.

This project is going to involve 487 man-days of program development. Using the ratio of eight to one, this means that development of the system test should require about 60 man-days, or 12 man-weeks. If we assume that, during the first five months, Miller will spend about half of his time on project management responsibilities, this will give him 10 man-weeks to develop the system test. All this is cutting things a little short, but we decided to go ahead and put this pressure on Miller.

Now that we had completed the task assignments for Miller, Fried, and Nazarevitz, we could see that, in addition to the remaining program development tasks, the tasks of developing the file conversion procedures and preparing the operations and user manuals were still unassigned, and consequently, we were going to have to assign four junior people to the project.

We had already selected all the senior personnel available, so we now decided to select the trainees, Catalfo and Tabbert. This left us with the requirement to select two out of the three programmers.

Each programmer had something to offer the project. Long had her English education, Kramer had more COBOL experience than anyone available for assignment to the project, and Nickelson was the only person available with any experience on the new computer. We felt that some experience with the new computer was needed on the project, and we wanted Long's English education for the user manual, so we selected Nickelson and Long.

We assigned Nickelson the tasks most directly related to the new computer. Thus, we had him prepare the operations manual, and develop the sorts and the file conversion procedures. We figured the file conversion could be accomplished by means of a program, so developing the conversion procedure amounted to developing a conversion program. Since Nickelson developed the conversion program, we decided to keep him on the project during the week when the file was being converted. Finally, on the assumption that a card to tape and edit program might be more hardware related than some other programs, we assigned program 2 to Nickelson.

We assigned the preparation of the user manual to Long. Since this task is primarily a matter of modifying the functional specifications to convert them into a user manual, we felt five weeks was plenty of time to do this task.

Since programs 12, 15, and 17 all handle the extracted tax master file, we felt one person should develop all three programs. Because she seems to be a self-starter, we assigned these tasks to Catalfo.

This left the development of programs 10, 11, 13, 18, and 25 to be split between Long and Tabbert. Long had some payroll experience, and on the theory that programs 13 and 18 were more payroll related than 10, 11, or 25, programs 13 and 18 were assigned to Long.

Neither Nickelson nor Long had any COBOL background. Consequently, one week each was set aside for their training.

The result of our arrangements was to develop a manpower plan in which each project member has a number of tasks to complete. The sequence in which each person completed his tasks was arranged so that, as soon as possible, several programs could be hung together for subsystem testing. Thus, if everything goes according to plan, at the end of week 12, programs 1–5, 7, 9, and 10 can be run as a subsystem, and at the end of week 13, programs 12, 14, and 15 can be run as a subsystem. Such plans for subsystem testing would have to be taken into consideration by Miller as he developed the system test.

## Chapter 10

1. During the construction phase, computer time is needed for acceptance testing, file conversion, system testing, and unit testing.

2. The major factor influencing the amount of system test computer time required is system type.

3. As far as amount of system test computer time is concerned, there are two system types.

   a. Batch sequential.
   b. Transaction responsive.

4. In Fig. S-3, we've shown our computer time projection for the manpower plan shown in the exercise statement. Again, we must say that the computer time plan we show is only one of many feasible plans. There are two possible variables here.

   a. If you based your computer time projection on your own manpower plan, rather than the one given in the exercise statement, your projection will necessarily vary from ours.
   b. In making your projection, you may have used different assumptions than we did.

   The assumptions we made are as follows.

   a. A person uses two shots a day during unit test periods.
   b. The sorts and the file conversion program are small programs—that is, test shot time is 10 minutes each.
   c. During system test, one hour of computer time per day is used.
   d. File conversion requires 5 hours.
   e. Acceptance testing requires 11 hours and 40 minutes.

   We also allowed 10 hours of computer time for contingencies. You should check your assumptions against ours and determine which you think are more reasonable.

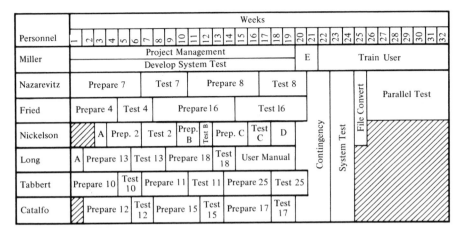

| Personnel | Weeks |
|---|---|

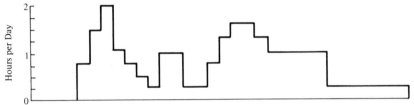

Fig. S-3  Computer time plan.

We admit that our computer time estimate is somewhat higher than it should be, since the test periods, shown in the manpower plan given in the exercise statement, include both:

a. A provision for developing a test plan, test data, and predetermined results, and:

b. A provision for unit testing.

Programmers would not be using two shots a day during the time they were developing their tests, yet we ignored this fact in our computer time plan and provided for two shots a day during the whole test period shown on the manpower plan.

In any case, we feel that you should come up with a total time estimate of between 90 and 130 hours. Otherwise, you're either being too stingy with your company's computer time (which means you aren't using your manpower efficiently) or else you're planning on some pretty sloppy program testing procedures.

## Chapter 11

1. The two parts of this question are really just different aspects of the same thing. There is little question that you can't commit to a fixed price and completion date on an incompletely defined project, because if you know only partially what the project is to accomplish, then you can't develop a complete list of the tasks to be done by the project. An incomplete task list for a job means that any plan for doing the job is going to be unreliable. And since schedules and cost estimates are just plans looked at

from a particular point of view, you must of necessity have a low level of confidence in any schedule or cost estimate you develop. Now, evaluate the typical analysis project in light of this discussion. How often is it that you can draw up a complete list of tasks to be done in analyzing a data processing system situation and have a high degree

COST ESTIMATE

| PROJECT NO. | | PROJECT PHASE Construction | |
|---|---|---|---|
| PREPARED BY      Tom      Gildersleeve | | | DATE |

SALARY

| NAME | WEEKS | SALARY | COST |
|---|---|---|---|
| Miller | 32 | 275.00 | 8800.00 |
| Mozorenitz | 32 | 225.00 | 7200.00 |
| Fried | 32 | 225.00 | 7200.00 |
| Mickelson | 23 | 175.00 | 4025.00 |
| Loup | 24 | 175.00 | 4200.00 |
| Tolbert | 24 | 162.50 | 3900.00 |
| Cotolfr | 23 | 162.50 | 3737.50 |
| | | | |

TOTAL  $\boxed{39,062.50}$

OVERHEAD _____  $\boxed{39,062.50}$

COMPUTER TIME

HOURS $\boxed{120}$      RATE $\boxed{100.00}$      COST $\boxed{12,000.00}$

TRAVEL AND LIVING EXPENSES _____  $\boxed{\phantom{xxx}}$

SUPPORT SERVICES                                              COST

| | |
|---|---|
| | |
| | |
| | |

TOTAL  $\boxed{\phantom{xxx}}$

GRAND TOTAL  $\boxed{90,125.00}$

**Fig. S-4   Cost estimate.**

of confidence in the reliability of your list? That's how often you can commit to a fixed price and completion date on a project to do the analysis phase.

2. System development cost categories are manpower (including overhead), computer time, travel and living, and support services.

3. We developed a cost estimate for the plan given in the exercise statement. If you costed out your own plan, you may have come up with a somewhat different total than ours, but your approach should parallel ours, which is shown on the form in Fig. S-4.

## Chapter 13

1. A cost estimate is a plan translated into dollars. Checkpoints are a device to see if progress is going according to plan and that, consequently, costs are staying within estimates.

2. The essential characteristic of good checkpoints is that their attainment be tied to the production of tangible outputs which are an integral part of the task. Other desirable characteristics are that they occur frequently, and that they be set in cooperation with the person who must meet them.

3. Most of the tasks the project members have to do are concerned with the development of programs. We'd require that a programmer develop a program by following the sequence of steps listed below.

   a. First the programmer would have to write a set of specifications for the program. This set of specifications is often called the program narrative, but we'll use the name "internal specifications."

   b. Once the internal specifications are complete, the programmer must make a logical analysis of his program. This logical analysis might be a flow chart or a decision table.

   c. When the logical analysis is complete, the programmer can start writing code.

   d. When he has completed his code, the next thing the programmer must do is prepare a test plan. This is a written description of how he plans to unit test his program.

   e. When the test plan is complete, the programmer can start developing test data and predetermined results.

   f. When the programmer has developed his test data and predetermined results, he's then in a position to do unit testing.

   As a consequence, we'd propose that the following products and events be used to signify the attainment of various checkpoints.

   a. The internal specifications document.

   b. The logical analysis document.

   c. All sheets of coding paper submitted to the keypunching department.

   d. The test plan document.

   e. All test data recorded in the form in which it's going to be used.

   f. The program correctly performs all the tests documented in the test plan.

   The shortest time span for developing a program in the payroll system is 28 days. As a consequence, we'd use all six checkpoints for each program development task. However, we wouldn't always propose using all six. For example, if development of a program is going to take two weeks, two of the six checkpoints are adequate for monitoring a person's schedule.

On the other hand, if a program development task is large enough, more than six checkpoints might be set up for it. What would these extra checkpoints be? Basically, subdivisions of the first six.

For example, suppose that after the logical analysis is complete, it's estimated that it will take two months to do the coding. It should be possible to analyze a program of this size into several modules, and a checkpoint can be set up for the completion of the coding of each module. Checkpoints for unit testing can also be set up on a module by module basis.

The other type of task to which persons on the payroll project are assigned is the preparation of manuals—the operations manual and the user manual. Products to which checkpoints can be tied for this type of task might be:

a. The table of contents.
b. A first draft ready for review and revision.
c. A final draft ready for production.

It can be seen from the above that most of the products developed on a systems and programming project are documents. To be used as a basis for setting up a checkpoint, a document must be produced as a necessary part of accomplishing the task. For example, a status report is a document, but a checkpoint can't be tied to it, because preparation of a status report isn't an integral part of any systems and programming task.

## Chapter 14

When a checkpoint is missed, you:

1. Determine the reason.
2. Take action to:
   a. Eliminate the reason.
   b. Recover the slippage.
3. If recovery is impossible, let the people depending on the deadline know.

## Chapter 15

1. The control techniques to use during the construction phase are:
   a. Testing.
   b. Internal specifications.
   c. Conventions.
2. The techniques to use during the design phase are:
   a. Design review committee.
   b. Standards.
   c. Alternative designs.
3. The control in the analysis phase is user approval of the functional specifications.
4. A general purpose control technique is communication between project members.

## Chapter 16

1. You should have a tickler file to remind you of future commitments, both by you and to you.
2. To make a tickler file work, you must:
   a. Make entries in it.
   b. Look at it.

## Chapter 17

1. No, a special effort doesn't have to be made to develop the documentation for a data processing system.
2. A special effort doesn't have to be made to develop the documentation for a data processing system because all the needed documentation is produced as an automatic by-product of the system development activities.
3. A table of contents for our system documentation volume is as follows.

   a. Analysis phase—functional specifications.
   b. Design phase—design specifications.
   c. Construction phase:
      1) For each program-module:
         a) Internal specifications.
         b) Logical analysis.
         c) Program listing.
      2) Regression test.
      3) Operations manual.
      4) User manual.
4. The operations manual is written to the computer center's specifications. This is a specific example of the general rule that the user of a product must take the responsibility for specifying the product.
5. Preparing the user manual isn't a major effort. It's basically a matter of modifying the functional specifications.
6. A regression test is a standard set of tests against which a system is run to demonstrate that it hasn't deteriorated. The purpose of the regression test is to detect inadvertent introduction of error into a system at the time a modification is being made to the system.

## Chapter 18

1. A status report should cover the following points.
   a. Accomplishments in the last report period.
   b. Overall progress toward long-term goals.
   c. Problems, current and anticipated, together with solutions, both being pursued and suggested.
   d. Goals for the next report period.

2. a. A status report provides the recipient with status information.
   b. A status report:
      1) Makes the sender review his accomplishments, evaluate his progress toward his long-term goals, and adjust his plans to maintain his best posture toward his long-term goals.
      2) Gives the sender an opportunity to remind the recipient of problems on which the sender needs help.
      3) Creates a historical record.

3. Constructing a project history consists of keeping a file of your status reports.

4. The specialty of the leader of a group is coordination.

5. The two forces pushing a group leader into communication with the group's environment are:
   a. The external force—the tendency of the people outside the group to prefer to communicate with the leader rather than any other group member.
   b. The internal force—the leader's need to maintain his credibility with the group as a coordinator whc knows what's going on in the world in which the group operates.

6. The two questions you should ask to determine if it's worthwhile for you to attend a meeting are:
   a. "Does the meeting have a purpose?"
   b. "Can I contribute to the meeting's purpose?"

7. Two general techniques for handling potentially disruptive communications are:
   a. Channel them.
   b. Formalize them.

8. You should prepare a comprehensive status report once a month.

9. You make sure all the significant things that happened this month get into this month's status report by keeping notes.

10. To a service organization you represent a user.


## Chapter 20

Some of the ways to motivate project members are:
1. Assign tasks that the project members have some reason of their own, such as challenge or interest, for doing.
2. Make your performance expectations clear.
3. Give credit for all performance meeting your expectations.
4. Give prompt, constructive criticism.
5. Submit honest performance appraisals.
6. Provide conducive working conditions.
7. Develop a team.
8. Give direction.

# Chapter 21

1. A form design specialist, who's someone other than the analyst. This is a specific instance of the general principle that the analyst is most effective when he confines himself to his area of expertise and exploits the expertise of other specialists.

2. He has none. The essence of system test data preparation is that it be done independently of the people who prepare the programs making up the computerized data processing system.

3. a. 1) Prepare good documentation.
      2) Develop well-organized programs.
      3) Develop a regression test.

   b. Good documentation and well-organized programs expedite the determination of what should be done where to implement a change. A well-organized program is easier to change. A regression test protects against the introduction of fortuitous error.

# APPENDICES

# A. DESIGN SPECIFICATIONS STANDARDS

## 1.0 PURPOSE

The basic document that constitutes the backbone of design specifications is the system flow chart. A system flow chart is a set of symbols representing manual, EAM, and computer operations connected together to show the sequence of operations making up a system. Thus, it shows the flow of data through the system.

The purpose of the system flow chart is two-fold.

1. As a kind of master plan of the system, it provides a convenient starting point and reference point when orienting oneself to the system.
2. As the fundamental document produced during system design, it provides the basis for system evaluation.

As will become clear in the following, to satisfy this second purpose, the system flow chart must be supported by certain backup information.

## 2.0 FORM

### 2.1 The Operation

The basic element of the system flow chart is the operation, which may be a manual operation, an EAM operation, or a computer program. A program is defined as that which accepts input and produces output, input and output here including tape and disk files

**231**

used within the system as well as the transaction input and report output with which the user deals. The only input/output not included in this definition is intermediary or scratch output later used by the same program as input. Thus, the strings of data produced and read by a sort do not make each pass of the sort a program. Instead, the entire sort is considered to be one program.

An operation is shown as a rectangle. Inside the rectangle, the operation is identified by:

1. Operation number.
2. Operation name.

For example:

## 2.2  Input/Output

All other symbols on the system flow chart show input/output.

### 2.2.1  Magnetic Tape

A magnetic tape file is shown as a circle with a tail. Inside the circle, the file is identified. For example:

### 2.2.2  Random Access Storage

A random-access-storage-device file, such as a disk file, is shown by the following symbol.

### 2.2.3  Punched Cards

A punched card file, read or punched, full or stub, is shown by the following.

### 2.2.4  Printed Reports

*2.2.5  Paper Tape*

Input or output. Paper or plastic. Chad or chadless.

*2.2.6  Keyboard*

Input or output. Identified by type of information being handled.

*2.2.7  Display*

For plotters and video devices. Identified by type of information being handled.

*2.2.8  Other*

If input/output other than that shown above is used, it's shown in the following symbol.

The symbol contains an identification of the device being used and the information being handled.

### 2.3  Indication of Flow

*2.3.1  On Site*

On-site data flow is shown by arrows. For example:

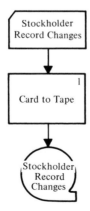

### 2.3.2 Communication Link

The automatic transmission of information from one location to another via communication lines is shown as follows.

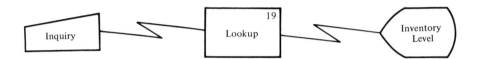

### 2.3.3 Cycle Flow

Output produced in one cycle of a system that is to be used as input in the succeeding cycle of the system is shown by a dotted line. For example:

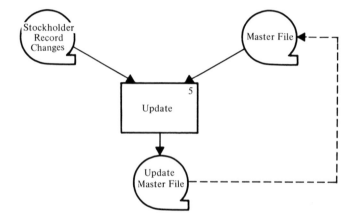

### 2.3.4 Page to Page Flow

More than one page may be required to draw a process chart. Flow between the pages is indicated by the following symbol:

If the symbol is leading off of the page, it has an arrow entering it, and it's labeled with:

1. The number of the operation that is going to use the file as input.
2. The number of the page on which the operation appears.

If the symbol is leading onto the page, it has an arrow leaving it, and it's labeled with:

1. The number of the operation that produced the file as output.
2. The number of the page on which the operation appears.

The file itself appears on both the "from" and the "to" pages. For example:

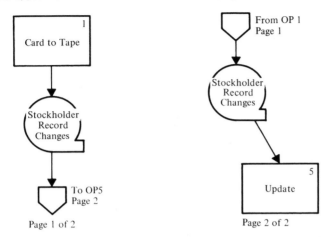

Page 1 of 2                                    Page 2 of 2

### 2.3.5  Page Flow

With the exception of cycle flow, on each page of the system flow chart, the chart is drawn to show the data flowing from top to bottom. Input flows into the tops of operations. Output flows out the bottoms.

### 2.4  Legends

Each page of a process chart contains a legend. Identified in the legend are the following.

1. System name.
2. System cycle (daily, weekly, monthly, etc.).
3. Number of pages in the process chart.
4. Number of this page.
5. Author's name.
6. Date.
7. Revision identification.
   a. Revision number.
   b. Reviser's name.
   c. Revision date.

### 2.5  System Restraints

As implied by the above description of the legend, each page of the system flow chart is confined to a cycle of the system. Generally speaking, to execute effectively each cycle of a system, the input from the user is required by a certain date and/or time and the output must be supplied to the user by a certain date and/or time. These input cutoff and output due times appear on the system flow chart.

### 3.0  EXAMPLE

A page from an example system flow chart is shown in Fig. A-1.

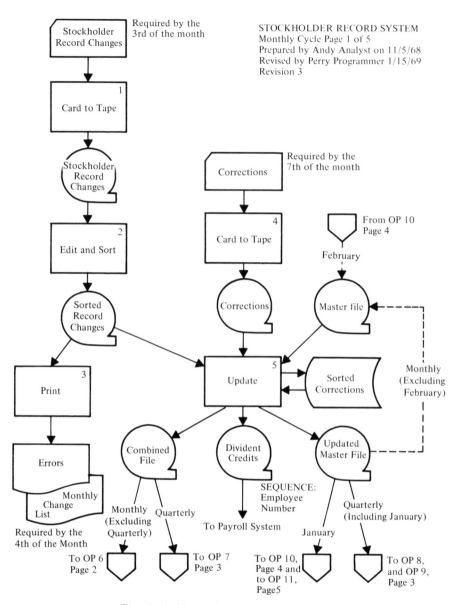

STOCKHOLDER RECORD SYSTEM
Monthly Cycle Page 1 of 5
Prepared by Andy Analyst on 11/5/68
Revised by Perry Programmer 1/15/69
Revision 3

**Fig. A-1   Example system flow chart.**

## 4.0   BACKUP

As can be seen from the example system flow chart, the chart provides insufficient information for purposes of system evaluation. Certain backup information for each operation is necessary for these purposes. This information describes the operation and each file that it handles as described below.

### 4.1  Operation

#### 4.1.1  Outline

For each operation on the system flow chart, the following is provided.

1. A gross description of the processing done. For example, if one of the operations done is a sort, the description so states, and the sort keys, from major to minor, are listed.
2. An estimate of:
   a. The core (region size) required, if the operation is a program.
   b. Running time.

#### 4.1.2  Example

The following is possible backup for operation number 5 in the example system flow chart.

DESCRIPTION
Monthly (Including Quarterly)

1. Read corrections and sort on disk.
2. Skip errors on change file.
3. Update master file.

Monthly (Excluding Quarterly)

1. Select accounts with over 500 shares and write on combined tape.
2. Write balance totals and posting errors on combined tape.

QUARTERLY

1. Calculate dividends and update year-to-date dividends paid.
2. Compute amount withheld and update year-to-date foreign withholding for non-resident alien accounts.
3. Select accounts with over 500 shares items, bank analysis, and dividend credits.
4. Prefix balance totals, posting errors, over 500 shares items, bank-analysis items, and dividend credit items with a sort key so they'll group on the output tape.
5. Sort.
   a. Balance totals, posting errors, and over 500 shares items by account number and certificate number.
   b. Dividend credit items by employee number.
   c. Bank analysis items by bank code.

ESTIMATED CORE REQUIRED—32K

ESTIMATED RUNNING TIME—30 minutes

### 4.2  Files

#### 4.2.1  Magnetic Tape

4.2.1.1  Outline

1. Record type (fixed or variable).
2. Record length (if variable: maximum, minimum, and average length plus a frequency distribution).

3. Block length in bytes (if variable length records, maximum block size).
4. File size, in number of blocks.
5. Recording density.
6. Reel size.
7. Number of volumes.
8. List of fields making up the record.
9. File sequence.

Where standard values for these parameters are adopted, only exceptions need be noted.

### 4.2.1.2 Example

The following is possible backup for the Stockholder Record Changes magnetic tape file in the example system flow chart.

*Record Type*—Fixed
*Record Length*—50 bytes
*Block Length*—100 bytes
*File Size*—550 blocks
*Recording Density*—800 bpi
*Number of Volumes*—1
*Fields*
   Account Number
   Transaction Type Code
   Certificate Number
   Certificate Type Code
   Certificate Class Code
   Number of Shares
   Date (Of Issue or Cancellation)
   Account Number with which This Account is Combined
   Account City Code
   Account State Code
   Employee Identification Number
*File Sequence*
   Major—Account Number
   Intermediate—Transaction Type Code
   Minor—Certificate Number

In this example no specification of reel size is made because a 2400-foot reel is standard.

### 4.2.2  Random Access

1. Equipment type.
2. Record type.
3. Record length.
4. File organization.
5. Block length in bytes.
6. File size, in terms of number of cylinders required.
7. Number of volumes.
8. List of fields.

9. Access method.
10. Access key or file sequence, whichever is appropriate.

### 4.2.3  Punched Card

4.2.3.1  Outline

1. Card types, if more than one.
2. File size, in terms of number of cards.
3. List of fields making up each card type.
4. File source.
5. Sequence, if any.

4.2.3.2  Example

The following is possible backup for the Stockholder Record Changes card file in the example system flow chart.

*Number of Card Types—*1
*File Size—*11,000 cards
*Fields*
   Account Number
   Certificate Number
   Certificate Type
   Certificate Class
   Number of Shares
   Date of Issue
   Date of Cancellation
   Account Number Combined With
   State Code
   City Code
   Employee Identification Number
*File Source—*Received from Clerical Control Room; cards are batched by control group and are accompanied by a control sheet.

### 4.2.4  Printed Report

4.2.4.1  Outline

1. Rough report layout.
2. Indication of form to be used (preprinted or not).
3. Number of copies.
4. File size, in number of pages.
5. File sequence.

4.2.4.2  Example

The following is possible backup for the Monthly Change List in the example system flow chart.

*Layout—*The validated, sorted Stockholder Record Changes are listed in a double-spaced, columnar form, one column to each field in the record.
*Form—*Standard two-ply 11 X 14 blank printer form is used.

*File Size*—375 pages.
*File Sequence*
   Major—Account Number
   Intermediate—Transaction Type Code
   Minor—Certificate Number

### 4.2.5  Paper Tape

1. Record type.
2. Record length.
3. Block length.
4. File size, in number of blocks.
5. Density.
6. Reel size or strip, whichever is appropriate.
7. Number of volumes.
8. List of fields.
9. File sequence.

### 4.2.6  Keyboard

1. Record length.
2. List of fields.

### 4.2.7  Display

Rough display layout.

### 4.2.8  Other Input/Output Devices

1. Indication of file content, in terms of:
   a. Fields.
   b. Records.
   c. Blocks.
2. Indication of file size.
3. Indication of relevant time-influencing factors, so that file size can be used as a factor in determining running time when appropriate.
4. Indication of file organization.
5. Indication of method of file access.

## 4.3  Communications

For an operation involving a communications network, backup information describes the following.

### 4.3.1  Coverage

1. Locations to be covered including building, office, and location within the office.
2. Shift coverage; by location if different.

### 4.3.2  Input/Processing/Output

1. System Cycle. Brief description of the system cycle in terms of operator/input-output/CPU functions and interfaces.

2. Input/Output Messages:
    a. Input/output form: punched card, typed, paper tape, etc.
    b. Message types and characteristics: length, format, field size, and fixed vs. variable characteristics.
    c. Message samples.
3. Teleprocessing Logic:
    a. Type
        1. Data collection.
        2. Inquiry.
        3. Message switching.
    b. Editing
    c. Auditing, including any message control totals or time-stamps.
4. Operational Mode. Conversational or nonconversational.
5. Response Times. Maximum allowable response times including application program process time.
6. Input/Output Volumes. By location, shift, and input/output device with identification of any peak and/or slack periods.

### 4.3.3  Hardware Requirements

1. Normal operational requirements.
2. Error response and error handling requirements.
3. Backup requirements in case of input/output device, transmission line or CPU failure.

### 4.3.4  Example

1. Coverage

| Group | Location | Shift Coverage | # Terminals |
|---|---|---|---|
| Materials Sched. | OBB-3 | 1st | 1 |
| Materials Sched. | L-Bldg. | 1st, 2nd, 3rd | 2 |
| Shop Dispatching | Marsh. Bldg. | 1st, 2nd, 3rd | 1 |
| Spares Follow-Up | L-Mezz. | 1st | 1 |
| Finished Stores | L-Bldg. | 1st, 2nd, 3rd | 1 |
| Assembly Floor | M-Bldg. | 1st, 2nd, 3rd | 1 |
| Materials | Middletown | 1st, 2nd, 3rd | 2 |
| Purch. Dispatching | L-Bldg. | 1st and 2nd | 3 |
| Materials | North Haven | 1st, 2nd, 3rd | 1 |
| P.I.C. Area 1 | | 1st * | 1 |
| P.I.C. Area 2 | | 1st * | 1 |
| P.I.C. Area 3 | | 1st * | 1 |
| P.I.C. Area 4 & 5 | | 1st * | 1 |
| P.I.C. Area 6 | | 1st * | 1 |
| P.I.C. Area 14 | | 1st * | 1 |
| | | Total | 19 |

*Limited usage possible on the 2nd and 3rd shift. Saturday coverage will be required.

2. Input/Processing/Output
   1. Terminal operators will key in a code and part #.
   2. Processing will be the extraction of the requested part of display.
   3. Output will be the transmission of the status record back to a terminal.
   4. Input/Output Messages
      a. Input/Output Form is a stock paper for a 13 1/8" pin feed platen.
      b. Message types
         1. Status type records, length of 75 characters.
         2. Error messages.
   5. Teleprocessing Logic
      Inquiry with some editing
   6. Operational Mode
      Nonconversational
   7. Response Time
      Not to exceed (20) seconds after inquiry has been submitted from a terminal.
   8. Input/Output Volumes

| Group | Location | Inquiry At Peak | Time | Slack Time |
|-------|----------|-----------------|------|------------|
| Materials Sched. | PBB-3 | | 3:00 pm | 5:00 pm–8:00 am |
| Materials Sched. | L-Bldg. | 400 | 1:00 pm | 12:00 M –7:00 am |
| Shop Dispatching | Marsh. Bldg. | | 11:00 am | 3:30 pm–7:00 am |
| Spares Follow-Up | L-Mezz. | | 7:30 am | 3:30 pm–7:00 am |
| Finished Stores | L-Bldg. | | 7:00 am– 4:00 pm | 4:00 pm–7:00 am |
| Assembly Floor | M-Bldg. | | 8:00 am | |
| Materials | Middletown | | 7:00 am– 1:00 pm | 3:30 pm–7:00 am |
| Purch. Dispatching | L-Bldg. | | 1:45 pm– 3:00 pm | 4:00 pm–7:00 am |
| Materials | North Haven | | 8:00 am | 4:00 pm–7:00 am |
| P.I.C. Area 1 | E. Hartford | | 10:00 am–11:00 am | 3:30 pm–7:00 am |
| P.I.C. Area 2 | E. Hartford | | 10:00 am–11:00 am | 3:30 pm–7:00 am |
| P.I.C. Area 3 | E. Hartford | | 10:00 am–11:00 am | 3:30 pm–7:00 am |
| P.I.C. Area 4 & 5 | E. Hartford | | 10:00 am–11:00 am | 3:30 pm–7:00 am |
| P.I.C. Area 6 | E. Hartford | | 10:00 am–11:00 am | 3:30 pm–7:00 am |
| P.I.C. Area 14 | E. Hartford | | 10:00 am–11:00 am | 3:30 pm–7:00 am |

3. Hardware Requirements
   1. Keyboard input and Typewriter output.
      2741 Terminals
      4790 Multipoint Local Line-Adapter
      6114 Record Check
      1313 Automatic EOB
      7479 Station Control
      9509 Pin Feed Platen
      9162 Line Feed Feature
   2. Error response is a message for action to re-submit.

3. Back up requirements.
   a. Spare Terminals
   b. Spare Lines
   c. Ability to tie with other transmission lines.
   d. Listings, as presently provided, to back up CPU failure.

# B. FUNCTIONAL SPECIFICATIONS STANDARDS

## INTRODUCTION

Many standards for a document try to describe, in as much detail as possible, what information is to be included in a document. The ideal is to provide a form on which the appropriate paragraphs, sentences and phrases are to be checked off. Because of the variable nature of the contents, the nearest approach to this ideal that has been achieved in the standardization of functional specifications has been the construction of an outline, or framework, which the system analyst is to fill out with content. Some such guideline is needed to assure that all pertinent points are covered in the functional specifications and excellent specifications are written which conform to the structure specified. Nevertheless, the disturbing fact is that many sets of functional specifications, written in conformance to the letter of the standards, prove to be unsatisfactory, while other specifications do perform according to expectations despite the fact that they vary significantly from the standards.

This situation arises from the fact that the systems analyst isn't filling out a checklist but is writing narrative. The extent to which this narrative ultimately proves satisfactory depends on the degree to which the system analyst understands the purpose of the document. Therefore, this description is divided into two parts, purpose and form. (It also contains two other parts, an example and a summary.) And because the functional specifications are a narrative, understanding the purpose of the document is considered essential to the preparation of a satisfactory product. Functional specifications are to be

**244**

recognized as a tool, and while ingenious individuals occasionally develop a more useful form of a tool, it's the case that, as long as production of the tool remains a custom job, the serviceability of each individual tool is a direct function of the degree to which the producer understands its purpose.

## PURPOSE

The functional specifications are the end result of the system analysis phase. They are the physical manifestation of the agreement reached between the Data Processing Department and the user as to what the system is going to do.

In a word, they're a "contract."

Therefore, they're written in such manner that:

1. Whenever a question of the form, "What did we say was going to happen in this situation?" arises between the Data Processing Department and the user, the natural reaction is to look for the answer in the functional specifications.
2. Whenever it becomes desirable to change the system function in a small or a large way, whether the suggestion for the change is initiated by the user or the Data Processing Department, the natural way to record the change is to modify the functional specifications.

The above is an ideal. No functional specifications will meet it perfectly. Questions will arise on which the functional specifications will not shed light. However, the fact that the ideal isn't attained does not negate the desirability of the goal.

## FORM

The functional specifications are a contract—the physical manifestation of the agreement between the Data Processing Department and the user as to what the system is from the user's point of view.

With respect to the form of the functional specifications, the most important phrase in the above definition is "from the user's point of view." The functional specifications are written to be understood by the user. This means that they're written:

1. In the user's words.
2. In a form that's easy to read.
3. In terms of what the system is going to do for the user.

These points are worth some expansion.

1. In any application area there's a nomenclature, a terminology. It's in this language that the functional specifications are written. If there's some fear that the specifications will, consequently, lose some of its comprehensibility within the Data Processing Department, it can have appended to it a glossary in which unfamiliar terms are defined. Functional specifications written in this language tend to guarantee that:

    a. The system analyst understands what the user is talking about.
    b. The user understands what he's getting.

2. Well-done functional specifications are generally a good-sized document. One of the most effective ways that has been found to make such a document readable is to design it in the same way an onion is constructed, so it can be peeled away a layer at a

time. This means that the first thing in the specifications is a relatively short, general description of the system which gives an overall picture of what's going on. This general description is followed by the detailed description. If the detailed description is large, it's divided into sections. Each section is organized into a general description of the information in the section followed by the detailed description. If the detailed description of a section is large, it's divided into subsections, each consisting of a general description and a detailed description, until the detail in any one subsection becomes small enough to be easily readable. What "small enough" is, isn't best defined in terms of number of pages. Information is organized into functional units, and the breaking of a functional unit into two subsections to conform to some maximum page standard doesn't contribute to readability. A better rule is to divide the document into as many levels of subsections as organization of the content will allow.

3. Installation of a data processing system isn't a painless task. For a user to agree to undergo this punishment, the system must offer him some significant benefits—advantages over not having the system. As the user is subjected to the dislocations and disappointments that generally attend the design and construction phases, these benefits may tend to grow dim. Therefore, it's useful to have them clearly and succinctly listed in the second section of the functional specifications, so they can be easily reviewed, and memories can be refreshed. This section is an explanation of why upper management and the user decided to institute the system in the first place.

The functional specifications are a description of what the system is designed to do and how the user goes about getting it to perform its function. The functional specifications describe:

1. Every system operation that can be performed in response to input introduced by the user. This includes the description of any output that may be produced.
2. Each possible input that the user can introduce.
3. Audit controls.
4. For some products, such input/output routines or compilers, time and space utilization. At first these will have to be estimates. Later they can be revised on the basis of experience.

Input is described in terms of its content and the way the user introduces it to the system. For example, if input is a form the user fills out, the final form doesn't have to be defined, but the meaning of each possible entry on the form and the way in which it's to be entered is spelled out. If the input is to be keyed in on a remote device, the exact nature of all key-ins doesn't have to be described, but a listing of possible key-in types, their meaning, and the general characteristics of their format does appear.

Similarly, output is described in terms of its contents, and the way the system presents it to the user. For example, if the output is a printed report, the final form doesn't have to be defined, but the meaning of each field on the report and the general form layout is spelled out. If the output is a display on a remote device, the nature of all displays doesn't have to be described, but a listing of possible displays, their meaning, and the general characteristics of their format does appear. In general, the more defined the input and output are, the better are the chances of delivering the system to a satisfied user.

System processing is described to the extent necessary to define the way each output field is derived. In many instances, the name of the field is sufficient to describe its source—for example, vendor name or employee badge number. In other instances, more detail is necessary—for example, the algorithm used to determine recorder quantity, or the priority with which deductions are to be applied to a man's wages.

A description of the contents of functional specifications raises the question: How much detail is necessary? The only possible answer is a functional one.

1. The functional specifications are the physical manifestation of an agreement between the Data Processing Department and the user.
2. To be a party to this agreement the user must understand what he's agreeing to:
   a. What he's getting.
   b. What he's not getting.
   c. What his obligations are.
3. Therefore, the functional specifications must be in sufficient detail so the user can understand them.

The point at which most functional specifications writers balk is the extent to which a description of the processing operations done by the system is required. However, most of this information already exists and doesn't have to be rewritten. All that's necessary is a reference to the appropriate document. For example, rules for computing wages are specified by citing the appropriate labor agreement, methods for computing withholding tax are described by referring to the appropriate government document, and the algorithm for computing reorder quantity in a new order system can generally be found in correspondence or reports documenting the development of the algorithm.

The quality of functional specifications is enhanced if a comprehensive set of test case examples is included. By the time a project enters design, considerations begin to get more technical and less functional in nature. As a consequence, the user's grasp of what is being specified may begin to suffer. Nevertheless, at the end of system construction it's the user who must be satisfied. The user may get lost in the technicalities of the design specification, but he should understand the data that's being processed. Consequently, he's in a position to pass on the accuracy of the test case examples developed, or even better, develop them himself. A comprehensive, user-prepared set of test data examples is a long step toward a satisfied user.

By way of illustration, if the discount policy is that no discount is given on invoices totaling $1000 or less, a 10% discount is given on that amount of the invoice which is more than $1000 up to $5000, and a 20% discount is given on amounts in excess of $5000, the following examples clear up any confusion as to what the discount policy is:

*Example 1*

| Invoice Gross Amount | $1,000 |
|---|---|
| Invoice Net Amount | $1,000 |

*Example 2*

| Invoice Gross Amount | $5,000 |
|---|---|
| Invoice Net Amount | |

$$\begin{array}{r} \$1000 \\ + .90\ (\$4000) = \underline{\quad 3600\quad} \end{array} \qquad \$4,600$$

*Example 3*

| Invoice Gross Amount | $10,000 |
| Invoice Net Amount | |

|  | $1000 | |
| + .90 ($4000) = | 3600 | |
| + .80 ($5000) = | 4000 | $ 8,600 |

Finally, functional specifications are identified by:

1. System title.
2. Author's name.
3. Date.
4. Revision identification
   a. Revision number.
   b. Reviser's name.
   c. Revision date.

## EXAMPLE

An example of functional specifications isn't presented here, but instead, reference is made to several, one of which everyone with other than machine level programming experience is familiar with—the Assembler manual or the Compiler (COBOL, FORTRAN, PL/1, etc.) manual. Of course, these manuals end up being revised, but as anyone with experience with a newly-marketed computer knows, they exist in a comprehensive form before the system, assembler, or compiler is designed or constructed. Consequently, at least chronologically, it's possible for them to be functional specifications. Let us see how any one of the documents meet the standards.

1. Users start programming from the document long before the language processor is operational. When they have a question as to how to code something, they go to the document for the answer. They propose changes to the document. And they react when the language-processor manufacturer proposes changes. They behave toward it as if it were a contract.
2. The document is written in the user's words. It contains no references to symbol tables, scramble tables, and so on, although all language processors contain these things. (The document does contain equipment configurations, but only because this is useful user information—the user wants to know what equipment he needs to take advantage of related language-processor features. But it contains no reference to how the language processor uses the equipment.)
3. Whether the document is easy to read is debatable, but the attempt has been made to make it so. It's divided into sections and subsections, and each consists of a general description followed by a detailed description.
4. The benefits to the user of using the language processor are described in the front of the document.
5. All possible inputs to the system are described in terms of its content and how it is introduced into the system. The coding form is described, and the bulk of the manual is concerned with what can be put on the coding form and where it can be put.

6. All possible outputs to the system (object code and listing) are described, and they are described in terms of what the language processor does to what input to produce what output.

7. Inputs that are treated as errors, and the system's reaction to these errors, are described (audit controls).

8. Time and space utilization figures are given.

9. The manual assumes a certain level of knowledge on the user's part and doesn't go into detail beyond that level. For example, it's assumed that the user knows how to get the input from the coding sheet to the computer, and no description is given in the manual. In the case of the Assembler manual, it's assumed that the user is familiar with the object computer, and no description of it is given.

10. It doesn't repeat what is explained elsewhere but instead makes reference to other documents, for example, the Link-edit manual.

11. Although the document is weak is this regard, it does contain examples, which are typically more comprehensible to the user than is the narrative.

The Assembler or Compiler manual meets all the specifications for functional specifications and consequently, can be considered an example of the same. Relatively speaking, they represent good examples.

## SUMMARY

1. The purpose of the functional specifications is to serve as a contract between the Data Processing Department and the user.

2. The functional specifications are identified by:
   a. System title.
   b. Author's name.
   c. Date.
   d. Revision identification:
      (1) Revision number.
      (2) Reviser's name.
      (3) Revision date.

3. The functional specifications are written:
   a. In the user's words.
   b. In a form that's easy to read ("onion formed," consisting of successively more detailed layers of information).

4. The first section on the functional specifications is a general description of the system.

5. The second section of the specifications is a listing of the benefits of the system.

6. The remaining sections of the specifications describe:
   a. Every system operation, particularly the production of output, performed in response to the introduction of input.
   b. Every possible input.
   c. Audit controls.
   d. If appropriate, time and space utilization.

7. Input is described in terms of:
   a. Content
   b. The way it's introduced to the system.

8. Output is described in terms of:
   a. Content.
   b. The way the system presents it to the user.
9. System processing is described to the extent necessary to define the way each output field is derived.
10. If required material exists in other documents, reference to such documents constitutes sufficient documentation.
11. The functional specifications are sufficiently detailed to be understood by the user.
12. Definitive examples are included.

# C. REQUEST
# FOR CHANGE FORM

Once a data processing system development effort has passed through the analysis phase, any user-originated requests for change to the definition of the system must be made on a request for change form (see Fig. C-1) and adhere to the following procedure.

The request for change form is initiated by the user. It's then submitted to the project leader, who acknowledges the receipt of and files for future action all postponable changes. For changes requiring immediate attention, the project leader spells out the impact of the change on the system and the project, and then estimates the change in schedule and budget required to institute the change in specifications. This information is transmitted to the user. When the user approves the changes in schedule and budget, the specifications change is implemented.

The request for change form, a four-part form, is completed in the following way.

1. The requesting department is identified.
2. The project is identified by project number.
3. The requested change is described.
4. The benefits to be derived from the change are listed.
5. The change is classified as:
   a. Immediate—a change that must be immediately incorporated into the design.
   b. Postponable—a change that's desirable but which can wait for implementation until the initial system is accepted.
6. The form is approved by the requesting department head.

REQUEST FOR CHANGE FORM

| REQUESTING DEPT. | PROJECT NO. |
|---|---|
| PROJECT NAME | |

DESCRIPTION OF CHANGE

BENEFITS

☐ IMMEDIATE            ☐ POSTPONABLE

| DEPARTMENT HEAD | DATE |
|---|---|

IMPACT

| DELAY IN SCHEDULE (IN WEEKS) | BUDGET INCREASE (IN DOLLARS) |
|---|---|
| PROJECT LEADER | DATE |
| DEPARTMENT HEAD | DATE |

ADD PAGES TO FORM AS REQUIRED

**Fig. C-1  Request for change form.**

7. The original and two copies are submitted to the systems and programming group.
8. If the change is classified as postponable, the project leader acknowledges the request by signing the form and returns the copies to the user.
9. If the change is classified as immediate:
   a. The project leader spells out the impact of the change. This description must include:
      (1) The new tasks, if any, that must be set up to effect the change and the man-hours required to complete these tasks.
      (2) The increase in man-hours required for each already existing task.
   b. The estimated change in schedule is entered.
   c. The estimated change in budget is entered.
   d. The project leader signs the form.
   e. The original and one copy are returned to the user.
   f. If the user accepts the schedule and budget changes, the form is approved by the requesting department head.
   g. The original is submitted to the systems and programming group.
   h. The change is implemented.

# D. PAYROLL APPLICATION CASE STUDY

I. Background

The Omega Corporation is a nationwide service organization consisting of several companies. Each company is organized into regions, the regions are subdivided into offices, and the offices into facilities. All employees to be handled by the payroll system are salaried, and transfer between facilities, offices, regions, and even companies is not only possible but is relatively common.

The corporation presently runs its payroll at a central location on a computer. Over the years both the corporation's business and organization have expanded to the point where the current payroll system no longer has the ability to reflect the levels of organization in the present corporate structure, transfers within the organization are becoming increasingly difficult to handle, and there are many local tax situations that must be handled outside the system. For these reasons the corporation has decided to redesign its payroll system on next generation equipment, which it already has installed on site. This equipment has 65K bytes of memory, four tape drives for data tapes, a reader, a printer, and a console typewriter.

The following is a description of the proposed payroll system.

II. General Description

A. Purpose

The Payroll System provides the Corporate Payroll Department with an automated system which:

1. Provides prompt and accurate payroll checks.
2. Develops and maintains records of employee earnings and deductions.
3. Records and reports various taxes and other statistical data as required by governmental agencies.
4. Produces other payroll-related management information.

B. Features

The system has the following features:

1. Only information directly concerned with payroll problems is required as input.
2. A Company, Region, Office, Facility (CROF) code structure is incorporated that allows additions of companies, regions, offices and facilities as easily as new employees.
3. Selective processing permits the user to process some CROF's and not others.
4. Modular programming is used so that routines may be altered or transposed with minimum difficulty.

C. Procedure

The system has been divided into four phases. The first three form the backbone of the system and must be run each payroll cycle, i.e., twice each month. The fourth phase contains programs which produce quarterly, annual, and supplemental payroll-related management information.

In Phase I the old master file, which contains historical payroll data for each employee, is read. Each employee is represented on the file by one record for each company for which he worked during the year. The records on the old master file are updated with data from the records on the transaction file. The transaction file includes personnel action data, payroll action data and header record data.

A transaction trail file of all updating actions which have been made to the master file is produced. It is edited and printed in Phase III. In addition, all transaction input data is edited and a list of diagnostics is produced. Accompanying the diagnostics is a run analysis indicating which CROF locations are being processed.

The input to Phase II is the updated old master file created in Phase I. Detail calculations are made on the first pass of the master file. Current deductions (such as Federal Income Tax, and FICA) and current income are calculated. Net pay and current vacation status are also calculated. Year-to-date fields are revised to reflect the new calculations. The completed record is written on an intermediate output tape.

On the second pass, the intermediate tape is read and copied onto the new master file. Current and year-to-date information is summarized to the CROF level and summary records are written on the new master file for each unique CROF break. In addition a withholding tax analysis is produced. This analysis shows how much tax was withheld for each tax body at each unique CROF break.

When errors which were undetectable in Phase I are found, these errors are listed for analysis before Phase III begins.

In Phase III the new master file is read and the cyclical reports and checks are produced according to the options available to the Payroll Department. These options allow selection of reports and the inclusion or exclusion of given CROF codes. Reports such as Payroll-Deduction Register and Checks will be required each payroll cycle. Other reports such as the Vacation-Register and the FICA Report will be required only once a month.

Payroll-related management information reports are produced in Phase IV. These reports include mailing labels and start-date lists. The programs in this phase are run on an as-needed basis. They may use any master file as input, but in most cases the most recent master file is used.

The new master file becomes the old master file when all of the desired reports have been produced and is retained for input to Phase I of the next payroll cycle.

III. Process Chart

A process chart for the proposed payroll system follows.

IV. Detailed Run Specifications

A. Run One—Sort Old Master

A standard manufacturer's software sort is used.

B. Run Two—Card to Tape and Edit

1. Purpose

The Card-to-Tape Edit is designed to validate all input to the Payroll System, to produce a list of records that contain errors or possible errors with appropriate diagnostics for each record, and to reformat valid input where necessary.

2. Discussion of Input

Transaction cards provide the information required to update the Payroll Master File.

Information regarding new employees or changes to existing employees is submitted to the Payroll Department on personnel action forms. These forms are edited by a payroll clerk and submitted to a keypuncher for punching. The form is designed so that punching can be done directly from it without an intermediate transcribing effort.

Errors introduced by over-payment, under-payment, deduction problems, etc. are corrected by means of cards punched from payroll action forms. Numeric values on the forms can be positive or negative depending on the cause of the original error.

C. Run Three—Sort Transactions

A standard manufacturer's sort is used.

D. Run Four—Reset and Update

1. Purpose

This program has two functions, to reset and to update the payroll master file. At each payroll cycle all current fields must be reset to zero; at the beginning of each quarter, quarter-to-date fields must be reset to zero; and at the beginning of a new year, year-to-date fields must be reset to zero. The master file can then be updated with new employee records and with changes to existing records. Updating is done with input prepared from personnel and payroll actions. Processing is selective, based on location request cards.

2. General Method

During housekeeping the ID and Date Card is read and the cycle number stored. The location request cards are read, edited, and stored internally in a table of requested location codes. Then an analysis of these cards is produced and the run continues.

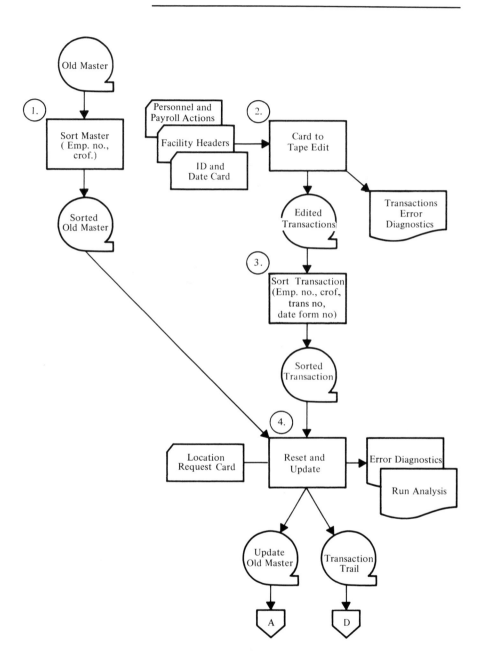

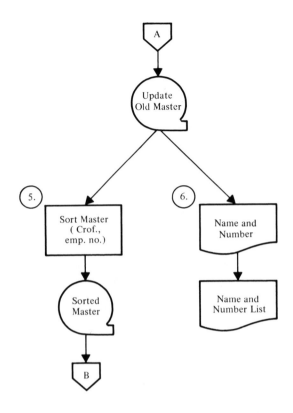

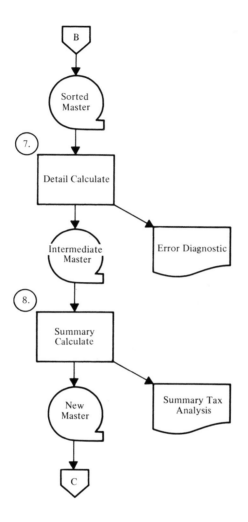

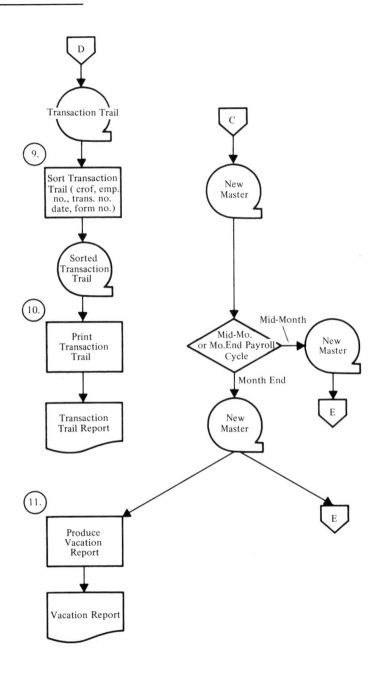

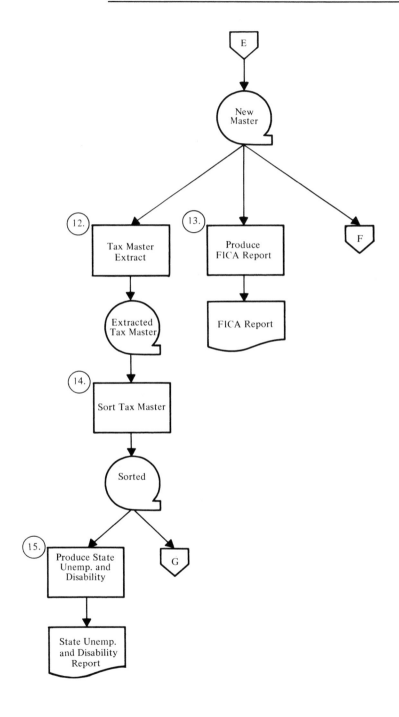

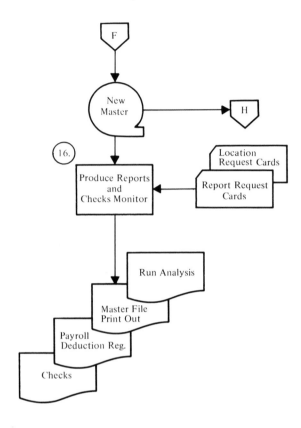

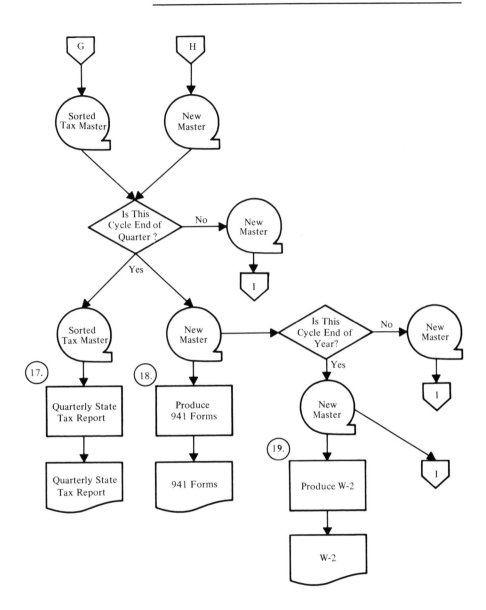

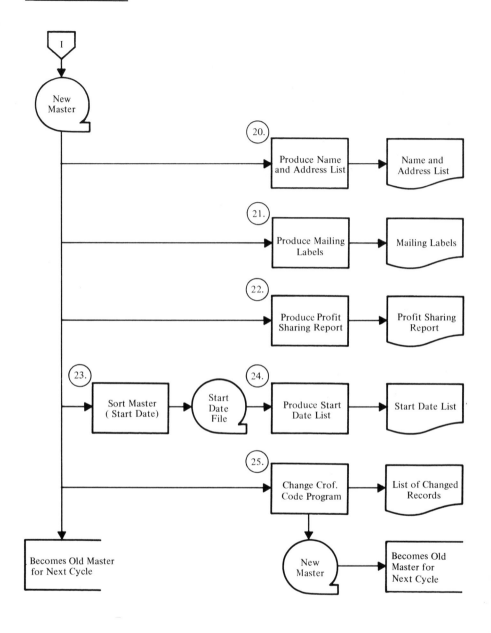

The two tape input files, the transaction file in employee-number, CROF, transaction number sequence and the old master file in employee-number, company-code sequence are alternately passed with resetting and updating of the master file being accomplished. The updated old master, the transaction trail file, and a list of diagnostics are produced as output.

File control is perhaps the most difficult part of this program, for only locations requested by location request cards are to be processed. The CROF code on the master file is used for this selection process.

3. Discussion of Input
   a. Old Master

   The main input to this program is the old master file in employee number, company code sequence. Three types of records exist on the file; header records, detail records, and summary records. All of these records contain 1600 bytes, but all do not have the same descriptions.

   All header records have employee number '00000' and, therefore, exist as a series of records at the beginning of the file.

   Detail records have employee numbers falling somewhere within '00001' and '99997.' These records are the ones which will be reset and updated.

   Two types of summary records can exist on the file. Employee number '99998' is a mid-month summary while employee number '99999' is a month-end summary. Whenever the cycle number is odd (from the ID and Date Card) both types of summary records exist. Whenever the cycle number is even, only type '99998' exists. All are passed on to the updated old master.

   b. Sorted Transaction File
   (1) Kinds of Records

   Three kinds of records may appear on the transaction file and are discussed below.
       (a) ID and Date Card

       Only one such record exists. It contains the number of the payroll cycle being processed in format YNN where Y is the year and NN is the actual cycle number. This record also contains other dates in various formats.
       (b) Facility Header Records

       These records supply titles, addresses, tax information, and work hours in each month for all companies, regions, offices, and facilities.
       (c) Personnel and Payroll Actions

       Personnel and payroll actions appear on the file whenever new employees are being added to the master file or whenever a change is being made to an existing employee record on the master file. Personnel and payroll actions are divided into four action types: new employee; personal data changes; current payroll; year-to-date payroll.

4. Discussion of Output
   a. Updated Old Master

   The updated old master contains all the records of the old master in up-dated form plus records for new employees for whom the required trans-actions have been entered. Records whose CROF were not to be processed, as indicated by the location request cards, have not had their cycle num-bers updated.

   b. Transaction Trail File

   The transaction trail file contains at least one record for each transaction that is input to the program except header transactions. Each record con-tains the new data input to the system for an employee and, for personnel actions, will contain the replaced data or a comment. For each transfer there are two records on the file: one for the CROF where the employee transferred from and one for the CROF where the employee transferred to.

   c. Diagnostics

   Diagnostics are printed during the running of the program to indicate errors which may need correction before continuing.

E. Run Five—Sort New Master

   A standard sort is used.

F. Run Six—Name and Number List

   This program produces a list of names and employee numbers for all employees on the file.

G. Run Seven—Detail Calculate

   1. Purpose

   This program calculates current pay and deductions for individual employees. These calculations are based on the payroll cycle, the codes pertaining to the individual, and the adjustments to pay and deductions which are supplied through the reset and update program. The results of the current calculations are reflected across year-to-date fields.

   2. General Method

   The program is a main program which uses a series of subroutines to calculate:

   a. Vacation accrual.
   b. State income taxes.
   c. City income taxes.
   d. State unemployment taxes.
   e. State disability taxes.

   The main program opens the files, reads and selects records to be processed, does certain calculations, links to the proper subroutine, updates year-to-date fields, and writes the record on an intermediate tape. State income taxes are calculated for California, the District of Columbia, Georgia, Indiana, Mary-land, Massachusetts, Michigan and New York. City income taxes are calculated for New York City, Detroit, and Maryland County.

H. Run Eight—Summary Calculate

   1. Purpose

   This program summarizes pay and deduction data calculated in the detail cal-culate program and produces two summary records for each CROF break. The first summary record is a summary of data for the current payroll period; the second is a summary of the current plus the preceding payroll period. The program also produces a current tax analysis which shows the amount of tax deducted for each tax body at each CROF break.

2. General Method

The program opens the files and reads records. It copies all header records and detail records onto the new master file, and in so doing summarizes these detail records. When a header or a summary record is found, a current-period summary record is written. The second summary record is created by adding the data from the current summary record to that of the summary record just read. This addition creates a record which contains summary data for the current period plus the previous period.

The tax analysis is printed for each CROF break. This analysis shows how much state tax was withheld, and for which states. The analysis does the same thing for city, unemployment, and disability taxes.

I. Run Nine—Sort Transaction Trail

Standard sort is used.

J. Run Ten—Transaction Trail Print

1. Purpose

The Transaction Trail Print Program is to print a trail of all transactions against the payroll master file for the inspection of the various office and facility managers concerned. The program edits all data showing replacing and replaced data and comments where appropriate.

2. General Method

This program reads the transaction trail records from tape, formats and prints them. Formatting for common data is done by a common routine, with many routines used for formatting the variable data.

K. Run Eleven—Vacation Report

1. Purpose

The vacation report provides the payroll department and the office managers with a breakout of vacation-pay and accrued vacation hours for each employee and a summary of that information for each facility.

2. General Method

An input parameter card is read and validated. The master file is passed and records which contain vacation information are printed. The vacation information is summarized and, when CROF breaks occur, printed. Duplicate summaries are suppressed.

L. Run Twelve—Tax Master Extract Program

1. Purpose

This program is designed to produce an extract of the master file containing all information necessary to produce state unemployment, disability, and withholding tax reports for each state. The design of the extract is such that it can be sorted to produce each of the reports with one pass of the file.

2. General Method

Multiple records are produced if an employee worked or resided in more than one state. The state code fields associated with applicable data are used to determine how many records to produce for an employee and for which states.

The header records contain a filler of two spaces in the sort field to force them to be sorted at the front of each group of records for a state.

M. Run Thirteen—FICA Report

1. Purpose

This run produces the FICA withholding report for the use of the payroll department.

2. General Method

An input parameter card is read and validated. The master file is passed and records which contain FICA information are printed. The FICA information is summarized and, when CROF breaks occur, printed. Duplicate summaries are suppressed.

N. Run Fourteen—Sort Tax Master

Standard sort.

O. Run Fifteen—State Unemployment and Disability Report

1. Purpose

The purpose of the state employment and disability report program is to print the unemployment and disability tax report for California and the unemployment tax report for other states that require them.

2. General Method

The page layout for all state reports will be the same with disability information being printed for California only.

P. Run Sixteen—Produce Reports and Checks Monitor

1. Purpose

The produce reports and check monitor controls the subroutines which produce the paychecks, the payroll-deduction register and the master print program, and determines which CROF's on the master file these subroutines may use.

2. General Method

This program reads and validates a report request card and a deck of location request cards. Errors in these cards are indicated on the printer and provision is made for reloading the card deck when errors occur. A list of the reports to be produced and locations to be included or excluded is also printed. One pass of the master file is required for each report. The ID-and-Date card is obtained from the header.

Every record on the master file is read and its cycle number is checked against that of the ID-and-Date card. Records whose cycle numbers disagree with the ID-and-Date cards are bypassed. Valid records are passed to the appropriate subroutines.

When all requested reports are produced, the user may request additional reports, or else go to end of job.

3. Subroutine Description

a. Master Print

(1) Purpose

The master print subroutine is an edited dump of the payroll master file and provides the accounting department and maintenance programmers with a meaningful picture of the contents of the file.

      (2) General Method

This subroutine receives a record from the payroll master file via the produce reports and checks monitor, identifies its type, and prints the information on the record according to the appropriate format. When the record has been processed, control returns to the produce reports and checks monitor.

    b. Payroll Deduction Register

      (1) Purpose

The payroll deduction register provides the accounting department with a record of the checks which have been issued, and year-to-date accumulations of payments and deductions.

      (2) General Method

This subroutine receives a record from the payroll master file via the produce reports and checks monitor and identifies its type.

When a record has been processed, control is returned to the produce reports and checks monitor.

    c. Checks

This subroutine produces the payroll checks for the corporation. The input record is processed if it will produce a meaningful check and control is returned to the produce reports and checks monitor.

Q. Run Seventeen—Quarterly State Tax Report

The purpose of the state withholding tax report program is to print state withholding tax reports for those states that require them and the District of Columbia.

R. Run Eighteen—941 Forms

    1. Purpose

This run produces the 941 Forms that are sent to the Federal Government.

    2. General Method

The master file is passed and federal withholding information is extracted from the detail records and printed on the 941 Forms. Totals are kept at the Grand, Company, and Office levels and are printed when breaks are encountered in those keys.

S. Run Nineteen—W2 Forms

This run produces the W2 forms that are sent to the federal government.

T. Run Twenty—Name and Address List

This program produces a list of names and addresses for all active and on-leave employees. In addition to names and addresses, the following data appears: tax codes, exemptions, additional withholding and percentage of time spent subject to the tax for federal tax, state tax, and city tax.

U. Run Twenty One—Mailing Labels

This program produces mailing labels from legal or mailing addresses for all active and on-leave employees.

V. Run Twenty Two—Profit Sharing Report

This program provides a list of all full-time employees who have had at least three continuous years of service at the end of a given fiscal year. It lists also the amount of regular pay they have earned for the first nine months of the calendar year.

W. Run Twenty Three—Sort Master
   Standard sort.

X. Run Twenty Four—Start Date List
   This program produces a list of all full-time employees in start date sequence.

Y. Run Twenty Five—CROF Code Change
   This program will change all CROF codes on the master file from a given code to another given code. The program is primarily intended to be used to promote a facility to office status and to allow realignment of geographical boundaries. Changes are entered through the console typewriter.

V. Job Descriptions
   Of the companies that make up Omega, one is in the business of providing programming and analyst services with respect to data processing. As a result, the personnel available to work on Omega's payroll have varied applications and equipment backgrounds, and they could be expected to be relatively used to moving into an unfamiliar environment to go to work. Job descriptions for the various analyst and programmer ranks follow.

   A. Analyst
      Broad experience on more than two stored program computers. Demonstrated ability in flow charting, coding, debugging, and documentation of complex programs, and ability to guide and train senior programmers and programmers in these areas. Ability to grasp total system concepts and to design systems including program specifications. Competency in successfully communicating with non-technical clients as well as with technical personnel assigned to project. May have responsibility for project leadership under direct supervision and cognizance of a staff analyst or above. Personnel in this category shall average more than 5 years EDP experience.

   B. Senior Programmer
      Personnel in this category shall have direct experience with at least two stored program data processing computers, ability in flow charting, coding, debugging, and documentation with minimum supervisory guidance. They shall have shown ability to teach and guide other programmers. Minimum educational requirement is a bachelor's degree or equivalent EDP experience. Personnel in this category shall average more than 3 years EDP experience.

   C. Programmer
      Training on more than one stored program data processing machine with direct experience on at least one stored program data processing machine, capability in flow charting, coding, debugging, and documentation. Minimum educational requirement is a bachelor's degree or its equivalent EDP experience. Personnel in this category shall average more than 18 months EDP experience.

   D. Programmer Trainee
      Minimum educational requirement is a bachelor's degree or its equivalent EDP experience.

VI. Available Personnel
    The following is a description of the people with which the project might be staffed.

    A. Henry Miller
       Rank—Analyst.
       Age—26.

Education—BA, Mathematics.

Experience—Mr. Miller's first commercial experience was with Omega, and he has been with the company for four years now. His experience has been in commercial applications, where he has worked in such areas as material accounting and land management. He has no previous experience on payroll applications, but in the last few months he has been working with the present payroll system to get as much as possible of what was necessary out of it. In this work he has been consulted from time to time on the design of the new system. Mr. Miller has three years of experience with the computer on which the present payroll is running and an equal amount of experience with the assembly language in which it is written. Although he has been studying the computer on which the new system is to be built, Mr. Miller has had no actual experience with it. He has three years of COBOL programming experience.

B.  Morgan Fried

Rank—Senior Programmer.

Age—31.

Education—BA, Education.

Experience—Mr. Fried taught public school for six years. He then worked for an insurance company for two years, where he got his first experience with computers. He then joined Omega and has now been with the company for two years. During this time his work has been in the area of commercial applications handling large files on large scale equipment. He has no previous experience on payroll, he does have two years of experience with the computer on which the present payroll is running and with the assembly language in which it is written, but he has no experience with the computer on which the new payroll is to be put. He has a half year's experience in COBOL.

C.  John Nazarevitz

Rank—Senior Programmer.

Age—28.

Education—BA, Speech; Masters, Speech.

Experience—Mr. Nazarevitz did some programming in the scientific programming and statistics area while in school. His first commercial experience was with Omega, and he has been with the company for two years. During this time he has worked on commercial applications, mostly programs that perform some type of calculation or summary operation. He has no previous experience with payroll, with the computer on which the payroll is presently running, with assembly language, or with the computer to be used for the new payroll. He has one half year's experience in COBOL.

D.  Charlene Long

Rank—Programmer.

Age—23.

Education—BA, English.

Experience—After graduating from college, Miss Long worked for a bank for two years, where she learned to program. Before leaving the bank, she did spend a short period of time working on the bank payroll. She then joined Omega, where she has been for the last month. During this time she has been training herself by reading manuals on the computer on which the new payroll is going to be installed. Her two years of experience has been with the computer on which the payroll is presently running and with the assembly language in which it is written, but she has no COBOL experience.

E. William Kramer
   Rank—Programmer.
   Age—23.
   Education—High School Graduate.
   Experience—After graduating from high school. Mr. Kramer spent four years in the Air Force, during the last three of which he was a programmer in the inventory control area. He has recently been discharged and is a new hire with Omega. He has no experience in payroll, with the computer presently being used, nor with the computer to be used with the new payroll system. He has three years of COBOL experience.

F. Norman Nickelson
   Rank—Programmer.
   Age—26.
   Education—BA, Mathematics.
   Experience—After college and the armed services Mr. Nickelson joined Omega, where he has been now for two years. He has done some commercial work, but most of his time has been spent in the area of statistics. He has no experience in payroll, or with the computer on which the payroll is presently being run. He has a year's experience with the computer on which the payroll will be installed. He has no COBOL experience.

G. Eva Catalfo
   Rank—Programmer Trainee.
   Age—24.
   Education—BA, Chemistry.
   Experience—After graduating from college, Miss Catalfo spent three years working as a laboratory technician. During this time she has taken both a home study and an evening school course on programming, on both of which she did well. She is now a new hire at Omega. Her courses have both included COBOL training, and in the evening school course she had some limited exposure to the computer on which the payroll will be installed.

H. Jules Tabbert
   Rank—Programmer Trainee.
   Age—21.
   Education—BA, Computer Science.
   Experience—Mr. Tabbert has recently joined Omega after graduation. His overall grade average, as well as his computer science grade average, was C+. He has taken a one semester course in COBOL, and the computer on which he worked at school is the same as the one on which the payroll is to be implemented.

# E. ACTIVITIES IN THE DEVELOPMENT OF A DATA PROCESSING SYSTEM

I. Analysis.
  A. Determine the facts.
    1. Methods.
      a. Existing documentation.
        1) Collect it.
          a) Procedure manuals.
          b) Working papers.
            (1) Reports.
            (2) Forms.
            (3) Files.
        2) Analyze it.
        3) Prepare an integrated description of it.
      b. Interview.
        1) Construct the interview guide.
        2) Determine who to interview.
        3) Hold the interviews.
        4) Prepare the interview reports.
      c. Observe the present system—Prepare a description of it.
    2. Alternative—Get heavy operating-managers participation.
  B. Determine the cost of the present system.

C. Survey the relevant literature—Prepare a summary.

D. Analyze similar systems—Prepare a summary.

E. Determine the organizational units that will use the system. Document the conclusions.

F. Determine the changes in organization and function that will be required. Document the conclusions.

G. Determine the data base manipulation requirements. Document the conclusions.

H. Determine the required operating statistics. Document the conclusions.
1. Volume.
   a. Input.
   b. Output.
2. Frequency.
   a. Input.
   b. Output.
3. System response requirements.
   a. Input cutoff time.
   b. Output deadlines.

I. Develop the acceptance test.

J. Write functional specifications.

K. Estimate the cost of the proposed system.

II. Design.

A. Develop alternative designs.
1. Design files.
   a. Tape.
      1) Fields.
      2) Record format.
      3) Record length.
      4) Sequence.
   b. Direct access.
      1) Fields.
      2) Record format.
      3) Record length.
      4) Organization.
      5) Access method.
      6) Medium.
2. Estimate file size.
3. Design source documents.
   a. Fields.
   b. Organization.
   c. Medium.
      1) Forms.
      2) Cards.
      3) Tape.
      4) Keyboard.
      5) Paper tape.
      6) OCR.
      7) MICR.

    4. Design output.
      a. Fields.
      b. Organization.
      c. Number of copies.
      d. Medium.
        1) Reports.
        2) Cards.
        3) Paper tape.
        4) Plotter charts.
        5) Displays.
    5. Design Programs.
      a. Specify functions.
      b. Estimate size.
    6. Design procedures.
      a. Input.
        1) Origination.
        2) Collection.
        3) Routing.
      b. Output.
        1) Handling.
        2) Distribution.
        3) Use.
    7. Construct controls.
      a. Validity checks.
      b. Batch totals.
      c. Control totals.
      d. Record count.
      e. Restart.
      f. File retention plan.
      g. File recreation plan.
      h. Document numbering.
    8. Estimate equipment requirements.
    9. Estimate system timing.
   10. Re-estimate system cost.
  B. Evaluate alternative designs.
  C. Develop process chart and supporting documentation.

III. Construction.
  A. Develop programs.
    1. Prepare internal specifications.
    2. Prepare flow chart or decision table.
    3. Code.
    4. Punch.
    5. Assemble or compile.
    6. Link.
    7. Develop unit test plan.
    8. Develop unit test data and results.

9. Write test operating instructions.
10. Perform unit test.
B. Prepare computer center operating procedures.
C. Procure forms.
D. Write user procedure manuals.
E. Publish user procedure manuals.
F. Develop subsystem test plan.
G. Develop subsystem test data and results.
H. Perform subsystem test.
I. Develop system test plan.
J. Develop system test data and results.
K. Train the computer center in operating procedures.
L. Perform system test.
M. Perform computer center operating procedures test.
N. Develop file conversion procedures.
O. Develop volume test plan.
P. Prepare volume test data and results.
Q. Perform volume test.
R. Convert files.
S. Train the user.
T. Perform parallel test.
U. Perform user procedure manual test.
V. Perform acceptance test.
W. Develop regression test plan.
X. Develop regression test data and results.
Y. Validate regression test procedures.
Z. Provide for maintenance.

# F. TIME-ESTIMATING STANDARDS

There are various types of time-estimating standards.

One type of standard is the determination of an average amount of time required to perform a task. This type of standard assumes that, if a person is capable enough to be assigned to the task, then difference in capability isn't varied enough to influence the amount of time required to do the task, and that therefore, task complexity is the only factor which has to be considered in making the estimate. This type of standard also assumes that the task is going to be done many times in completing the overall job, and that even though the time required to do the task any particular time may vary, over the long run, the use of an average time will yield a reliable estimate overall. Some examples of this type of standard taken from *Project Control Systems for Data Processing* (Brandon Systems Institute, 1967), are as follows.

1. Analysis of existing documents.
    a. One man-day per report or form.
    b. Four man-days per file.
2. Conducting interviews.
    a. One and one half man-days per interview at the management level.
    b. Two man-days per interview at the supervisory level.
    c. Three man-days per interview at the technical level.
    d. One and one half man-days per interview at the clerical level.

A second type of standard is one that establishes a relationship between the time required to do one task and the time required to do another task. One such standard says that it takes about as long to test a program (develop the unit test plan, test data, and predetermined results; prepare the test operating instructions; and do the unit test) as it does to prepare the program (write the internal specifications, do the logical analysis, and write the code). Such a standard can be used in a variety of ways.

1. If you've estimated the time required to prepare a program, you can also use it as an estimate of the time required to test the program.
2. If you've estimated the time required to prepare and test a program, half of this estimate will be a good estimate of the time required to prepare the program.
3. If you've estimated the time required to prepare a program as being equal to the time required to test the program, and you seriously overrun your program preparation estimate, you'd better adjust your plans to anticipate an equally serious program testing overrun.

Another example of this second type of standard says that the ratio between program development time and system test development time is about 8 to 1. That is, if you estimate that it's going to take 40 man-months to develop all the programs in a system, then you should plan on another five man-months to develop the system test for the system.

A third type of standard involves assignment of values to various characteristics of a task and the person assigned to it. An example of this kind of standard is given in Appendix G.

# G. ESTIMATING PROGRAM DEVELOPMENT TIME

Listed below are the functions to be included under program development and those functions which are assumed to have been accomplished before program development begins.

Prior to development and considered as design activities (not included in program estimate):

- Delineation of program functions as shown on a general systems flow chart.
- Design of all input and output record formats.
- Design of all data layouts, code tables, and field descriptions.
- Design of file specifications.

It is anticipated that all these may change slightly during program development, but the need for major changes will require reworking the estimate.

During development (included in program estimate):

- Program logic:
  Program description.
  Program flow charts and/or decision tables.
  Any corrections or changes to the above which may be necessitated by program or design changes.

- Coding and developing test data:
    Coding computer program.
    Developing test data.
- Testing and debugging:
    Program assembly.
    Desk checking.
    Machine testing.
    Processing test data.
    Analysis of post list and dumps.

Program estimating is a determination of man-days required to develop the program. The estimate is made by assigning values to this formula:

$$
\underset{\substack{\text{Program} \\ \text{Complexity}}}{\textit{Step 1}} \times \left[ \underset{\substack{\text{Programming} \\ \text{Know-how}}}{\textit{Step 2}} + \underset{\substack{\text{Programmer Job} \\ \text{Knowledge}}}{\textit{Step 3}} \right] = \underset{\substack{\text{Program} \\ \text{Development Time}}}{\textit{Step 4}}
$$

### Step 1   Determine Program Complexity

The complexity of the program depends upon input and output characteristics (Table 1) and the processing functions which take place. To some extent these processing functions depend upon the program language used. Table 2 reflects options used and displays three grades of weighting points. Step 4 shows how these weightings are used to produce man-days.

**Table 1   Input/Output Characteristics**

| Input | Weighting Points[a] |
|---|:---:|
| Card: Single format | 1 |
| Multiple formats | 2 |
| Each tape file | 1 |
| Each disk file | 1 |
| *Output* | |
| Print per record format (headings plus data) | 1 |
| Each tape file[b] | 1 |
| Card: Single format | 1 |
| Multiple formats | 2 |
| Each disk file | 1 |

[a]Included under I/O weightings are such program requirements as input/output subroutine calls, establishing work areas, and data movement commands.

[b]When tape is completely formatted for slave printing by a lesser machine, assign weightings as though output were print.

Table 2  Major Processing Functions

| Programming System | Function | Weighting Points | | | Range[a] | |
|---|---|---|---|---|---|---|
| | | Simplex | Complex | Very Complex | Min. | Max. |
| COBOL | Restructure data | 1 | 3 | 4 | | |
| | Condition checking | 1 | 4 | 7 | | |
| | Data retrieval and presentation | 2 | 5 | 8 | | |
| | Calculate | 1 | 3 | 5 | | |
| | Linkage | 1 | 2 | 3 | | |
| | Total | 6 | 17 | 27 | 4 | 27 |
| BAL | Restructure data | 4 | 5 | 6 | | |
| | Condition checking | 4 | 7 | 9 | | |
| | Data retrieval and presentation | 4 | 7 | 9 | | |
| | Calculate | 3 | 5 | 8 | | |
| | Linkage | 2 | 3 | 5 | | |
| | Total | 17 | 27 | 37 | 12 | 37 |
| Utility or package programs | Control card changes only | 1 | N/A | N/A | | |
| | Own coding required | 2 | 3 | 4 | | |
| RPG | | 2 | 8 | 13 | | |

[a]Range represents the minimum and maximum weighting which can be developed from the proper use of these tables as applied to a single program.

### Step 1A   Weight Program Input and Output Characteristics

Assign weights to input and output as shown in Table 1.

### Step 1B   Weight Program's Major Processing Functions

The processing functions which occur within a program fall into several or all of the categories shown in Table 2. Keep in mind that these categories are general in nature. When written, the program will comprise a series of logic and arithmetic coded instructions which implement these functions. When estimating program development time it is not known, of course, which, or how many, of these coded instructions will be needed. By a consideration of functions rather than number of program steps, the program's complexity can be more accurately gauged.

The estimator must first determine whether a function applies to the program he is estimating; second, if it does apply, he must determine whether its function is simple, complex, or very complex. For example, a program may involve one complicated calculate routine and may rate a "complex" calculate. On the other hand, another program might involve many simple calculate routines but also be rated "complex." A function within a program, such as calculate, should always be viewed as a whole, when determining weighting points. For example, if a function will perform five simple calculates, the total of its weighting points is equal to that of one simple calculate, or that of one complex, or of one very complex calculate, and not five times the weight of a simple calculate.

The categories of processing functions are described as follows:

- Restructure Data. Combining, condensing, rearranging, or deleting data. Do not consider building output formats as this consideration is provided for under I/O weightings, Table 1.
- Condition Checking. Control checks such as header and trailer label routines, reasonableness checks, limit checks, and error routines associated with these procedures.
- Data Retrieval and Presentation. File search, table lookup, randomizing techniques for record access, and indexing associated with these activities.
- Calculate. Arithmetic computations of all types excluding simple steps taken in connection with one of the other categories (for example, add 1 to a counter).
- Linkage. Program overlay routines, checkpoint and restart procedures, routines required to permit program to interface with a programming system or with another program or program module.

On occasion, table values have been selected between simple and complex or between complex and very complex. This is to emphasize that these weightings are not precise and are not intended to preclude the use of judgment.

### Step 2   Determine Programming Know-How

This step in the estimating technique is an attempt to recognize the degree to which staff experience affects program development. Each programmer assigned to the project should be assigned an experience factor based on the type of program(s) he will be responsible for writing. When the estimator does not know the individuals who will be assigned, he will have to use a group average. Table 3 gives the weighting points for various degrees of experience.

Table 3   Programming Know-How

| Overall Programming Experience | Man-Days Per Program Weighting Point |
| --- | --- |
| Senior Programmer | 0.50 to 0.75 |
| Programmer | 1.00 to 1.50 |
| Apprentice | 2.00 to 3.00 |
| Trainee | 3.50 to 4.00 |

### Step 3   Determine Programmer Job Knowledge

Job knowledge, as used in this context, refers to the degree to which the programmer must understand the subject to be programmed. Table 4 gives the weighting points for various degrees of job knowledge.

Table 4   Job Knowledge

| Job Knowledge Available | Job Knowledge Required | | |
|---|---|---|---|
| | Much | Some | None |
| Detailed knowledge of this job | 0.75 | 0.25 | 0.00 |
| Good general knowledge of this job with fragmentary detailed knowledge | 1.25 | 0.50 | 0.00 |
| Fair general knowledge of this job but little or no detailed knowledge | 1.50 | 0.75 | 0.00 |
| No job knowledge but general knowledge of related subjects | 1.75 | 1.00 | 0.25 |
| No job knowledge, no general knowledge of related subjects | 2.00 | 1.25 | 0.25 |

**Step 4   Determine Program Development Time**

Program development time is determined by multiplying the program complexity weightings from Step 1 by the man-day factors for programming know-how + job knowledge, developed in Steps 2 and 3. For example:

| Run XXXXX | Weighting | | Man-Days Per Program Weighting Point |
|---|---|---|---|
| Input (Step 1A) | 2 | Programming Know-How (Step 2) | 1.00 |
| Output (Step 1A) | 4 | Job Knowledge (Step 3) | 1.25 |
| Processing Functions (Step 1B) | 8 | | |
| Total | 14 | Total | 2.25 |

Programming time = 14 X 2.25 = 32 man-days

Overall Programming Experience (in Table 3) is defined in the following list:

• Senior Programmer—Written and implemented many programs on different types of equipment. Very experienced with particular configuration and programming system.

- Programmer—Written and implemented programs of various complexities. Experience with particular configuration and programming system.
- Apprentice—Written and implemented several programs. Limited experience with particular configuration and programming system.
- Trainee—Completed programming school. Written training program. Very limited experience on operating program.

Job knowledge required (in Table 4) is defined as follows:

Much: Detailed knowledge is required and subject is complex and difficult to understand; and/or job requires knowledge of complex mathematical or statistical formulas; and/or job requires application of special program concepts not in common use (such as linear programming).

Some: Detailed job knowledge is required but subject either is not complex, or is complex but can be easily explained; and/or job requires knowledge of standard mathematical or statistical formulas.

None: Job can be understood with little or no background on the part of the programmer (similar to a classroom problem).

(This example has been adapted in a substantially unchanged form from *Management Planning Guide for a Manual of Data Processing Standards* by International Business Machines Corporation.)

# H. INTERNAL SPECIFICATIONS-CARD TO TAPE EDIT PROGRAM

## CARD TO TAPE EDIT PROGRAM

### Purpose

The card-to-tape edit is designed to validate all input to the payroll system, to produce a list of records that contain errors or possible errors with appropriate diagnostics for each record, and to reformat valid input where necessary.

### Discussion of Input

I. Transaction cards provide the information required to update the payroll master file.
   A. Information regarding new employees or changes with respect to existing employees is submitted to the Payroll Department on personnel action forms. These forms are edited by a payroll clerk and submitted to a keypuncher for punching. The form is designed so that punching can be done directly from it without an intermediate transcribing effort.
   B. Errors introduced by overpayment, underpayment, deduction problems, etc. are corrected by means of cards punched from payroll action forms. Numeric values on the forms can be positive or negative depending on the cause of the original error.

II. Record types and formats.

A. ID and Date Card

|  | Column | Information |
|---|---|---|
| 1. | 2–8 | PAYROLL. |
| 2. | 21–26 | End of the pay period in MMDDYY format. |
| 3. | 36–53 | The date the payroll is being run; example: July 24, 1967. |
| 4. | 54–5 | Date to appear on checks in MMDDYY format. |
| 5. | 61–65 | Cycle |
| 6. | 67–69 | Three digit cycle number. The first digit of the cycle number is the last digit of the current year. The next two digits of the cycle number is the chronological number of the payroll being run that year. Example: The fifth payroll cycle of 1967 would be cycle 705. |

B. Facility header cards.

1. Common Information.

| Column | Information |
|---|---|
| 1–5 | 00000 |
| 6–13 | CROF |
| 14–19 | Last six digits of CROF |
| 21–26 | Effective date in MMDDYY format |
| 80 | A |

2. Variable Information

| Card Type | Column | Information |
|---|---|---|
| 1 | 20 | 1 |
|  | 36–75 | Company name. |
| 2 | 20 | 2 |
|  | 36–75 | Region name. |
| 3 | 20 | 3 |
|  | 36–75 | Office name. |
| 4 | 20 | 4 |
|  | 36–75 | Facility name. |
| 5 | 20 | 5 |
|  | 36–75 | Mailing name. |
| 6 | 20 | 6 |
|  | 36–75 | Second line of mailing address. |
| 7 | 20 | 7 |
|  | 36–75 | Third line of mailing address. |
| 8 | 20 | 8 |

| Card Type | Column | Information |
|---|---|---|
| | 36–37 | Unemployment code. |
| | 38–42 | Unemployment rate; example; 2.2% = 00220 |
| | 43–44 | Disability code. |
| | 45–49 | Less than 5 year vacation hours; example: 10.00 hours = 01000. |
| | 50–54 | Greater than 5 year vacation hours; example: 13.33 hours = 01333. |
| | 55–61 | Work hours in year; example: 2080 hours = 0208000. |
| | 62–66 | Work hours in month of January including holidays; example: 176 hours = 17600. |
| 9 | 20 | 9 |
| | 36–40 | Work hours in month of February. |
| | 41–45 | Work hours in month of March. |
| | 46–50 | Work hours in month of April. |
| | 51–55 | Work hours in month of May. |
| | 56–60 | Work hours in month of June. |
| | 61–65 | Work hours in month of July. |
| | 66–70 | Work hours in month of August. |
| | 71–75 | Work hours in month of September. |
| A | 20 | A |
| | 36–40 | Work hours in October. |
| | 41–45 | Work hours in November. |
| | 46–50 | Work hours in December. |

C. Format for personnel and payroll action records.

| Column | Information |
|---|---|
| 1–5 | Employee number. |
| 6–13 | CROF. |
| 14 | Transaction type. |
| 15–20 | Effective date in MMDDYY format. |
| 21–29 | First nine characters of name with last name first. |
| 30–33 | Form number. |
| 34–35 | Card number. |
| 36–75 | Input data (exact information and format can be obtained from the personnel and payroll action forms). |
| 80 | B |

III. Record Sequence.

The only sequence restriction imposed on the input records is that the ID and Date Card must be the first record read.

## Discussion of Output

I. Type: 9 track magnetic tape.
II. Record length: 80 characters.
III. Blocking: 40 records.
IV. Sequence: As specified for input.
V. Volume: Variable.
VI. Format.
    A. Personnel and payroll actions. The first 35 positions of personnel and payroll actions are reformatted to facilitate the sort.

Personnel and payroll record reformatting.

| Position on Output | Position on Input |
|:---:|:---:|
| 1–14 | 1–14 |
| 15–16 | 34–35 |
| 17–20 | 30–33 |
| 21–26 | 15–20 |
| 27–35 | 21–29 |
| 36–80 | 36–80 |

    B. Header records. Header records are not changed on output.
    C. ID and Date Card. The ID and Date Card is not changed on output.

## Procedure

I. ID and Date Card.
    A. The first record read and processed must be an ID and Date Card. It is validated as follows:
        1. Positions 2–8 must be PAYROLL.
        2. Positions 68–69 must be numeric and between 00 and 25.
        3. If positions 68–69 equal 01 and
            a. position 26 is not = 9, position 67 must be 1 greater than position 26.
            b. position 26 = 9, position 67 must be zero.
        4. If position 68–69 is not equal to 01, position 67 must be equal to position 26.
        5. Positions 54–59 must be a valid date.
        6. Positions 36–53 must not be blank.
        7. Positions 21–26 must be a valid date.
    B. When errors are found on the ID and Date Card, a message is displayed on the console identifying the error and requesting a corrected ID and Date Card.
    C. When a valid ID and Date Card has been read
        1. The following information is saved:
            a. Cycle number, positions 67–69.
            b. End of the pay period, positions 21–26.
        2. The ID and Date Card is written as the first record on the output tape.

II. Validation of transactions.

Whenever validity errors occur, the record is printed and all diagnostics pertaining to that record are printed afterwards. There are two types of diagnostics: fatal and warning. If a record contains an error that produces a fatal diagnostic, the record is dropped from the file. All other records are written on the output file unless the validation for that particular record specifies otherwise.

A. If column 80 contains an *A*, the record is a facility header and is validated as follows:

1. 1-5 must contain 00000 (zeros)

   Diagnostic—**FATAL FACILITY HEADER MUST HAVE EMPLOYEE NUMBER 00000

2. 6-13 must be numeric

   Diagnostic—**FATAL NON-NUMERIC CROF CODE

3. column 20 must be 1-9 or A

   Diagnostic—**FATAL INVALID HEADER CODE

4. If the header code (column 20) is

   a. 1-7, columns 36-75 should not be blank.

      Diagnostic—WARNING NO TITLE ON THIS FACILITY HEADER.

   b. 8, all columns 36-75 must not be blank but individual fields may be blank. Each individual field that is not blank must be numeric. Other validation, if any, for each individual field is listed below as well as the appropriate diagnostic.

      (1) Tax code, columns 36-37, must be less than 57

          Diagnostic—**FATAL INVALID LOCAL UNEMPLOYMENT CODE

      (2) Local unemployment rate (columns 38-42) must be greater than 0.09 and less than 10.01

          Diagnostic—**FATAL LOCAL UNEMPLOYMENT RATE INVALID

      (3) Local Disability code (columns 43-44) must be less than 57.

          Diagnostic—**FATAL LOCAL DISABILITY CODE INVALID

      (4) Less-than-5-year vacation hours, columns 45-49 must be greater than 7.99 and less than 20.01

          Diagnostic—**FATAL INVALID LESS-THAN-5-YEARS VACATION HOURS

      (5) Greater-than-5-years vacation hours, columns 50-54, must be greater than 7.99 and less than 20.01

          Diagnostic—**FATAL INVALID GREATER-THAN-5-YEARS VACATION HOURS

      (6) Work-hours-in-year, columns 55-61, must be 1885 or 2080

          Diagnostic—**FATAL INVALID WORK-HOURS-IN-YEAR

      (7) Base-hours-in-month, columns 62-66, must be greater than 99 and less than 201.

          Diagnostic—**FATAL INVALID BASE-HOURS-IN-MONTH.

   c. 9, columns 36-75 must be numeric.

      Diagnostic—**FATAL INVALID BASE-HOURS-IN-MONTH

   d. A, columns 36-50 must be numeric.

      Diagnostic—**FATAL INVALID BASE-HOURS-IN-MONTH

B. If column 80 contains a *B*, the record is a payroll or personnel action. It is reformatted into output form before validating but in case of error, the original record is printed.

1. General validation for all records in this group is

 a. Employee number, columns 1–5 must

 (1) be numeric.

 (2) not be

 (a) 00000

 (b) 99998

 (c) 99999

 Diagnostic—**FATAL INVALID EMPLOYEE NUMBER

 b. CROF code, columns 6–13, must be numeric

 Diagnostic—**FATAL NON-NUMERIC CROF CODE

 c. Transaction number, columns 14–16, must be within one of the following ranges:

 (1) 001–015

 (2) 101–115

 (3) 201–230

 (4) 301–327

 Diagnostic—**FATAL ILLEGAL TRANSACTION NUMBER.

 d. Form number, columns 17–20, should not be blank.

 Diagnostic—WARNING NO FORM NUMBER.

 e. Effective date, columns 21–26 must be

 (1) a valid date in the form MMDDYY

 Diagnostic—**FATAL INVALID EFFECTIVE DATE

 (2) equal to or earlier than the stored date from the ID and Date Card

 Diagnostic—**FATAL EFFECTIVE DATE PUTS TRANSACTION IN LATER PAY PERIOD.

Specific validation for input data is done by form type as well as card type. If the form:

a. Is a personnel action (column 14=0 or 1) and the card type (column 15–16) is

 (1) 01, the record is for assignment or transfer

 (a) column 36–43 must be numeric.

 Diagnostic—**FATAL ASSIGNMENT OF CROF CODE NOT COMPLETE

 (b) If the employee is new, column 14=0, columns 36–43 must equal columns 6–13.

 Diagnostic—**FATAL FOR NEW EMPLOYEE. COLS. 6–13 AND COLS. 36–43 MUST BE EQUAL.

 (2) 02, the record is for name and martial status

 (a) column 36–65 should not be blank

 Diagnostic—**FATAL NO NAME GIVEN

 (b) column 66 must be M or S. If it is neither, move S to column 66.

 Diagnostic—WARNING ILLEGAL MARITAL STATUS, ASSUME SINGLE.

 (c) there must be one and only one comma in columns 36–65.

Diagnostic—**FATAL THERE MUST BE ONE AND ONLY ONE COMMA IN NAME

(3) 03 or 04, the record is for address, columns
- (a) 36–65 should not be blank
  Diagnostic—WARNING NO ADDRESS GIVEN
- (b) 71 must be
  - aa. M
  - bb. L
  - cc. B
  If not, move L to column 71.
  Diagnostic—WARNING CANNOT DETERMINE IF MAILING OR LEGAL. ASSUME LEGAL.
- (c) If col. 15–16 = 04, 66–70 must be numeric
  Diagnostic—WARNING NO ZIP CODE GIVEN

(4) 05, the record is for home telephone and columns
- (a) 36–38 should be numeric
  Diagnostic—WARNING INVALID AREA CODE GIVEN
- (b) 39–45 must not be blank and 41–45 must be numeric
  Diagnostic—**FATAL INVALID PHONE NUMBER GIVEN

(5) 06, the record is for social security number, birth date and sex.
- (a) col. 36–44 must be numeric or blank. If not, cols. 36–44 are blanked
  Diagnostic—WARNING SOCIAL SECURITY NUMBER IS ILLEGAL. NONE USED.
- (b) Birth date, cols. 45–50 must be a valid date in the form MMDDYY or blank. If not, blank 45–50.
  Diagnostic—WARNING DATE IS BAD. NONE USED.
- (c) If record is for new employee (col. 14=0), col. 51 must = M or F. If record is a change (col. 14=1), col. 51 must be M, F, or blank.
  Diagnostic—**FATAL CANNOT DETERMINE SEX.

(6) 07, the record is for status and salary.
- (a) column 51 must be F, P, or blank.
  Diagnostic—**FATAL CANNOT DETERMINE NEW STATUS
- (b) If column 51 = F, 52–55 must be numeric and 56–59 must be blank. If column 51 = P, 56–59 must be blank. If column 51 is blank, either 52–55 must be numeric and 56–59 must be blank or 56–59 must be numeric and 52–55 must be blank.
  Diagnostic—**FATAL SALARY IS INCORRECT.
- (c) If column 51 is blank, 52–55 is numeric and 56–59 is blank, move F to column 51.
- (d) If column 51 is blank, 56–59 is numeric and 52–55 is blank, move P to column 51.

(7) 08, the record is for rank and title.
- (a) Columns 38–39 must not be blank.
  Diagnostic—**FATAL NO RANK ASSIGNED.
- (b) Column 40–54 should not be blank.
  Diagnostic—WARNING NO TITLE GIVEN

(8)  09, the record is for hospital coverage.
  (a)  Column 36 must be blank, or contain Y, N, or zero.
       Diagnostic—**FATAL INVALID LIFE INSURANCE CODE
  (b)  Column 37 must be
       aa.  blank
       bb.  numeric
       cc.  less than 5
       Diagnostic—**FATAL CANNOT DETERMINE TYPE OF HOS-
       PITAL COVERAGE
  (c)  38–41 must contain a date
       aa.  in the form MMYY
       bb.  for the current month of the following month. If the date is
            further in advance, the following diagnostic will appear.
            Diagnostic—**FATAL HOSPITALIZATION SCHEDULED
            TO START MORE THAN 1 MONTH IN ADVANCE. If the
            date is prior to the current month the following diagnostic
            will appear.
            Diagnostic—WARNING HOSPITALIZATION WILL START
            THIS MONTH.
(9)  10, the record is for federal tax. Columns
  (a)  38–39 must be
       aa.  blank or
       bb.  numeric.
       Diagnostic—**FATAL INVALID EXEMPTIONS.
       If numeric, columns 38–39 should be less than 13,
       Diagnostic—WARNING QUESTIONABLE EXEMPTIONS
  (b)  43–48 must be
       aa.  blank or
       bb.  a positive number
       Diagnostic—WARNING INVALID ADDITIONAL WITHHOLD-
       ING. ZERO USED. If numeric, columns 43–48 should be less
       than $100.00
       Diagnostic—WARNING QUESTIONABLE ADDITIONAL
       WITHHOLDING
(10)  11, the record is for state tax. Columns
  (a)  36–37 must be
       aa.  blank or
       bb.  numeric
       Diagnostic—**FATAL ILLEGAL TAX CODE
  (b)  38–39 must be
       aa.  blank or
       bb.  numeric or
       cc.  left digit M or S and right digit numeric
       Diagnostic—**FATAL INVALID EXEMPTIONS.
       If numeric, columns 38–39 should be less than 12.
       Diagnostic—WARNING QUESTIONABLE EXEMPTIONS.

(c) 40–42 must be

aa. blank or

bb. numeric in the range of 0.00 to 1.00. If not, make equal to 1.00

Diagnostic—WARNING BAD PERCENTAGE. 100 PER CENT USED.

(d) 43–48 are validated as in (9) (b).

(11) 12, the record is for city tax. All columns are validated as in the state tax records.

(12) 15, the record is for termination,

(a) If the cycle is month-end (odd) or column 51=Y, fields are made zero.

aa. regular hours (columns 41–45)

bb. overtime hours (columns 36–40)

cc. vacation hours taken (columns 46–50)

(b) If the cycle is mid-month (even) and column 51 is not Y, columns

aa. 36–40 must be a positive number. If not, this field is made zero.

Diagnostic—WARNING INVALID OVERTIME HOURS. AS-SUME ZERO

bb. 41–45 must be a positive number

Diagnostic—**FATAL NEED TO KNOW HOURS WORKED UNTIL TERMINATION

cc. 46–50 must be a positive number. If not, this field is made zero

Diagnostic—WARNING INVALID VACATION-HOURS-TAKEN. WILL ASSUME NO VACATION USED.

(c) column 51 must be Y or N. If not, this column is made N.

Diagnostic—WARNING MANUAL CHECK INDICATOR IS IN-VALID. WILL ASSUME NO MANUAL CHECK WRITTEN.

(13) None of the above, no coding exists for this type of transaction

Diagnostic—**FATAL NO CODING HAS BEEN IMPLEMENTED FOR THIS TYPE OF TRANSACTION

b. a current payroll action (column 14=2) and the card type (columns 15–18) is

(1) 01–10, 18–28 and 30, columns 36–42 must be numeric.

Diagnostic—**FATAL NON-NUMERIC VALUE IN NUMERIC FIELD.

(2) 11–17 the following conditions are valid

(a) columns 36–42 numeric and 43–49 blank

(b) columns 36–42 blank and 43–49 numeric

(c) columns 36–42 numeric and 43–49 numeric

If the record is valid and one of the fields is blank, zeros are moved to the blank field.

Diagnostic—**FATAL NON-NUMERIC VALUE IN NUMERIC FIELD.

(3) 29, columns 36–41 must contain a valid date in MMDDYY format.

Diagnostic—**FATAL INVALID LAST DAY OF LEAVE.

c. a Year-to-Date payroll action (column 14 = 3) and the card type (column 15-16) is

    (1) 01-26, the record is validated as a current payroll action.

    (2) 27, columns

        (a) 36-37 must be

           aa. numeric

           bb. in the range 01-06

               Diagnostic—**FATAL INVALID TAX TYPE

        (b) 38-39 must be numeric.

           Diagnostic—**FATAL INVALID TAX CODE

        (c) 40-60 contains 3 fields and the following conditions must prevail:

           aa. all three fields must not be blank on the same card.

               Diagnostic—**FATAL INVALID ADJUSTMENT

           bb. gross (columns 40-46) must be

               aaa. blank or

               bbb. numeric

               If blank, move zeros to this field. If nonnumeric (other than blank), print the following diagnostic.

               Diagnostic—**FATAL NON-NUMERIC GROSS

           cc. the same validation that is used for gross is used for taxable gross (columns 47-53).

               Diagnostic—**FATAL NON-NUMERIC TAXABLE-GROSS.

           dd. the same validation that is used for gross is used for withholding (column 54-60)

               Diagnostic—**FATAL NON-NUMERIC WITHHOLDING

C. None of the above, the following diagnostic is printed:

    **FATAL THIS CARD INVALID OR OUT OF SEQUENCE

## Controls

I. Totals

    A. At the end of job the following is printed.

        1. Number of fatal diagnostics.

        2. Number of records dropped.

        3. Number of warning diagnostics on records that were dropped.

        4. Number of warning diagnostics on records that were not dropped.

        5. Number of records read.

        6. Number of records written.

    B. ID and Date Card

        1. The ID and Date Card is written as the first record on the output file for identification.

        2. All effective dates are compared to the end of pay period on the ID and Date Card and are validated relative to it.

II. Console Messages

    A message indicating the beginning of the run is printed.

# I. INTERNAL SPECIFICATIONS –SCAN SUBROUTINE

**SCAN SUBROUTINE. IDENTIFICATION: CFAAC**

**Program Definition**

*Purpose and Usage*

To assist command routines in stepping through the variable fields of a command, in validating input parameters, and in writing error messages and prompting for corrections.

*Description*

The scan subroutine performs a number of functions. The basic one is the scanning routine itself. It provides for the caller a pointer indicating the start of the current field, and a character count. A terminator code defines the separator (comma, slash, or end-of-command) encountered by the scan. The CLI Director is responsible for setting the pointer to the first character after the command verb. An option permits the scan subroutine to move the current field to an area specified by the caller.

A group of checking functions validate the form of a command parameter. Each of these scans the character string, starting at the first pointer and going to the end of the field. If an invalid character for the field type appears, a parameter, which is actually the number of a standard error message, is set in a register for return.

An error printing function is also part of the scan subroutine. On entry to the subroutine, an error code is used to select and issue a standard error message. This subroutine recognizes two kinds of error codes: those involving a reply (prompting type) and those to be issued for the user's information. For a prompting message, the subroutine waits for the reply, then returns to the caller with a pointer set to the reply.

### Error Checks

For the errors detected by the scan subroutine, see Exit Points.

### Program Interface

### Entry Points

NEXTPAR (CFAAC1)—Entry point for the next parameter. On entry, register 3 is set to the starting location for scanning. Register 2 is set either to zero or to the location to which the field is to be moved after scanning.

CHEKDS (CFAAC2)—Entry point to check for a valid data set name. Input parameters are the pointer to the start of the character string, (in register 3) and the length of the string (in register 0).

ALFNUM (CFAAC3)—Entry point for checking a string of alphameric characters. The string should contain no blanks or special characters. The length of the string is supplied in register 0; the pointer to the start of the string is in register 3.

NUMSTG (CFAAC4)—Entry point to check a string of numeric characters. The string should not contain blanks or alphabetic or special characters. The length of the string is supplied in register 0; the pointer to the start of the string is in register 3.

CHKNUM (CFAAC5)—Entry point to check and convert (integer conversion) a string of numeric characters. String length is supplied in register 0; maximum value in register 2; and the pointer to the start of the string is in register 3.

ALBET (CFAAC6)—Entry point to check an alphabetic string. No numerics, blanks, or special characters permitted. String length is supplied in register 0; the pointer to the start of the string is provided in register 3.

ERROUT (CFAAC7)—Entry point to put out an error message and, perhaps, await a reply. Register 1 contains the error code used to select the error message. If the code is positive, the message is issued and control returned to the caller. If the code is negative, the message is issued and a response is requested. In the latter case, register 2 contains a pointer to the location in which the response is to be placed.

### Subroutine Calls

NEXTPAR may call the Gate subroutine if the command is to be continued on the next line. If so, the next line of the command is read in immediately after the current string.

ERROUT calls on the Gate subroutine, either at the write or the write-with-spontaneous-response entry. For the latter, the pointer to the input area (given in register 2) is supplied in the form Gate expects.

### Exit Points

NEXTPAR returns to the caller with the pointer in register 3 set to the first nonblank character of the current string, a character count in register 0 (this does not include the terminator character or any blanks preceding the terminator), and a terminator code in register 1. This code is one of these:

1—Comma.
2—Slash.
3—End of command.

CHEKDS returns to the caller with the input parameters unchanged. Register 1, however, is either set to zero (indicating no errors) or to one of the following codes:

1—member of a generation data group (GDG).
2—member of a partitioned data set (PDS).
3—member of PDS which is a member of a GDG.
4—normal data set, name 35 characters.
5—member of a GDG, name 35 characters.
6—member of a PDS, name 35 characters.
7—member of a PDS of a GDC, name 35 characters.
−11—data set qualifier has more than 8 characters.
−12—data set qualifier first character not alphabetic.
−13—data set qualifier has invalid characters.
−14—data set name has more than one contiguous separator.
− 5—data set name contains more than 44 characters.
− 6—GDC relative number is invalid.
− 7—module name does not start with an alphabetic character.

ALFNUM returns to the caller with register 1 set either to zero (no error) or to one of the following codes:

−1—field has more than 8 characters.
−2—first character not alphabetic.
−3—field contains invalid characters.
−4—field is empty (either no characters or all blanks).

NUMSTG returns to the caller with register 1 set either to zero (no error) or to one of the following codes:

−8—blank, alphabetic, or special characters found in string.
−9—field is empty.

CHKNUM returns to the caller with register 1 set either to zero (no error) or to one of the following codes:

−10—number greater than maximum allowed.
−18—blank, alphabetic, or special characters found in string.
−19—field is empty.

Register 2 contains the value of the converted quantity (integer conversion).

ALFBET returns to the caller with register 1 set either to zero (no error) or to one of the following codes:

−15—string is empty
−16—numeric or special characters in string

ERROUT returns to the caller. If the input code was negative, the user response is in the location to which register 2 pointed. There are no other outputs to the caller.

**Comments**

It will be possible to add to the number of checks in the scan subroutine. The one described here are needed for the current commands; added commands may require other checks to be written. Experience will show what added facilities should be provided within the scan subroutine.

**Applicable Documents**

Command language functional specifications.

# J. FUNCTIONAL SPECIFICATIONS EXAMPLE

## PREPARATION OF PERSONNEL ACTION FORMS

### General Instructions

These forms are designed to be typed with a typewriter. The typewriter is set in the expand position and the triple space bar is used when spacing. The forms are also designed to allow the use of tab stops which should be determined and set by you where appropriate.

Information submitted on these forms will replace the information currently on file. If only part of a transaction on a line is applicable, only that part should be filled out. Thus, if someone changes his marital status but did not change his name, only position 36 of transaction type 2 would be filled in.

All forms must be signed by a person authorized to do so.

### Specific Instructions

#### Top Section

Enter the date on which the form is executed in the upper right hand corner in the space marked "Today's Date."

#### Position Numbers

1-5   Enter current employee number or newly assigned number preceded by a 0, since the system uses 5 character employee numbers.

6-13 Enter company, region, office and facility numbers that have been assigned to your office in the table of CROF numbers which appears in the appendix.

14 Designate a new employee with a 0 and a change for an existing employee with a 1.

15-20 Enter effective date of transaction in month, day, year order. Thus an effective date of March 1, 1967 would be entered as 03 01 67.

21 Enter the employee's name in the following order: Last name followed by a comma, first name, middle initial. Last names which are made up of two parts should have a space between the two parts. In addition, put a slash (/) after the first nine characters of the name since these are the control letters for identifying each employee. For persons with last names with less than nine characters, part of the first name will be used. The following examples show special cases:

| *Name* | *Name to be Shown on Form* |
|---|---|
| John J. Smith | Smith, Joh/n J. |
| Charles Allen Anderson | Anderson, / Charles A. |
| James Edward St. Clair III | St. Clair /III, James |
| Nicola M. D'Ippolito | D'Ippolit/o, Nicola M. |
| Omar L. Dickerson, Jr. | Dickerson/ Jr., Omar L. |
| George Mc Queen | Mc Queen, / George |

30-33 These four digits are the form number and are preprinted.

*Lower Section*

The type of transaction to be processed should be indicated by an "x" in the appropriate box in the left hand margin. Forms enclosed should be designated by an "x" in position 49 on the appropriate line.

Transaction Numbers

01 Assignment or Transfer
New employees in your office should be given the CROF number for your office. Transfers from your office to other offices should be assigned the CROF number of the office to which the employee is being transferred.

02 Name, Marital Status
Indicate marital status in position number 36 using M for married and S for single. It is most important to send the form in when marital status changes, since the withholding tax depends on marital status. Starting in position 37 enter the employee's name in the same order as in the top section of the form except delete the slash. It is most important to put a comma between last and first names since this is used in the system.

When an employee changes his or her name the old name is to be entered starting at position 21 of the top section of the form exactly as the old name appears on your records. The new name is to be entered in transaction 02 in the order described above.

03 Address
Enter (B) in position 36. In instances where an employee anticipates that he will be out of town for an extended period of time and wishes Company mailings to be sent to him, submit a separate Personnel Action form indicating the mailing address (M). Enter street address starting in position 37.

04  City, State, Zip Code
    Enter (B) in position 36. Starting in position 37 enter the city and state. Enter the
    zip code in positions 67–71. It is most important that the zip code be entered. How-
    ever, if you cannot obtain the correct code, enter 00000.

05  Home Telephone
    Enter phone number. If you do not have the number, enter zeros.

06  Social Security Number, Birth Date and Sex
    Enter social security number as it appears on individual's social security card. Enter
    the birth date in month, day and year order. Thus, a birth date of March 1, 1940
    would be entered 03 01 40. Indicate male with M and female with F.

07  Status, Salary, Date Last Raise
    For new employees only the information required in positions 51–59 is necessary.
    For changes in status or salary positions 36–50 must also be filled in.

    Positions
    36      To be used only when a person is switched from full time to part time or
            vice versa. The opposite entry should be made in position 51. For example,
            a full time person going to part time would have an F in position 36 and a P
            in position 51.

    37–40   To be used for full time employees only. Salary is to be expressed in dollars
    52–55   only using all 4 positions. Thus $500 would be shown as 0500.

    41–44   To be used for part time employees only. Salary is to be expressed in dollars
    56–59   and cents using all 4 positions. Thus $6.75 per hour would be shown as
            0675.

    45–50   Enter date of last raise using all 6 positions. Again date is in month, day,
            year sequence.

    51      For new employee enter status, using F for full time and P for part time.
            For change of status for existing employee enter appropriate designation; be
            sure that position 36 contains the old status.

08  Rank Title
    Indicate old rank in position 36–37 and new rank in position 38–39. The new title
    should be indicated starting in position 40 using the abbreviations and ranks which
    appear in the appendix.

09  Hospital Coverage and Insurance
    Position 36 is to be used for contributory life insurance and position 37 for hos-
    pitalization insurance.
        A "Y" is to be entered in position 36 if employee desires contributory life insur-
    ance and an "N" is to be entered if he does not want the insurance.
        The following codes are to be used for hospitalization in position 37:

| | California Offices | All Other Offices |
|---|---|---|
| Employee only | 0 | 0 |
| Employee and one dependent | 3 | 1 |
| Employee and more than one dependent | 4 | 2 |

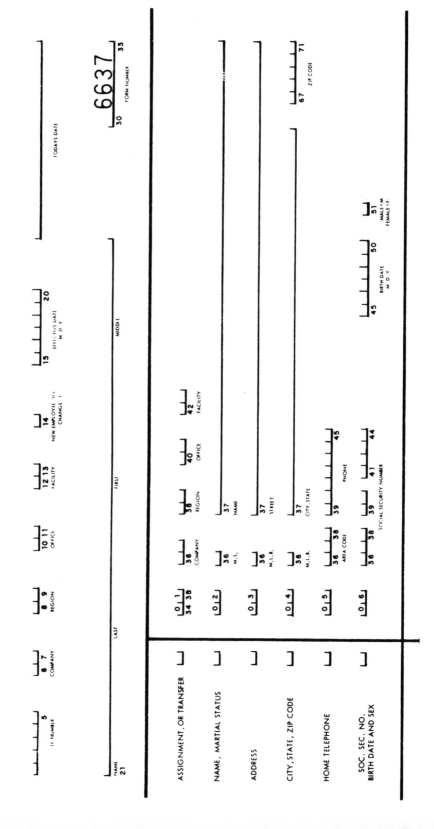

# PERSONNEL ACTION

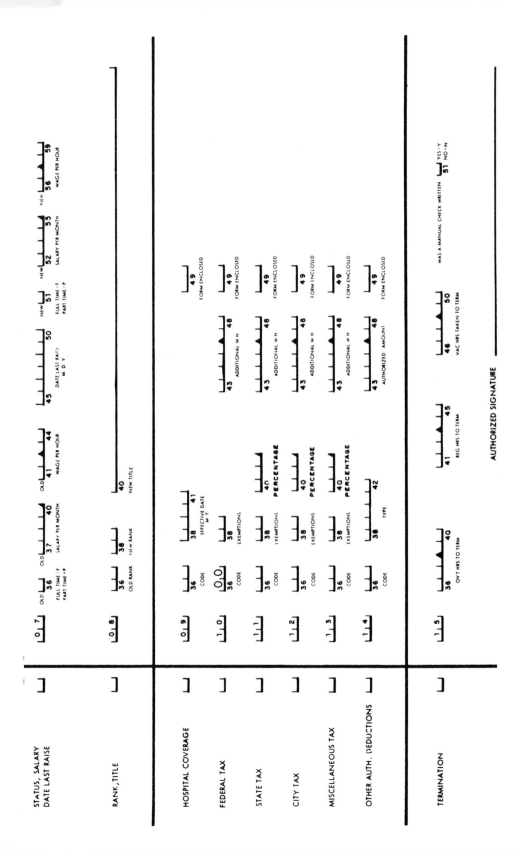

The effective date will be the first day of the calendar month coinciding with or following date of employment or change.

This will be indicated in fields as follows:

March 1, 1967      0367

The appropriate insurance forms must be enclosed and an "x" entered in field 49.

10  Federal Tax

Indicate number of federal exemptions in positions 38–39. Thus 3 exemptions would be 03 and 10 exemptions would be 10. Any additional withholding desired each pay period should be expressed in dollars and cents using all positions. Thus an amount of $25.00 would be shown as 002500. A W-4 form and/or an additional withholding form must be enclosed and indicated by an "x" in field 49.

11  State Tax

Enter proper state income tax code in positions 36–37. The acceptable codes are listed in the State Income Tax appendix.

When transferring employees from your office to an office in another state, enter the new state tax code in positions 36–37. If no tax code is applicable to the new office, "00" should be entered in positions 36–37.

The number of exemptions to be entered should be the number used for federal purposes or a different number if the employee so desires. In the latter case, a state withholding form must be enclosed.

Enter 100 in positions 40–42 except in the case of a nonresident of a state who is allocating only a certain percentage of time to the state. In this latter case that percentage should be entered to the nearest percent in positions 40–42. Thus if a nonresident estimates he is going to work in the state approximately 65% of the time, 065 should be entered in positions 40–42. For all employees, resident or nonresident, transferring to your office from another office you must indicate 100% for residents or an amount ranging from 000 to 100 for nonresidents.

This is necessary to clear the existing fields for the employee.

Any additional state income tax withholding desired should be entered in positions 43–48 following the instructions for additional withholding.

The appropriate forms must be enclosed and an "x" entered in position 49. In cases where the same federal and state exemptions are used and no state form is enclosed the "x" should be entered in position 49.

12  City Tax

Enter proper city income tax code in positions 36–37. The acceptable codes are listed in the City Income Tax appendix.

The instructions for positions 38–49 for state income taxes should be used for those positions pertaining to city tax.

13  Miscellaneous Tax

Not to be used. Leave blank.

14  Other Authorized Deductions

Not to be used. Leave blank.

15  Termination

The information required here is necessary so that we can pay terminating employees. The information called for pertains to time within the current month only.

All fields are to be used and the amounts entered should be correct to the nearest quarter hour. Since the form is our source for keypunching, it is not sufficient to send only a telegram. Personnel Actions should be sent to Corporate no later than the termination date.

The address the terminating employee specifies that his W-2 should be mailed to should be checked against your address listing, and if different, this new address should be indicated on the Personnel Action form which is prepared for termination.

Overtime hours to termination should be entered in positions 36–40 for persons who qualify for overtime. These hours should also be included in regular hours worked to termination called for below.

Regular hours worked to termination should be entered in positions 41–45. This should include vacation time which is recorded in positions 46–50.

Vacation hours taken to termination should be entered in positions 46–50.

If the state law required a manual check to be written and this was done, enter a "Y" in position 51. If no Manual check was written, enter an "N" in position 51.

The termination date must be intered in the top section under effective date.

# K. TIME REPORT

The purpose of the time report is to contribute to a data base for task time-estimating standards refinement.

The time report is completed by each project member and submitted to the project leader.

Time is reported in tenths of hours and is distributed over categories created by a three-tier accounting number scheme. From major to minor, the tiers are:

1. Project
2. Function
3. Activity

These tiers are defined below.

**PROJECT**

If time was spent working on a project, enter the identification number of the project. It is recognized that time is spent on activities unrelated to projects, and to account for this time, special time allocation numbers, to be used in lieu of a project number, are provided. These special allocation numbers are as follows.

00001–Holidays.
00002–Vacation.

00003–Sickness.

00004–Excused absence.

00005–Education, recipient. To be used when being educated.

00006–Education, donor. To be used when conducting an education program.

00007–Meeting attendance. To be used when attending a meeting for other than education purposes. Note that this account number is not to be used for project related meetings. Such time is to be charged to the project.

00008–Lost time. Time that is unproductive because of reasons beyond your control. For example, software malfunction during a computer session. (Explain under remarks.)

00009–Other. (Explain under remarks.)

These special allocation numbers do not require an entry for function or activity.

## FUNCTION

These are the functions into which the project is divided. For example, the card to tape program might be a function. Function numbers are assigned by the project leader. There may be instances in which a function number is not assigned to a task, in which case all zeros are entered, and the task is identified by activity alone.

## ACTIVITY

These are the categories into which systems and programming work falls. Activity numbers are as follows.

001–Analyzing existing documentation.

002–Conducting an interview.

003–Surveying literature.

004–Analyzing systems.

005–Developing acceptance test.

006–Writing functional specifications.

050–Designing systems.

100–Preparing internal specifications.

101–Doing a logical analysis (flow chart or decision table).

102–Coding.

103–Developing unit test plan.

104–Developing unit test data and results.

105–Unit testing.

110–Preparing computer center operating procedures.

111–Writing user manuals.

112–Developing system test plan.

113–Developing system test data and results.

114–System testing.

115–Developing file conversion procedures.

116–Converting files.

117–Training user personnel.

120–Project meetings.

TIME REPORT

NAME

EMPLOYEE NO.

DATE

| PROJECT | FUNCTION | ACTIVITY | SAT | SUN | MON | TUES | WED | THURS | FRI | TOTAL | REMARKS |
|---------|----------|----------|-----|-----|-----|------|-----|-------|-----|-------|---------|
|  |  |  |  |  |  |  |  |  |  |  |  |
|  |  |  |  |  |  |  |  |  |  |  |  |
|  |  |  |  |  |  |  |  |  |  |  |  |
|  |  |  |  |  |  |  |  |  |  |  |  |
|  |  |  |  |  |  |  |  |  |  |  |  |
|  |  |  |  |  |  |  |  |  |  |  |  |
|  |  |  |  |  |  |  |  |  |  |  |  |
|  |  |  |  |  |  |  |  |  |  |  |  |
|  |  |  |  |  |  |  |  |  |  |  |  |
|  |  |  |  |  |  |  |  |  |  |  |  |
|  |  |  |  |  |  |  |  |  |  |  |  |
|  |  |  |  |  |  |  |  |  |  |  |  |
|  |  |  |  |  |  |  |  |  |  |  |  |
|  |  |  |  |  |  |  |  |  |  |  |  |
| TOTAL |  |  |  |  |  |  |  |  |  |  |  |

Project leaders may request the manager to assign additional activity numbers to suggested definitions.

The time report is completed as follows.

1. The time report is identified by the project member's name and employee number, and the date of the Friday ending the week being reported on.
2. Time is reported in tenths of hours and is distributed over days. Time is to be reported as it was used. If you worked on Saturday, report it. If you worked 12 hours on one day, report it. Similarly, if you worked only five hours on a given day, report only five hours.
3. Time is totaled by day and by account number, and is then crossfooted.
4. A space is provided for any appropriate remarks.

# L. REQUEST
# FOR SERVICES FORM

The request for services form is initiated by the user. It is then submitted to the systems and programming manager. The systems and programming manager has the privilege of rejecting the request, in which case it is his obligation to enter into negotiations with the user, the outcome of which may be:

1. Reconsideration of the rejection on the part of the systems and programming manager.
2. Acceptance by the user of the rejection.
3. Modification of the request to be mutually acceptable to the systems and programming manager and the user.
4. Placement of the request in a pending file for future consideration.

On acceptance of the request, the work to be done is classified by the systems and programming manager as project or maintenance. For project work the systems and programming manager assigns a project leader. In either case, the systems and programming manager assigns a work identification number.

The request for services form, a three-part form, is completed as follows.

1. The requesting department is identified.
2. A short description of the problem that led to the decision to make the request for the data processing system work is entered.

R E Q U E S T   F O R   S E R V I C E S

| |
|---|
| REQUESTING DEPARTMENT |
| PROBLEM STATEMENT |
| OBJECTIVES |
| SCOPE |
| BENEFITS |
| DATE DESIRED |

| | | |
|---|---|---|
| DEPARTMENT HEAD | | DATE |
| ID NUMBER | PROJECT LEADER | |
| SYSTEM AND PROGRAMMING MANAGER | | DATE |
| PROJECT LEADER OR SYSTEM MAINTENANCE SUPERVISOR | | DATE |

ADD PAGES TO FORM AS NECESSARY

3. The objectives to be met by the system work are listed.
4. The scope of the proposed work is described. This description should specify all departments and operating areas affected by the proposed work.
5. The benefits to be derived from the new data processing services provided as a result of the proposed work are enumerated. Each benefit must be quantified.
6. The date on which the user desires the new services to be in operation is entered.
7. The form is approved by the requesting department head.
8. The original and one copy are submitted to the systems and programming group.
9. If the systems and programming manager accepts the request, he:
   a. Assigns a work identification number.
   b. If the work is to be handled on a project basis, assigns a project leader.
   c. Approves the form.
10. Approval of the form is completed with the signature of the assigned project leader in the case of project work, or the signature of the system maintenance supervisor in the case of maintenance work.
11. The copy of the approved form is returned to the user.

# M. SYSTEM ACCEPTANCE FORM

The data processing system developed by a project requires acceptance by the user, the computer center, and system maintenance. The system acceptance form is initiated by the project leader. A project stays in the construction phase until its product is accepted.

The system acceptance form, a six-part form, is completed as follows.

1. The project identification number is entered.
2. The original and five copies are submitted to the user.
3. User acceptance is made by the user department head.
4. The original and four copies are returned to the project leader.
5. The original and three copies are submitted to the computer center.
6. Computer center acceptance is made by the computer center manager.
7. The original and two copies are returned to the project leader.
8. The original and one copy are submitted to system maintenance.
9. System maintenance acceptance is made by the system maintenance supervisor.
10. The original is submitted to the systems and programming group.

## SYSTEM ACCEPTANCE FORM

Project Identification Number _____

I and those members of my department appointed by me have reviewed the above referenced systems and programming product and agree that:

1. The product meets the acceptance test previously set forth for it and agreed to by us and the systems and programming group.
2. Acceptable procedure manuals have been prepared and are available to us for use in utilizing the product.
3. Our personnel have been provided with adequate instruction in the utilization of the product.

_____     _____

User Department Head                                                                    Date

I and my staff have reviewed the above referenced systems and programming product and agree that:

1. The operating instructions have been prepared in accordance with computer center standards.
2. Computer center personnel have been provided with adequate instruction in the operation of the product.

_____     _____

Computer Center Manager                                                             Date

I and my staff have reviewed the above referenced systems and programming product and agree that it conforms to systems and programming standards for:

1. Documentation
2. Program organization.
3. System testing
4. Regression testing.

_____     _____

Systems Maintenance Supervisor                                                   Date

# N. PROJECT LEADER CHECKLIST

1. Prerequisites.
   a. Find out who your user is—find out who represents him.
   b. Determine the phase the system development is in.
      1) Are there functional specifications? (If not, development is in the analysis phase—your estimate error is at the 100% level.)
      2) Are there design specifications? (If not, development is in the design phase—error is at the 50% level.)
   c. Establish what constitutes system acceptance.
2. Planning.
   a. Manpower.
      1) Enumerate the tasks making up the job.
      2) Determine the dependency between tasks (bubble chart).
      3) Determine the external restraints.
      4) Allocate personnel to tasks.
      5) Estimate the time to do each task.
      6) Construct a bar chart.
      7) Allow for contingencies.
   b. Computer time.
      1) Unit test.
      2) System test.

3) File conversion.

4) Acceptance test.

c. Travel.

d. Support services.

e. Develop a cost estimate.

3. Monitoring the schedule.

a. Establish checkpoints.

1) Tie them to the production of tangible outputs that are an integral part of the task.

2) Establish them in cooperation with the person who must meet them.

3) Keep them close together (not separated by more than a month).

b. If a checkpoint is missed:

1) Take action to recover.

2) If you can't recover, notify the people depending on the deadline.

3) Determine the cause.

4) Take action to eliminate the cause.

4. Controlling performance.

a. Analysis—user approval of functional specifications.

b. Design.

1) Standards.

2) Alternative designs.

3) Design review committee.

c. Construction.

1) Conventions.

2) Internal specifications.

3) Testing.

d. General—Communication.

1) Keep people informed.

2) Make documentation and status reports generally available.

3) Hold project meetings.

4) Seat people working on related tasks together.

e. If a technical problem beyond you and your people's abilities to solve arises, get advice, from either within or without your company.

f. Require documentation.

1) Analysis—functional specifications.

2) Design—design specifications.

3) Construction.

a) For each program-module:

(1) Internal specifications.

(2) Logical analysis.

(3) Program listing.

b) Regression test.

c) Operations manual.

d) User manual.

g. Use a tickler file.

5. Communication.
   a. Prepare status reports.
     1) Accomplishments in the last report period.
     2) Overall progress toward long-term goals.
     3) Problems.
     4) Goals for the next report period.
   b. Report significant happenings immediately.
   c. If you have problems you can't solve, ask for help—loudly, clearly, and repeatedly.
6. Motivation.
   a. Allocate tasks among people in such a way that the people have some reason of their own, such as challenge or interest, for doing their assigned tasks.
   b. Make your performance expectations clear.
   c. Give credit for all accomplishments that meet expectations.
   d. Give prompt, constructive criticism—help the person improve himself.
   e. Submit honest personnel appraisals, both positive and negative, so the system of rewards (raises, promotions, and opportunities) stay in synchronization with performance.
   f. Provide conducive working conditions—keep contingencies down.
   g. Develop a team.
     1) Keep people informed.
     2) Make documentation and status reports generally available.
     3) Hold project meetings.
     4) Seat the people working on the project together.

# INDEX